WOMEN
OF
CRISIS

RADCLIFFE BIOGRAPHY SERIES

WOMEN OF CRISIS

Lives of Struggle and Hope

Robert Coles and Jane Hallowell Coles

A Merloyd Lawrence Book
DELTA/SEYMOUR LAWRENCE

A MERLOYD LAWRENCE BOOK
A Delta/Seymour Lawrence Edition
Published by
Dell Publishing Co., Inc.
1 Dag Hammarskjold Plaza
New York, New York 10017

Excerpts from this work first appeared in *Redbook* Magazine
and *The New York Times Magazine*.

Delta ® TM 755118, Dell Publishing Co., Inc.

Reprinted by arrangement with Delacorte Press/Seymour Lawrence

ISBN: 0-385-29169-8

Manufactured in the United States of America

9 8

VB

Foreword

Radcliffe College is pleased and proud to sponsor the Radcliffe Biographies, a series of lives of extraordinary American women.

Each volume of the Radcliffe Biographies serves to remind us of two of the values of biographical writing. A fine biography is first of all a work of scholarship, grounded in the virtues of diligent and scrupulous research, judicious evaluation of information, and a fresh vision of the connections between persons, places, and events.

Beyond this, fine biographies give us both a glimpse of ourselves and a reflection of the human spirit. Biography illuminates history, inspires by example, and fires the imagination to life's possibilities. Good biography can create for us lifelong models. Reading about others' experiences encourages us to persist, to face hardship, and to feel less alone. Biography tells us about choice, steadfastness, and chance.

The women whose lives are told in the Radcliffe Biographies have been teachers, adventurers, writers, scholars. The lives of some of them were hard pressed by poverty, cultural heritage, or physical handicap. Some of the women achieved fame; the victories and defeats of others have been unsung. Some of the women lived and died years ago; others are our contemporaries. We can learn from all of them something of ourselves. In sponsoring this series, Radcliffe College is responding to the renewed interest of our society in exploring and understanding the experience of women.

The Radcliffe Biographies project found its inspiration in the publication in 1971 of *Notable American Women,* a scholarly encyclopedia sponsored by Radcliffe's Schlesinger Library on the History of Women in America. We became convinced that some of the encyclopedia's essays should be expanded into full-length biographies, so that a wider audience could grasp the many contributions women have made to American life—an awareness of which is as yet by no means universal. It seemed appropriate that an institution dedicated to the higher education of women should initiate such a project, to hold a mirror up to the lives of particular women, to pay tribute to them, and so to deepen our understanding of them and of ourselves.

We have been joined in this project by two distinguished publishing houses and by a remarkable group of writers. I am grateful to them and to the editorial board—and particularly to Deane Lord, who first proposed the series, both in concept and in detail. Finally, I am happy to present this volume of the Radcliffe Biographies.

MATINA S. HORNER
President
Radcliffe College
Cambridge, Massachusetts

To the women we have met and come to know in various parts of the United States, and to others like them—relatives, neighbors, friends, fellow citizens.

And to the memory of Marian Ladd Hallowell, 1885–1968

Some have felt that these blundering lives are due to the inconvenient indefiniteness with which the Supreme Power has fashioned the natures of women: if there were one level of feminine incompetence as strict as the ability to count three and no more, the social lot of women might be treated with scientific certitude. Meanwhile the indefiniteness remains, and the limits of variation are really much wider than any one would imagine from the sameness of women's coiffure and the favourite love-stories in prose and verse. Here and there a cygnet is reared uneasily among the ducklings in the brown pond, and never finds the living stream in fellowship with its own oary-footed kind. Here and there is born a Saint Theresa, foundress of nothing, whose loving heart-beats and sobs after an unattained goodness tremble off and are dispersed among hindrances, instead of centering in some long-recognizable deed.

George Eliot, in Prelude to Middlemarch

Contents

Introduction

The first person we met when we started our work in New Orleans was Leontine Luke, a black woman of fifty. She took us to the homes of the four children who were initiating school desegregation during the autumn of 1960 against terrible odds —daily mobs full of heckling, threatening talk, and not a little inclination toward physical violence. We were beginning work with American children—work which would continue for nearly two decades. During that time our own three sons would be born, and grow, and do some traveling with us; together we saw various parts of a wonderfully diverse and almost endlessly complicated nation. During that time we would sometimes wonder whether there weren't, through all the travel and home visits and school visits and observation and writing and more writing, some important lapses, some blind spots, some failures of understanding, appreciation, or critical judgment. And during that time we often found ourselves hearkening back to a particular, rather dramatic moment in our work, not to mention the lives of a family we had come to know. One of the four black children— all aged six—who were braving the mobs of New Orleans' eastern, industrial-canal neighborhood had started to have an occasional second thought about the desirability of attending a totally boycotted school, day after day. The mobs were showing no signs of relenting; if anything, they were becoming more frenzied and vicious. Why persist?

The woman mentioned above, who had, in the first place, introduced us to the girl, Ruby, listened carefully to the child's restrained words. Yes, her worries and reservations were understandable, were well stated, were (needless to say) thoroughly realistic. But there was more to what was going on than Ruby could be expected to realize, so Mrs. Leontine Luke told her—and told us, the nervous and confused white Yankee visitors. Suddenly the child and the two of us were asked to listen to some words about one person's life, about the life of a people, and not least, about the life of a woman—as well as, more broadly, the lives of black women: "I will tell you Ruby, there is no turning back—not for you, and not for your mother, and not for me, and not for my daughters. I hear what they call you; every day I hear. Even the federal marshals are disgusted, and they're supposed to be tough men. But we're tough, too. That's what we are, and that's what we have to show every single member of that mob. Yesterday that white boy told you to stop putting on airs, and be a nigger girl. Well, you *are* a nigger girl, and that's a lot to be, let me tell you. And I'm a nigger woman; and that's a lot to be. It means to be a nigger, and it means to be a woman. It means to be strong, when people think you're weak. It means to be so strong you can cry and cry to yourself, then go out and meet the world and smile, and say yes, sir, to the world, to all the white people, who think they're so wonderful, and so smart, and so the tops. And it means to say yes, sir, to the niggers, too—the men. I'll tell you, it means that, too."

Abruptly, she stopped. The child, Ruby, seemed not only surprised by what she heard, but perplexed, even frightened. She left the room: thirst prompted a need for a Coke. When she came back there was silence for a moment, followed by Ruby's terse comment: "I'll think of what you said, Mrs. Luke, when I go by the mob next time." But Mrs. Luke had reconsidered, if not retrenched. She began an apology. She was sorry she used the word *nigger*. She was sorry she had sounded so bitter, cynical, angry. Wasn't Christmas coming? Ought one not to be full of compassion for others? Had not Negroes (at that time it would have been unthinkable for her to describe herself as "black") suffered long and hard, and therefore were they not especially obliged to think of others, hold their tongues, step in the shoes, even, of their persecutors, as Jesus Christ had done?

When that particular line of self-criticism, if not self-effacement, had been duly spoken, a further brief silence was interrupted by a comment of Ruby's which we have never forgotten: "But Mrs. Luke, Jesus Christ was a man." Mrs. Luke was not sure what she had heard or, maybe, was all too sure. She looked puzzled, looked to us for clarification, looked away, perhaps because she needed no clarification whatsoever. We were the last ones to be in a position to offer help. We sat there in a bit of a daze—at that time, for both of us, a constant mental state. What did this girl mean? What, alas, might be happening to her—that she would suddenly react so to a sermon not unlike the kind we had heard repeatedly in various black New Orleans churches?

The girl took the measure of all of us rather quickly. She, who had been learning to manage with screaming, ranting men and women crazily obsessed with their white skin, was not going to be overwhelmed by more friendly grown-ups: "If you're a man, you can be nice to your enemy, and get away with it. If you're a woman, you probably *have* to be nice to your enemy, but you may not get away with it." At that point, Mrs. Luke decided that we all ought get away—*from* "it." She changed the subject. She immersed herself and Ruby in a discussion of a forthcoming movie trip. Then came a television program Ruby liked to watch, and our departure. Mrs. Luke left with us, but we had come in

separate cars so there was only a chance for a few words—
exchanged under a heavy New Orleans late-afternoon thunder
shower. We never directly discussed the earlier remarks of
Ruby's, but Mrs. Luke, as she got in her car and arranged with
us the time for our next visits with the four black children,
observed that Ruby was "a deep child," and added a terse after-
thought: "I hope she doesn't suffer later. The more you think
and the deeper you are, the more you feel."

She wanted no further discussion. She had started her car. We
hurried back to ours, and sat in silence for a while as we worked
our way through the quickly formed puddles of an unpaved
street. Later, we talked about Ruby's constant trial: how long
could she possibly endure such severe harassment? Neither of us,
that evening or for some considerable time afterwards, mentioned the words we had heard, words about the implications of
sex rather than skin color—a prophetic message of a six-year-old
girl, we now realize. Only in 1965, when we began trying to
figure out what lessons we'd been taught over the years, did we
go back to that particular moment—a critical one, we now realize, in our education. A first-grade student, born to exceedingly
poor, uneducated, hard-pressed parents, and herself living under
the most extreme of circumstances during school days, had
managed to see beyond her own predicament—had managed,
arguably, a moment of transcendence. She had supplied us one
of those "contexts" social scientists so often call upon. She had
brought us up short; let us know that the issues confronting her
were not only racial, however obvious that side of her struggle
continued to be. She was a girl, and by that fate her life was also
circumscribed.

We came back North in 1965 and continued our work. Eventually we moved out West to New Mexico; then, back to New
England. Always it was children we were meeting, talking with,
trying to learn from. But, as Ruby had known to remind us, they
were boys and girls, and they had mothers and fathers, and these

sexual distinctions were as significant as those of race, class, region—the "variables" we tended to consider our primary concern. There is so much, of course, that one can say about individuals, never mind those "groups" of people whom observers "study" and write about, sometimes all too conclusively. In the five volumes of *Children of Crisis* different kinds of children were brought to the reader's attention in the hope of unraveling the significant aspects of their lives as blacks, as Appalachian whites, as Chicanos, Eskimos, Indians, as individuals born to migrant farm workers or tenant farmers, born to parents who live in our cities' ghettos or working-class neighborhoods, or who live in town houses, on plantations and estates. But Ruby's reminder stayed with us; and sometimes we wondered how to respond to it. She had not, it turned out, simply stumbled on a "truth," then forgotten it. We have continued a friendship with her over the years, and have heard from her lips many observations that have given us much pause. When Ruby was sixteen and aware that we had three sons, the youngest only recently born, she had this to say: "It'll be different for you, bringing them up; if you'd had three girls, you would think differently about the world, I'll bet."

She has never been one for long statements, and was not about to render one then. She was no member of a "liberation" group. She had not experienced any "heightening" of her "consciousness." She was a high school student, much preoccupied with friends, a job in a nearby supermarket, and the science courses which for her were the prelude to a planned career in nursing. She was also an active member of her church's choir. She loved to sing—found music a more congenial form of expression, actually, than long, wordy exchanges. When she made her observation about our family life she was telling us what was on her mind, what ought be on our minds; but, as one hears it put in the South, she was not inclined "to make a federal case out of it."

Others, however, have wanted to do just that—spell out the

broader implications of her remarks, her sense of things, and by no means only hers; and do so legally, politically, and not least, with many more words than she has ever had in mind to use. The result, as she began to realize when she became of high school age, is a significant number of books devoted to American women: their situation as it has been, is, and, given various changes, might one day turn out to be. Ruby has read some of those books and, from time to time, kept prodding us to add yet another to their number. Once we asked her why she wanted us to do so. Her reply was characteristically modest and brief, but not without a certain force: "You've met the kind of people who aren't mentioned in a lot of the books we've been reading in our high school social studies course." Later, in college (she was the first of her family to attend) there was still a certain insistence, perhaps more than matched by our stated reluctance: "I'd still like to read about some of the women you've met here in the South." Then, anxious to make a connection she felt we were not pursuing sufficiently (if at all), she pointed out: "There comes a time when some 'children of crisis' become 'women of crisis.' That's important—what happens to us, then."

We were in agreement, but not sure whether or how to follow her suggestion. In the various volumes of *Children of Crisis,* a number of women had appeared. In *The Old Ones of New Mexico* and in *Still Hungry in America* there were other women who spoke, sometimes with considerable candor. We would have gone no further had not Radcliffe College decided to encourage a series of books devoted to particular women. The point was to indicate through narrative and analytic presentations what it has been like and continues to be like for women to pursue their lives, their interests, their careers. Still hesitant to become involved in the project, whose importance we did not question, we discussed the matter with President Matina Horner of Radcliffe; with an able, warm-spirited colleague of hers, Deane Lord; with Seymour Lawrence; and with Merloyd Lawrence. We were especially taken with the college's interest in connecting any literary effort made with ongoing teaching: a seminar for those students who might be interested in reading and responding to what was being written. Moreover, President Horner kept reminding us that the students at Radcliffe, like most people who regularly purchase books, are not likely to meet the women we have spent time with these past decades. It would be helpful, she thought, for young women intent as never before upon coming to terms with themselves and their world to get some idea how it has gone and still goes for women quite different in important respects.

We agreed to join up, and the result is this book, yes; but the result also for us has been just the kind of education Ruby Bridges of New Orleans, Louisiana, long ago had in mind for us. The more we went over our experiences, the longer we thought about what we'd heard and seen, the more apparent it became to us that we had not really done justice to what a number of women had urged us over and over again to consider: the particular complexity of their lives as poor or working-class *women*. For a year before we began writing this book we went through our notes, transcripts of tape-recorded interviews, summaries of observations or conversations. We also went back to the homes of certain women, this time with a new angle of interest and, maybe, vision. It was touching and sometimes dramatically revealing to be told, as we often were, that it was "about time" we asked one or another question aimed at pursuing quite another line of discussion than on previous visits. We were, consequently, presented with the task not only of going over past work, but making sense of new work out in that "field" mentioned by anthropologists or sociologists—the world, of course, inhabited by individual human beings. In that latter regard, we were helped by various young women at Radcliffe to think a bit more carefully than might otherwise have been the case—think about what it is that certain American women have to struggle for or against as a consequence of their "background," and what it is they share (in the way of concrete realities, or hopes and fears) with other women fated to live quite differently.

The heart of this book, of course, is the lives of particular women who have lived, during the second half of the twentieth century, in the United States of America. As always, we have drawn upon years of work, dozens of talks. The "method" of work we pursue has been, perhaps, all too thoroughly discussed in the *Children of Crisis* volumes, and elsewhere as well. We try to get to know the members of a particular family. We visit them regularly—to start with, once or twice a week. We keep track through notes of what we have heard. We use a tape recorder from time to time—we hope casually and not with any intent to intimidate others, make them self-conscious, and not, we also earnestly hope, with ritualistic arrogance or in the illusion that we are "scientists" because a small Sony machine happens to be near at hand. Eventually, we pull together the words of others and our own observations into what (we can only pray) is a reasonably coherent and suggestive series of portraits, comments, reflections. We change the names of the people we are presenting to the reader. We edit statements; condense remarks; juxtapose assertions made on different occasions; choose selectively in the interests of clarity and understanding and, just as important, overall truthfulness to a given person's life. As many of the people we know have reminded us, they (like writers or scholars) have certain major preoccupations, which ought be kept in mind rather than undercut with distracting asides, even if supplied by the very individual whose life is the subject of attention.

We have, as always, tried to indicate some of our own responses (of thought and feeling) to the people we have visited and, upon occasion, been fortunate enough to live with. We have, in this book, tried to suggest links between the work we have previously described and the work that has gone into this book—links, too, between the experience of black people, mi-

part
ONE

LIVING
ON THE ROAD

We began to get acquainted with Ruth James in 1964, in the course of our studies of the children of migrant farm workers. She was the considerably older sister of one of those children. We recall asking to talk with her one day because she had been such a strong influence on all her younger sisters and brothers. She was willing to answer our questions, but quite convinced that she had nothing at all to tell us. Moreover, she emphatically denied that she was, in fact, doing quite a lot to bring up the family's young ones: "I'm not a mother. The public health nurse came here to give everyone in the camp some shots, and she said I was the mother of my brothers and sisters. I told her no. How could I have kids that old and be my age? She asked how old I am. I told her, sixteen. She said 'anything is possible, where migrants are concerned.' I remember the words, each one of them. I've been wondering what kind of nurse she is! And she knew my sister, the next one down from me, is fourteen! I bore her when I was two!

"She was just trying to be smart with me. She figured that because I was holding my little sister's hand, I was her mother.

And when a white person says something, and she's a nurse, too, and she thinks she knows so much, she isn't going to back down. She probably thought my sister who's fourteen is a mother, too. She told me migrant 'girls' start having kids when they're ten years old. I didn't answer her. It's best to keep quiet. She'd just call me sassy, pick up the phone, and get the foreman to come over. And he'd say 'yes ma'am, yes ma'am,' and tell us all, the whole family, to *git.* When he says *git,* we move as fast as our legs will carry us.''

Usually it was her arms, not her legs, that were kept busy. She had been picking beans for years—so far back that she had no memory of any introduction to the experience. But after a number of talks, she admitted that she was not without hope: "I'd like to have a different life. I'd like to work in a beauty shop. I would settle down and stop the traveling life. I wouldn't want to own a car. I'd walk to work. Who wants to drive! I'm sick of being in cars and trucks and buses! I'm sick of moving from place to place. I've asked my mother how she got into this life. She said: A woman marries a man, and that's how she gets into her life. Her life is his life, a branch of his tree. I don't know if that's right, but that's how my mother said it happens, and she knows. She's seen a lot!

"She's seen more than I want to see! The nurse is right; some of us do get tied up with a man when we're pretty young, and that's the beginning for us—a kid, then another one. I'm not sure I really want to have children—ever. It's wrong to talk like that according to the ministers who come here to the camp and preach to us. But they don't really preach to *you.* They preach to hear themselves. There's a difference! I'll be picking beans, and I'll see a plane flying, and it's bringing the rich people down to Palm Beach. We're in Palm Beach County, just like the rich people are. I follow the plane with my eyes, and I wish I was a rich woman and I had a home on the ocean. There's a beautiful beach in Palm Beach, but we've never seen it. I heard from the crew leader. He says he would take us there, but the police would drive us away. If you're colored, they might drive you away, even if you have a lot of money. I guess the civil rights people are fighting for us. They want us to be able to go into a white place and get fed, or swim on the white people's beach. I hope they win, but I'm not sure it'll make any difference to us. There will still be us migrants, living our own life, out here. My mother says that when they get the white man off our backs, there will always be the crew leader, one of our colored folks. He's a bad person—a bad man.''

She came up with that last qualification for a good reason. The crew leader dominated the migrants like a despot; they yielded to his every demand—or whim. He controlled their finances, their working arrangements, their housing accommodations. And if they were women, he also sought their favors. Ruth had known him for a long time; had been treated comparatively well by him; had learned rather a lot, listening to him recite his social knowledge—and had developed a seething hatred for him, which she kept, always, under strict control: "I'll be looking out the window, when we're on the bus going North to do the harvesting, and I'll catch myself looking up front—at him. He's driving. He's smoking. He's looking at the women on the side-walk of the town we're passing through. He's a brazen one. He's a fat, sassy nigger, that's what he is. He'll look at the white as well as the colored—any woman with pretty legs and a good rear. I can read his mind. I wish he'd stop the bus and get out and approach one of those white women. Then we'd be all through with him. They'd come after him, the whites would, and they'd get him and kill him on the spot, and leave him there, in some ditch, for the flies to land on and feed off. I wouldn't mind that. I know how bad he is. He's out for himself and no one else.''

But she has second thoughts. What would the migrants do without their crew leader? What would she and her family do without him? And moving back from the specific to the general:

What would women do without men? She asks the question rhetorically rather than out of personal confusion, or because she badly seeks an answer. She provides her own reply: "I guess we'd be in trouble, if there wasn't that crew leader around. I can't imagine a woman being a crew leader. Maybe there's a woman somewhere in the world who is as bad as the crew leader. I hope I don't meet her—ever. You need men because they are the ones who are tough, and the world is plenty tough, I've sure learned that already. The growers treat us like animals. The sheriff is in their pocket. They pull him out like a handkerchief. Every time a grower sneezes, the sheriff is right there, trying to be a help. He helps all right; he arrests us, calls us crooks because we complain that we're not getting the money we've worked for. The crew leader fights for us. Well, to be exact, he fights for himself. The only reason he wants us to be a little happier is because he needs us to work, so he can get money. We get some —just enough so that we show up for work!

"That crew leader is no better than the growers, though. He'd kill if it meant he could make more money, and if he thought he could get away without going to jail. The world is run by people like him—men who like to boss people around. His wife—she won't breathe without asking his permission first. She knows he fools around, and she knows he lies to her all the time, and she knows he lies to us. But she doesn't care, so long as she has that Cadillac of hers, and the green stuff in her alligator pocketbook. I've seen her peeling out those ten-dollar bills; she keeps them together with a gold clip he bought for her. She doesn't ask any questions and she doesn't want to know any answers. She just wants to get her hair straightened every week, and dyed red. The growers call her 'the red nigger,' but she doesn't hear that. They talk behind her back. They talk nice to her, when they see her, because they need her husband to supply the migrants. If it wasn't for her husband, they'd laugh at 'the red nigger' right to her face. I hear she's carrying on with one of the foremen—a white man who says all niggers are no good! He sneaks over in the afternoons. He has honest-to-goodness red hair! I think it's against the law for white and colored to have sex, but that's another law no one pays any attention to. The only time the law really cracks down is when a migrant asks for a little more money, or a colored person wants to vote, or a woman says she's tired of being pushed around by some man and she wants to leave him or leave the job some boss-man has given her.

"It's a man's world. You need the men, if you're going to have some money. Women don't make the money they should. Sometimes I wonder if there will ever be a time when it's all changed, and a woman can live her life and not need a man to fight for her, or to give her something, or to protect her, or speak for her."

Still at that time a teenager, though for years (since the age of ten) a school dropout and harvester of various crops, she was not without an interest in young men. So long as they were about her age, she saw them as different, as relatively honest and trustworthy, as uncorrupted by the world of commercial agriculture she knew so well. She had a boyfriend who, in fact, shared her dream of an escape from the migrant life. But by the age of sixteen he was fast losing any hope that it would ever be possible for either of them to settle down, find stable work, live like other people. They knew their limitations all too clearly: their race, their lack of education, their situation as Southerners in the early to middle 1960s. They told one another that there was always a chance—that miracles happen. But each of them harbored reservations, silent but grimly realistic social and economic appraisals.

In 1965, when Ruth James was seventeen and her boyfriend, Edward Thomas, the same age, they contemplated marriage, but after weeks of discussion decided no. It was, ironically, a decision prompted by a desperate kind of optimism which they did not want, either of them, to give up: "I told Ed that if we get married, we'll never, never have a chance to get out of this no-good, traveling life. We'll be stuck in it forever. Not only that, we might end up wandering all over Hell in the next life! God would take one look at us when we came to Him, and He'd say to Himself that we're a mess, and all we're good for is moving and moving and moving. That's what will happen, maybe. But I'm not ready to lie down and die, not yet. Ed says I'm kidding myself, and he's right, I know. He says we might just as well stop living with our families and start our own family—him and me and the kids we'll have. I told him I don't want kids—none. He laughed. He said I have big ideas. I told him he was wrong. But I do have a plan; I want to save money, and get a job in some beauty parlor, and have a little house that I stay in all year–no working 'on the season'–with the crops. It would be a short walk from the house to the beauty parlor.

"I don't have any money put away. I once hid five dollars, but I had to spend it on food. We ran low, and there was no work for weeks. You can't save and live this life of ours. I hear you have to go to school to be a beautician. There's a lady in Belle Glade who operates out of her house; she does your hair, and she told me once she'd teach me some things. But she changed her mind. She said she doesn't want the competition. Ed says she takes in men, besides the women she has come over. She fixes women's hair in the day, and she does favors for her men customers at night. She's rich. Ed asked me if I wanted to be like her. That's when we had a fight. I said that men sell themselves one way, and women do another way. Men cheat and lie and crook people, and no one is surprised. But if a woman does a few tricks, she's called no good. And what about the men paying for the tricks! Where did they get the money? A lot of them took it away from their wives. The woman works in the field, and the man collects her money as well as his own, and his wife is supposed to smile and call him Mr. Wonderful, and be as good as the day is long. Meanwhile, he's in Belle Glade drinking wine and visiting a woman. Men never have enough of anything; they always want more. That's what I told Ed, and he didn't like what he heard. But he still wants to marry me."

She has, actually, wanted to marry him, from time to time. When she was nineteen she almost did. Among migrants, young marriages predominate. It is a brief, mean time, "the traveling life." At thirty-five, many migrants have teen-aged children—and are feeling tired, weak, sad. They are likely to receive little, if any, medical care; they live under appalling circumstances, so far as housing and sanitation go; they are paid low wages. The toll becomes apparent in their early twenties—and they know it themselves. They may be removed from the ordinary world, but they are not unable to appreciate what they lack or others possess. When Ruth James was nearly twenty, she reminisced about the last year of her life, and wondered what was ahead for her: "I'm getting old. That's what I keep hearing from everyone. My mother wants to know why I don't stop 'dreaming.' My younger sisters, two of them, are married. My friends keep asking me why I have no man. I tell them I have Ed. They know that! They mean: Why don't you have children and call him your husband. I tell them that if I learned anything from my mother, it was not to have children just because you don't know how *not* to have children.

"That nurse who comes here and teaches us how to use pills or get fitted is the best friend we have. No wonder the crew leader wants to get rid of her and her program. He says she's an outsider, that nurse. He says she's white, and she doesn't understand us. But she understands all right—she understands him; that's what has him worried. He keeps asking me when I'm going to have a baby. He looks at me as if to say I'll never be a real slave of his until I come up with that kid! Then I'll be hooked! That's the one big lesson I've learned. I was never good in school, and I never liked those people who came to the camps and wanted to teach us and get us 'organized.' But the nurse who gave us the story on birth control, she was the biggest help of my life.

"I don't think Ed agrees. He'd like to pin us down with kids. Sometimes I'm ready to surrender. I'll be on my knees moving up and down, up and down, the rows of beans or the lettuce, and I want to go away and never come back, but I don't know where to go, so I just wish I was pregnant, *so* pregnant that I couldn't do any picking. Ed keeps telling me that if I don't watch out, I'll be an old woman whose hands are wrinkled from picking vegetables, but have never touched a baby. I suppose he thinks I'd be happy with five or ten children around me, helping me pick vegetables, the way I have helped my mother all my life. The first memory I have is rolling over and landing on a bed of beans. I remember my mother worrying that I'd fall in the irrigation ditch. I remember her telling me to follow her while she moved up and down the rows of beans and lettuce and tomatoes. That was my fun—keeping up with her. My toys were the no-good vegetables—the ones overripe! When I see those television programs telling kids to get all those toys, I laugh. I've never even seen a store where they sell that stuff.

"If I had kids, I'd be even more upset than I am now. What would I say to them? Would I lie, the way my mother used to lie to me? I remember asking her why we didn't stop moving all the time, from farm to farm, and state to state. She said we're lucky, we have work and there's food to eat. That was what I believed, that we're *lucky*. When I got older, I asked my mother why she kept telling us we're lucky. She said I should go and visit some of our people who have stayed in Alabama, in Lowndes County, and see how they live. They can't take a breath without checking it out to see if the white man will approve. And they haven't got a penny to their name. And they don't have a crew leader to make sure they get some food. My mother thinks the crew leader is a nice man because he feeds us. He's using the money we made for him to feed us, but my mother doesn't want to hear me talk like that! She tells me it's about time I had kids. She tells me how good Ed is for me."

The mother tells her other things, too; tells her that her father "died in his soul" when he was about ten or twelve and realized what the future held in store; tells her that she, too (the mother), long ago became "a walking, kneeling shadow"—a person without any real hope, without any conviction that there is a point to life beyond "breathing and eating and sleeping—and working, always working." The daughter asks the mother to reconcile such sad confessions to the suggestion that a marriage take place —Ruth and Ed, the obvious younger counterparts to an older couple. There is no hesitation on the mother's side. She responds expansively, with apparent melancholy, but with a certain toughness as well. And the daughter finds that what she has heard is unforgettable, if not entirely persuasive: "I can't sleep after I hear her talk. I hear her and hear her. I toss, and I grab the mattress, and I sit up and think. I close my eyes tight and try to forget. I can't, though. I put paper in my ears, but I still hear her. You can't get rid of a voice, if it's said something that's touched your heart! My mother says she and my father are 'dead,' but dead people don't say things that get to living people, and won't leave them for days and days and nights and nights. My mother is not 'dead'; she's alive and preaching! I'll be trembling in bed, on a warm night, after one of my mother's talks. I'll be shaking and asking myself why I was ever born.

"I ask God that question a lot, especially during a night when I can't sleep. I talk with Him. I don't know if I really believe in Him, but I talk with Him. I wish He'd let us know what His plan is. He must have had some reason for His son, Jesus Christ, to come here and say the poor are the lucky ones, and the rich are headed nowhere fast. He must have some reason for us to keep living this way and for the growers to keep having a great time for themselves. Maybe it'll be in my lifetime that God comes and changes the world, like the minister says He will one day—the

Second Coming. Maybe you've got to hold on to your religion, and pray that if it's hard now, it'll get better in the next life. My mother and father *must* believe in the next life. Why else would they keep living this way and working this way, if they didn't believe in the next life? They both have told us a lot of times that they could just go and give up and die, but they're waiting on the Lord. I'm not sure they believe what they say, though."

She is, in fact, quite sure of her parents' essential ambiguity of attitude toward their lives. She, too, moves from stoic acceptance or resignation to grim prophesy mixed with a quiet grief that can be devastating to behold—not to mention experience. One day she is happy to be the person she is. There will be a dance that night, and she plans to have a good time. Another time she is speculative in the way well-to-do, well-educated people are when a sudden tragedy or a disappointment of one kind or another has prompted a release from the everyday constraints of living a life. "Why is it," Heidegger asked, "that we usually stop and think about the purpose of our lives, when we are in trouble—and not otherwise?" Ruth James is almost always in trouble, and knows that to be the case. Perhaps she has, upon occasion, come up with an answer or two for Heidegger: "The worse it gets, the more you stop and ask yourself how long you can last. We had bad weather this winter—a freeze, and no work. We earned no money. We borrowed from the crew leader, more and more. He owns us. He has us in such debt, we'll never get out from under his power. Who said they freed the slaves! We should run away. But we don't. Why?

"I ask a lot of whys sometime. I ask why I was born. I ask why I was born the person I am, and not someone else. I ask when you should say *enough*— and go and drown in the irrigation ditch. I don't want to die because that's the end of being yourself, when death takes you. But it's no fun being myself, not now. With no work and a stomach that's not too full, I end up going on walks, and staring at the sky, and asking myself a lot of questions about what will happen to me and why I'm staying here; and the answers I give myself aren't very nice. I just say nothing good will happen to me, and I'm here because I'm stuck here, and I'll never get out, except to go North with the crew leader and come back with him. If I wanted to turn a trick with him two or three times a week, I suppose I'd stop asking myself questions, because I'd be spending my time choosing dresses and eating all the barbecue chicken I want from the best place in town."

When she was twenty, nearly twenty-one, she was almost ready to give up—yield to the insistent offers of that crew leader. Why not? What difference would it make? The answer to the latter question was obvious: a lot. She didn't, however, know how to deal with her considerable reservations—which, she realized, prevented her from doing something that seemed to be in her own best interests as defined by herself. The more she stopped and looked carefully at her present situation and future prospects, the more she felt inclined to say yes, once and for all, to the propositions being made her. And they were, she realized, becoming more and more substantial. She knew why, too: "He's a businessman. He wants all he can get. If he can't get something, it becomes more valuable to him. He tries harder to get it. He offers more money. That's the way he thinks, all the time. You can't rob and steal all day, the way he does, and turn it off at night. He looks at people as if they're animals. He buys and sells people. He says that's what it's like in the world—you win or you lose. His wife is a little doll he's got tucked away in a pretty little bungalow. She spends her time straightening her hair and trying to look lighter. She bleaches her skin. She wears white all the time. She listens to her records, 'mood music,' and watches television. She doesn't care what her husband does, as long as he gives her money and lets her spend every penny. She's been told he has girl friends. So what!

"She's the mother of that daughter of his, and the son. Those two spoiled brats! They are the lousiest kids I've ever seen. The girl is eight, and she's dopey because she has everything. She doesn't know what to ask for anymore. The boy is a liar, a bully. He is seven, and he pushes and shoves everyone. The school-teachers say they want to kill him, but they're afraid of the crew leader. He has the white people behind him. He can get a colored teacher fired, if he wants. The boy told some kids he's going to be a millionaire when he grows up. The girl wants to be on the cover of *Ebony*. That's the crew leader, speaking through his kids. I hear about all that because my little sister goes to school with the crew leader's daughter. He doesn't like his children going to school with 'migrants.' He's said so a lot. But he can't turn his kids white, and there aren't enough rich colored for a separate school for them. Too bad, I guess.

"If I gave in to him, I guess I'd become a lot richer colored gal than I am now, that's for sure! The only problem is I'd hate myself. I spent yesterday—we were doing oranges—asking myself why I'm so worried about my opinion of myself. Who am I to be so worried? I'm nobody. I'll always be a nobody. The minister says we're nobodies, but we're going to inherit the earth. My cousin had been drinking, and he spoke up; he said that was a big joke, to tell us such a story. The minister tried to ignore him, but my cousin repeated himself, and finally the minister shouted that he'd call the sheriff if there was one more thing said by anyone. I guess he was letting us know that he's a somebody and not a nobody, like the rest of us.

"There's another man who's been after me—the minister! He calls me to him, and tells me he wants to pray for me; and he wants to pray with me, and then I'll be saved. I tell him thank you, but I've got to go to work, or I'm so tired from having been at work that I'd best go and sleep. He gives me that fishy look. His eyes start warming up. His face begins to move. I can see his nose getting wider. His mouth opens. I know what's crossing his mind. He's told me once that the Lord smiles on people, and

I'm one the Lord has smiled on. I asked him what he meant. He
said I'm pretty, and that's because the Lord likes me. Then he
said it would be a sin to be selfish with yourself. I didn't know
what he was saying at first. I asked him what he meant. He came
to me, and took my hand, and stared into my eyes and said I am
'real pretty' and I should be generous, like the Lord was. Then
I began to catch his point. I moved away from him, fast. I told
him I had some work to do, and I was going. He followed me.
He said I was fleeing from the Lord. I said no I wasn't. He said
he knows the truth, and I was fleeing. Boy, did I run away, as
quick as I could."

She had not been all that surprised the first time, nor was she
surprised when, again and again, the minister approached her
with his peculiar mixture of Biblical piety and frank sexuality.
She had been reared on hard-praying fundamentalism, yet had
lost faith in God at an indeterminate age. That is, she remembered no specific, dramatic moment when disbelief seized her.
Rather, she recalls a growing cynicism with respect to religion
—a sense of incredulity, which she estimates acquiring as far back
as her seventh birthday. She remembers that day especially well,
because one of her sisters was born then. She remembers the
event, too. The family was with the crew leader in South Carolina, headed for vegetable picking in eastern North Carolina.
They stopped by the road at the mother's urgent request. Ruth
James remembers the crew leader saying no, there was plenty of
time and he would stop later. Eventually he became convinced:
the cries of a woman actually delivering a child in his bus. They
all got out, and within minutes a baby girl was born. The crew
leader wanted his passengers to get right back on the bus and
head north for work. But in a rare display of unity all the men
and women said no, they wanted Ruth's mother to have a rest,
wanted her to stop bleeding, wanted to go find, somewhere, "a
colored nurse."

They did so; but it took many hours, and the crew leader was enraged. He cursed the entire entourage, told them they were all fired, drove off. Rather soon, however, he was back—not repentant or apologetic, but silent and observant. What were "they" up to? Might they be seriously considering a "stand" against his authority? Had he best let them be, at least for a few hours? He asked himself such questions with considerable seriousness, all the while taking care to be exceptionally polite and respectful to the men, women, and children he (at other times) was wont to call "freight" without the slightest sign of embarrassment. By the late afternoon, when a nurse had come and cleaned and bandaged Ruth's mother, who declared herself ready to "go picking," the crew leader had decided that there was no reason for further caution or restraint. He resumed shouting, issuing unequivocal orders, speaking obscenities, mocking and degrading various individuals with personal remarks. The girl Ruth would never forget the one thrown her way: "That mother of yours sure served you up a nice birthday present. Have you looked at the ugly, noisy cake that came out of her insides?"

Word for word, years later, the two sentences, the statement and question, would be remembered—and much else: "He was the same then as now: a selfish man who never thinks of the people who listen to him talk and work for him and put up with him. He gave me a wink years ago; I was just beginning to be a woman. He had his eye on me, I guess, when I was a kid. He told my mother a long time ago that I would be a 'sexy number.' She didn't answer him. She told me later she was making supper, and she had the knife in her hand. She tightened her grip on the handle of the knife, but she didn't move. I think I knew I'd never really be a Christian when I heard her tell me that—and then add that she prayed to God for forgiveness later that evening. I wish she had killed him! If there was the God I think there should be, He should have struck the crew leader dead a long time ago— and a lot of other people, too. What's He waiting for up there? Why does He let the poor suffer, and the rich have a good time?

Why did He let my mother suffer so much that evening, after my sister was born, in South Carolina? I was a little girl, but I can hear her, right now, asking God to spare her, to let her go, to take her to Him—anything so she wouldn't stay in the pain and so the little baby would stop screaming. It was sick, real bad sick.

"The crew leader didn't care whether the baby died or not. He didn't care that my mother was crying. He just wanted to get us to North Carolina. He wanted us at work that next morning, early. I remember my mother holding the baby, and looking at me and my brother and my sister, and telling us that 'it's a mistake.' I asked her what was a mistake. She said all of us should die; God made a mistake, putting us here. My uncle told her to shut up. He said she'd been drinking. My father said no, she hadn't touched any beer or wine. He was going to get into a big fight with my uncle. My mother stopped them. I remember her saying it: 'Why are you fighting each other? Why don't you two go up to the front and take the wheel from him—the devil driving this bus? Why don't you throw the crew leader into a ditch, and step on the gas pedal and keep going, as fast as you can?'

"They weren't going to listen to my mother. I knew why then. I know why now. They were scared. They're always going to be scared. They were born scared. It's not that they have anything to lose. They don't. They could have gone and killed that crew leader. No one would have known what happened. They could have put a knife to him, and dropped him in some irrigation ditch. If a colored man found the body later, he wouldn't say a word. If a white man found the body, he'd have laughed and been happy: one less of the colored around! But that crew leader is the colored boss-man, and no one dares say a word back to him. He's God. He's the Devil, but he's God to us. He tells me I'm an 'uppity one,' just because I don't go along with him. Even my *mother* has been scared that I'm going to get us all in trouble by not going along.

"I never told her anything. I knew what she'd say: there are worse people than the crew leader. She's never given us any examples of who is worse, but she keeps telling us there are plenty of them, in case we want to know. My little sister was five when she told me she'd figured out that no one dared argue with the crew leader. She meant no one she knew—our parents. I was about nine or ten and near to my first period when I saw the crew leader eyeing me seriously, real seriously. I told my mother that night. She looked frightened. I told her not to worry. I told her I could take care of myself. My mother didn't say anything for a while. Finally, she asked me if I'd had anything to do with him at all, the crew leader. I said no. She said that when I did, just to let him get his way and forget what happened, and we'd all be just fine. That's what she told me!

"I ran away; it's the only time I did. I started walking, and I got all the way to Bean City. I was going to try to hitchhike to Palm Beach, and see if I could find a place to sleep and get a job. Then they pulled up beside me, my mother and the crew leader, in his big, black Buick. I thought I was dreaming! I wiped my eyes. It was dark. I thought I'd died, maybe, and I was in Hell, the place the preacher is always telling us about. But no, it really was my mother and the crew leader, and he was asking me what was the matter with me, and why was a 'nice, pretty girl' like me going on such long walks, and was I looking for something—and if I was, I could find it right at home, he'd make sure of that! I didn't answer him—not one word. I tried to catch my mother's face. But she wouldn't look at me; she was staring down at the floor of the car. I didn't look back at her anymore. I watched the cars coming toward us. It was then that the crew leader called me 'uppity.' He put his hand on my knee. I moved away. He said 'uppity.' That was the last word spoken on the trip back to Belle Glade."

She had, since then, broken off her friendship with Ed, and maintained without interruption her "uppity" nature—no matter what initiatives have been taken by various men. On that account, she became known as "strange." When she was twenty-one and still 'uppity,' her mother received an earnest, talkative visitor: the crew leader. He was, he took pains to make clear, a disinterested party. He worried about all "his people." Ruth was a particular puzzle and source of concern. She seemed so "man-shy," so reluctant to involve herself with "the other sex." The mother pretended ignorance, naïveté: really? The crew leader became talkatively explicit, the mother persistently evasive. Eventually the crew leader assaulted the pretenses they both had been keeping up. He told her that he was quite interested in Ruth, and intended to do something about that interest. If he were, yet again, rebuffed, he would not be able to contain his resentment and outright anger. He would take out his feelings on "other people." The mother said nothing, shook her head, looked at him for a second or two eye to eye, and lowered her eyes. She did not lift them until he had left. There was no farewell exchange. The crew leader simply turned and walked away.

Ruth had been peeking, listening in. She had heard every single word. She had caught the significance of every single stretch of silence—the faces, the eyes, the gestures of assertive-ness, of retirement and vulnerability. She had wanted to come storming out with a machete used to cut cucumbers. But no, she would not do so. Besides, the machete was dull, and what if she failed in her assault! She stood behind the door of her parents' bedroom, staring at the knife, imagining its use, paying close attention to what was happening in the next room. At one point her hand touched the door. (She recalled that moment vividly the next day.) She was ready to make her move and, if necessary, die. (The crew leader, she knew, carried a gun.) She had even started turning the knob, but suddenly had a change of mind: "I thought to myself that if I went after him, I'd be putting myself in his power. He'd have me arrested. He'd tell the sheriff that

I was a threat to him. Then the sheriff would ask him what he wanted to do; and he'd say that he didn't want to see me arrested or put in jail—just let go, in his custody! That's what he says to the sheriff every time one of 'his' migrants gets into any kind of trouble. He loves having a threat of jail to hold over us. He'd watch me all the time, and I'd become even more his property than I am now. I moved away from the door."

When the crew leader left, she charged out of the bedroom, crying and shouting at her mother. Why was she so quiet, so acquiescent? What was her obligation to the crew leader? Had she been lying to everyone—maybe even betraying her husband? The mother was surprised, hurt, but not without understanding. She told the daughter that there would never be a chance that she would speak back to the crew leader, speak up to him, let him know what she felt. She told the daughter that it was foolish for them to argue; they both knew the truth—and were turning on each other for lack of an opportunity to go after their real enemy. The daughter was impressed, but still quite suspicious: "I can't even believe my own mother, I realize that now. She is so tired and scared. She says whatever she thinks will give her five minutes of peace. When my father comes home with too much wine, my mother nods, agrees with his every stupid, crazy word—the crazy talk of a migrant wino. When my uncle tells my mother to come and help his wife because she's 'sick,' my mother goes over and feeds the children. She knows that his wife is selling herself for a few dollars in Belle Glade, but my mother won't try to stop her. Is that helping anyone? My mother has lost track of herself; she thinks of herself as someone's echo. It is too bad for her. And she is the one who tells me I am too proud, too independent. She is the one who tells me I can't afford to be like that. I can't afford *not* to be like that!

"I told her I couldn't trust her. I told her I didn't really believe she had been sleeping with the crew leader. It hasn't been her body that he has won; it's been her soul. (I'm sure that he'd have

gotten her body, if he'd wanted it!) She never disagreed with me.
She just tried to change the subject. She asked me if I wanted her
help with my clothes—to wash them. I said no, no help. My
mother has told me many times that the one thing a poor woman
can do, no matter how bad people treat her, is have children. I
wanted to tell her that day how disappointed in her I felt. I
wanted to say that I'd rather not have children than fool them
and lie to them. But I felt bad, thinking bad of my own mother.
I know what she has put up with. I know what my father does
when he's drinking. I know how hard she works. I've heard her
crying in the middle of the night. No one was supposed to be
listening. I was half-awake. I've heard the noise. I've thought I
was dreaming. It wasn't a dream, though.

"It was my mother, talking to herself, and talking to God. She
was asking Him when He'd treat us better. She was asking Him
what we'd done to deserve the treatment we were getting. Then
she'd sob and sob. Then she'd ask Him another question. It made
me want to cry. It made me want to go and sit with her and try
to be of comfort to her. She wouldn't have wanted me hearing
her, I knew that. I just kept still, still as could be. The next
morning she was smiling at us, and trying to be extra nice. She
cooked us the grits, and made the toast, and put a lot of jam on,
and told us we're lucky to be alive and to have the energy to go
out and work. She told us we had to thank God every morning
for keeping an eye on us, and looking out for our best interests.
She said we should never give up hope, and never feel sorry for
ourselves. It's a weakness, the ministers say, to feel sorry for
yourself. Of course, the ministers are doing better than we do.
They manage to live pretty good, as a matter of fact. They get
their prayers answered; we don't get very good answers to ours.
But I can't remind my mother of something like that. She'd start
crying right in front of us. She has, when I've spoken what's on
my mind in the past."

She was always the relatively candid one—at five, ten, fifteen,

twenty, and beyond. As a child she dared turn her back on the
foreman, the crew leader, the sheriff who swaggered into the
migrant camps, shouting at anyone around. As a youth she glared
at those same people. One grower in Virginia told her father that
she had the most hateful look he'd ever seen. She most certainly
had directed her utter contempt at him—the stare of someone
who would like to commit murder, but is afraid even to say a
word. As a young woman she got the reputation of a strangely
aloof, hard-to-figure person—unfriendly to just about everyone,
it seemed. She was called by some "the one without friends." She
had friends, but she argued with them, especially when the subject came up of crew leaders, foremen, and growers—the way
they treated migrants. She believed that her friends all too readily yielded to the power of others, though she was frank to
acknowledge, when pressed, that she had no plan or recommen-
dation that would make life any different for migrants.

When almost twenty-two and increasingly a "strange one" to
some of her former friends, she wanted desperately to get out of
the migrant life. The crew leader had given up being seductive
or sarcastic with her; he told her repeatedly that she was the only
one he respected in the entire migrant camp, and that he wanted
very much to be her friend. They began having talks, much to
the interest of the other migrants, who assumed an affair had at
last begun or soon would be on its way. On the way from farm
to farm, county to county, state to state, she sat beside him and
listened to his views, his beliefs, his strongly held and spoken
opinions. She began to feel a reluctant admiration for him and,
as a consequence, a sense of worthlessness about herself. Was she
behaving like a fool—falling for a "line"? Was she rather pleased
to be his favorite person; and was she kidding herself when she
insisted to everyone that there were no strings attached, that he
only "liked" her, and only wanted to have someone to listen
while he worked off his obvious spleen? She knew better than
to defend herself too strenuously. She had achieved, over the

years, a fine sense of ambiguity, a certain detachment, a capacity to smile at herself and even mock herself. She had no intention of getting caught in his corner by virtue of the requirements her conscience set for herself. She realized that if she kept apologizing to herself, never mind others, she would be lost, be his.

When he gave her several pairs of stockings for her twenty-second birthday, she told him there was no chance she'd accept them. She did not, however, want to lose him as a friend: "I know what's going on. I know what he wants. But he knows what I want: I don't want him! I want to get a job in some city and stay there, and maybe learn how to be a beautician. He owns some stores. He says he'll buy me a store, and set me up as a beautician. I laugh at him. He thinks I'm crazy for saying no. But I'm not going to become his mistress. He'll lose all interest in me, anyway, once he hears me say yes, suh, yes suh, Mr. Colored Boss-man. I've learned to enjoy talking with him. He's smart. He's been all over. He knows the world. And when the mood hits him, he can be friendly and funny—and not because of any designs on me.

"He'll sit there driving, and he'll remember his life. He was born as poor as anyone who ever lived. His daddy was a share-cropper in Alabama. The owner of the plantation would threaten to shoot him, and he'd get down on his knees and pray for his life. The crew leader says he'll never forget seeing his father on the ground, crying and begging. Later, the father gathered his kids and told them to leave—as soon as they're old enough. That's what the crew leader did. He walked away one day. He didn't say good-bye, even though he knew he'd never be seeing his mother and father and brothers and sisters again. He never has seen a single one of them either; he sends them money, but he hasn't wanted to go back to Alabama, and he doesn't want any of them going up and down the coast with him. I guess he stole a ride on the railroads and got to Florida somehow and got a job picking oranges. He did that for a year or two, and then he began to see that he was doing the work, but others were getting the money. He got friendly with a crew leader. The man had no sons, only two daughters. I guess he adopted the kid (he was about sixteen) and made him his partner. The crew leader took the man's name: John East. But I don't want to call him by his name. I don't want to call him John or Johnnie or Jack, or even Mr. East. He's been after me to do that. I tell him he's 'the crew leader' or Mr. Crew Leader to me, and that's that!"

She stops abruptly—as if to continue would undermine the firmness of her conviction with respect to the manner of addressing a particular person. She becomes abstract and impersonal when she resumes talking. She points out that one can be mean and deceitful some of the time, but decent at other moments. She points out that a man can apparently be quite prosperous and influential, yet have suffered rather a lot in his life. She points out that she is prepared to feel sorry for anyone—even a crew leader or a grower—if there's a sign of goodwill on the part of the person. The crew leader has shown her that sign, the gossip among the migrants notwithstanding: "He's a lonely man. He says so, and I believe him. His wife has bad asthma. She fights for her every breath. She looks weak and tired all the time. One of his sons got hurt being born, and his brain doesn't work right. He's in a state hospital, I think. Most people don't know he exists. The other son has asthma, like his mother. He has three daughters, and he never talks about them. Two have disappeared. The third is the one we see all the time—the bossy brat. He said he always wanted sons, so he could have some friends who are men. But he doesn't get on well with his son. He says he has no friends. He doesn't trust any man; and he's always got an eye out for a pretty woman, but after he wins her, she doesn't become his friend. He'll sleep with her, and then he can't believe a word she says. He thinks all women are out for money from men.

"I've never said I'm high and mighty. I've never bragged that

I don't want any of his money. He's told me that I'm a little crazy, and he wonders what my 'purpose' is, my 'angle.' I've told him I don't have any angle—except to get away from him and all the other people in the crew. I don't want to live the migrant life all my life. He says there's no way out, but then he admits that he got away from Alabama, and he knows some people who used to pick crops, who work in Palm Beach. He's promised to take me there and show me around. He says I could try to get a job in a restaurant. I could clean dishes. I could learn to be a waitress. I could go to a supermarket and try to get a job. They must need someone who's willing to work—somewhere. You learn to use your hands when you're on the road; you learn to use your legs, too. You learn to take orders."

She does not, however, want that kind of life indefinitely. Why move to Palm Beach, why risk Palm Beach, when she can be told what to do, where, and when as a member of John East's crew? The more time she spent talking with him, the more she came to realize that he was someone intriguing to her as well as a rather malicious and exploitative man. She would find herself thinking of him at odd places and times: at work, on the bus, while fixing her hair or tying her shoes. Once, while doing the last, she untied the two knots (only seconds before secured tightly), quickly took off the shoes, and scrutinized her mind's motives. She did so out loud, and her mother heard part of what was said. Later, Ruth tried to sort out her mother's words, her own, and, not least, her early-morning interruption of what had been for so many years an automatic act—shoes on, the last step in readiness for the fields: "I've been talking with the crew leader too much, I guess. Everyone is curious. Everyone can't figure out what is going on. They think I've given in to him. But at the same time they know I haven't. They're as mixed up as I am! They've been his 'children' for so long, they understand him as well as he understands them. They're on to him. They hear him talking a lot to me, and they're sure that he hasn't got me. If he'd got hold of me, he'd be silent with me. He'd treat me like dirt. That's the way he treats women. He throws ten-dollar bills at his wife. He throws them at his women. In his head, a ten-dollar bill means sex, or it means cooking the barbecue he likes.

"He never looks at women straight in the eye, face to face. He looks at their rears or their fronts or their necks. He likes to bite, I hear. That's all it'll ever be—that I'll *hear*. I'll never *know*—not unless I'm arrested and put in chains. He knows that. He told me he's given up on me. He told me I'd better watch out because I'm going to end up as his only real friend! I laughed and said he was trying to lull me, so he could get me! I keep my both eyes open all the time when I'm with him. I'll see the water in him boiling. I'll see him moving his hand toward me. I move away a little. He moves his hand back. I don't know if he's even aware of what's going on. I'm not sure I am either. One time I realized afterwards what had happened. Maybe I'm in a daze a lot of the time. Maybe I should think more about what's going on around me. Maybe I'm getting as confused as my father gets when he drinks a lot of wine."

She was referring to the casual personal authority she had achieved in her friendship with the crew leader. They had regular conversations; they enjoyed teasing each other or talking quite seriously about work or "life." Like members of a ballet company, each had an act of sorts, and occasionally the acts confronted each other—silently, with controlled emotion, subdued drama. Each of them had a sense of the other, and a sense of the other's sense: "I know what that crew leader is like; I think I know more about him than he does about himself. He doesn't trust anyone. All he knows how to do is push people around, boss them, cheat them, steal from them, trick them, be nice to them so they'll fall asleep, and he'll pounce on them. He's a cat, a big black cat, a cougar. He's smart, and he knows the jungle! The only reason he's spending a lot of time with me is because he can't figure out what will work with me. He's testing me; all the time he is. But he's finally realized that all he can do is talk, and then I'll listen, and I'll talk.

"If he moves his paw toward me, I push it back. I guess I have *my* paws! Maybe I'm a cougar, too! He told me that last week. He said I was a 'tough customer,' just like him. I laughed. He thought I might be 'softened up.' He put his hand on my shoulder. I chewed my gum harder. I made the noise I had to make. He pulled his hand away. I stopped chewing completely. He started telling me a funny story, and I took the gum out of my mouth and put it in a piece of paper. He was watching me out of the corner of his eye and driving too fast and looking at the crew through the rear-view mirror and doing his storytelling, all at the same time. I decided to test him. I opened the window and threw the gum out. I sat back and relaxed. I laughed a little louder at his jokes. Soon that hand was out again, trying to squeeze my shoulder. I took out a new stick of gum and worked real hard on it—and the hand went back pretty fast. I thought to myself: he's learned a lesson—the one thousandth one. He sure likes to learn his lessons!"

When she was twenty-two, she began to realize that there were also some lessons for her to learn. She had been asking herself some questions in response to questions put to her by the crew leader. She hadn't come up with many answers—only more questions and a nagging sense of uncertainty about her future. She began to feel "old," "tired," "wasted." All her friends were married and mothers. Her two younger sisters were also married and mothers. One of her younger brothers had a son and a daughter, the latter named Ruth, after her aunt. Meanwhile, the aunt was beginning to be called an "old maid." On her twenty-third birthday she was told by her father that she would never marry, that there was something wrong with her, that she should go talk with the Catholic priest and sign up with his religion, become a nun—the better to be fed, clothed, and housed. She thought seriously of doing just that—if only she could get paid, save up her salary, leave when in possession of enough money. She wasn't sure how much was "enough." She wasn't sure what she would do when "enough" became available. She only knew that she was indeed getting older and becoming withdrawn from her own family, from those once considered close friends—from everyone, it seemed, except the crew leader.

She despised him; she knew she did. At times when she thought of him her stomach rolled. She was sure she would vomit. At other times a headache came on and would not go easily. He asked her what was wrong. *You,* she thought to herself; but she knew that, bad as he was, it was not fair to saddle him with her life's frustrations. He was a slave owner, a slave driver, but she was, she increasingly said to herself, peculiar. She wondered why. She walked under the Florida moon and asked herself why. She talked to the citrus trees, the tall pines, the squat palms; surely they had answers for her. One evening her mother saw her walking, talking, staring upward, raising her arms. Ruth, poor Ruth! She *was* in bad trouble. Best to go toward her, touch her, hold her, console her, ask her those questions outright: Why doesn't she stop keeping herself apart, and when will she stop, and yes, isn't there a man who would please her, comfort her, make her *free?*

She would not easily forget her mother's suggestions, meant to be a plea for accommodation, for conformity—through marriage, or the politely worded equivalent used in the migrant camps all the time, "going steady." A week after her mother's evening approach, Ruth James was smiling at what had gone on and expressing her extreme scorn: "She tried to be my mother, and I guess I began to melt. I thought there'd be nothing left of me. I thought I'd become a puddle, and she'd wonder where I went. Then she told me I needed to be 'free,' and there was only one way for that to happen, through a man. I thought I was hearing things. I thought my mind was playing tricks—putting words into her mouth. I put my finger in one ear, then the other

—but I knew better. My mother has been patting herself on the back for years: she 'got' my father, and he brought her freedom! Boy, did he! I began to laugh. She told me to stop acting 'strange.' All the time I'm 'strange,' she told me. I wouldn't let her forget that word or the one she got me going with: 'free.' I said it was *strange,* the way she looked at her life, her *free* life: my father's beatings of her, the drinking that turns him into a madman. I said it was *strange,* the *free* time she has—working and getting no money, and moving all over, and living where we do. I told her it was *strange,* the way she pushes me toward men, but then later tells me she hates them.

"She would drink a lot herself a few years ago, and tell all of us girls that men are the devils, and we should stay clear of them. When the boys asked her what they could do to prevent themselves from turning into devils, she would tell them there was *nothing* they could do. They ran out of her sight when she said that word *nothing.* She was hissing at them. She was ready to claw them. She would start crying, and she'd swig the wine in, and she'd tell us it would be her wine against Daddy's wine, and she hoped she won. I asked her how we'd know who the winner was. She said that the dead one would be the loser. But she stopped drinking; and since then she has forgotten every word she spoke when wine went to her head and opened up the doors of the truth. She's buried the truth deeper than any roots of those orange trees go. She's buried the truth so deep that she doesn't know where she did the digging, never mind what's down there.

"That's why she doesn't understand me. She thinks I am 'strange'—when actually I am just being her daughter. She taught me what I know about men! She tells me now that I should love my father, I should respect him. I asked her if she loves him and respects him. She says yes, and I see in her eyes, even though it may be nighttime, that she means every word. She is in the hands of that devil she used to talk to us about. It is darker in her head than it is at midnight in Bean City or Pahokee. It is darker in her head than it is on a night when it's cloudy, and there's no moon trying to sneak through. The more she talks, the more I want to chase mosquitoes away. I slap them. I get them: blood on my hand, my arm, my bosom. She looks at me; she wants me to rush back into her arms, and say 'yes, Mother.' But I want to go running and never come back. I walk toward the irrigation ditch. I think to myself: jump in. What difference do I make to the world? If I died, there'd be one less 'migrant girl' around. The public health nurse calls all of us women that: 'migrant girls.' I almost have done it; I almost have slipped into the dark water, but I still have some fight in me. I tell my mother I am going to vomit, and I walk away."

Once after such a bad argument, she walked into Belle Glade; walked past the "loading zone," where each morning migrants are bid for by "publicity men," who shout the prevailing piece-work rates; walked up to the street that has bars, one after the other. She considered entering one, starting to drink, waiting for a man to join her, buy her wine and more wine. She hated the smell of wine, hated the spectacle of its power. Her father was one of many, she knew. There were few who shunned wine or beer altogether; in that respect, too, she was peculiar. Why not, though; why not plunge into a wine bottle, a beer can, rather than some irrigation ditch? Why not find out, once and for all, what her poor, ranting, crying, moaning, crawling, retching, shaking father must have felt. Had he not once, wiped out by wine, tried to grab her, assault her—screaming all the while that she "had to know," that she had to "join up," become "a true member" of his family? She, who was so aloof and self-preoccupied that alcohol seemed unnecessary, kicked the man, brought him to the floor, took his wine bottle outside, smashed it with a rock, walked away with her hand on her forehead—a headache. The crew leader had told her the next day that she was a "cruel bitch" who got her "kicks" by seeing others "down." She had never forgotten the comment; now that she stood motionless, but quite alive, outside a bar, The Long Night Lounge, the crew leader's face, his voice, his words came back to her. Did she want to knock a few people around, push them against the ropes, step all over them? Or was she, rather, ready at last to let someone try doing exactly that with her?

A week later she knew the answer to those questions: "I went inside that lounge, and I saw the world I'd been wondering about, off and on, since I was a little kid, and I'd see my daddy coming home drunk. He was drunk from the sun and the pain in his knees, 'picking drunk' we call it, and then he'd go and finish the job with wine. I knew from listening to him that there was something more than wine that got Daddy going. He couldn't stay away from those lounges. I thought it was the women, but after spending a few hours in The Long Night Lounge, I think I discovered why my father did his drinking in places like that.

"It's the darkness; it's the air conditioning; it's the music coming from that jukebox. It's another world—for those poor migrant people. All day they're crawling on their hands and knees, and sweating, and chasing away flies or trying to kill ants. All day they're hearing their own voices, counting the baskets or the boxes or the bags, counting the money—and knowing it won't really go to them. And all day they hear the crew leader or the foreman or the grower: keep moving, keep picking, stop loafing, stop wasting time, go, go, go, *let's go*. Then there's night, and in that lounge it was much darker than night. It was a delicious black. The lights in the ceilings were stars. The music—it didn't just sound good; it took you over. You forgot yourself, and you sang and drank. It was cold in there; I felt myself shivering. We're slaves of the sun. We're never free of the sun. In that lounge, the sun was an outlaw! I could picture my father there, and I was glad he'd gone there and all the other places! You can *sit* there; you can *stand* there; and no one to tell you to hurry up fast and get down on your knees and pick, pick, pick for the crew leader, pick for the foreman, pick for the grower—and for all those people going to the supermarkets. I felt the stools, and they were cold and smooth, and they felt good to my rear, as good as a beer to my mouth. I don't know why I left when I did. I wanted to stay there forever. I wanted to die there."

She left abruptly, one glass of wine and two cans of beer in her. She left after enjoying being by herself, then enjoying a long talk with a woman—who said, however, that she couldn't spend an entire evening without doing her "work," making some money. She left after having a talk with a man who wanted her to leave with him—and stay with him, he insisted, not for a night, but "for always." She was puzzled by his sense of time, his willingness to commit himself so quickly, so wholeheartedly. She asked him how much he had "taken in" that evening. He laughed at her derisively. She was asking the wrong question, "sweetheart" though she was. What mattered was his life; what mattered was how much of *that* he had "taken in." She was no stranger to tough living, so she laughed back at him, long and hard. She asked him a lawyer's questions, and got back a suffering defendant's reply. His wife and children had died in an accident. A bus full of migrants had plunged into an oncoming truck; there were a few survivors, but not any kin of his. He had not been on that bus because he had been in The Long Night Lounge all night, and had decided to take the following day off. Let "the woman" and "the small fry" go out on one of those daily jaunts. Let them sit in the bus, inhale the gas fumes, get bumped and jogged. Let them bring home their one-dollar bills, ten of them between six working human beings, if they were lucky—if, that is, the crew leader was in a generous, nonargumentative mood. He'd be there in the early evening, waiting for them with some hashed browns he'd cooked up and the streak-o'lean and the Cokes and all the bread and gravy any little or big mouth would want for itself.

When the sheriff came to his cabin, an hour or so before the sun set, the man contemplated running, but sized up his chances and stayed put. He was sure that the crew leader was going to have yet another "wino" migrant put behind bars for a day's drying out—the better to work during the next few days. But immediately the news was announced, and the man told it to Ruth James as he heard it, and she would never be able to forget his words—or the sight of him telling her about the sight of that sheriff: "He stared at the ceiling. I thought he was drunk. I thought to myself: Get away from this man; he's nuts. Then he looked at me and he told me: 'I lost my wife and my kids, all of them, in an accident. I'll never have another wife, and I'll never have any kids.' He stopped, and I thought he wasn't really telling the truth. My daddy would get so drunk every once in a while that he made up all kinds of stories. I figured this guy was doing the same. But his eyes kept looking at my eyes. Wherever I looked, he was there, following me. His lips were twitching. Then I saw his eyes fill up. He didn't really cry: no sobs, no noise at all—just the water coming out of his eyes.

"I've never seen anyone behave like that. He lost interest in me; he stopped talking; he stood there, the water coming and coming. I asked him if there was something I could do. He said no. He told me he would be spending the rest of his life in The Long Night Lounge—except for the picking he needed to do to pay for the wine. I think the grower gave him a hundred dollars to bury his family. He said he'd chosen the Lounge over his family that day, and now he had no family, so the Lounge was his wife and children. He asked me the strangest thing; he said he wanted to take me in his arms, if I'd let him, just for a few seconds. He said I was 'clean,' he could tell; and he didn't want to make me 'dirty.' He said I reminded him of one of his daughters—my nose and my chin. She was younger, but he could tell she was going to turn out 'clean.' I told him I really felt sorry for him, and I'd like to help him, but I didn't know what to do. I would have liked to hold him and hold him, until I'd squeezed all the sorrow out of him. He's too young to live the rest of his life like that. There won't be much more life, if he continues like that. He saw I wasn't going to hold him, unless he asked me again —and maybe started the tears flowing. I felt like a real 'tightwad.' That's what the crew leader calls me. But the man told me to forget what he asked of me. He apologized. He said he gets 'silly' sometimes. That was when I suddenly moved up to him and held him. I couldn't believe that I was there holding on tight to him in front of everyone. I didn't want to let go, either."

She stops, and takes a long time to resume. She lowers her head. She shakes her head. She lifts her head up high—her eyes seemingly reaching for the horizon. She comes back to her immediate situation. She begins to wonder out loud, rather than carry on a conversation. Why had she felt so close to that man? After all, she has been witnessing or hearing of tragedy for years. Her uncle fell into an irrigation ditch and drowned. Her two cousins died suddenly of a mysterious "infection." One of her brothers was killed by a migrant run amok with a gun. Two sisters died as infants. Her mother experienced several miscarriages. Her father had never really been sober for years. And there was more, much more—the stuff of her dreary, if not wretched, life. She was bewildered by what she had experienced.

The crew leader had always described her as "cool," but now she was alternately agitated and dreamy; and she was smitten, knew it, fought her feelings, couldn't banish them: "I sit here thinking of that man. He's probably out there working. I should be working, but I don't feel like it. I have forty dollars, and I'll just wait until it's gone, and then start with the beans again. That's what he does, that poor, poor man—pick beans. If I was in his shoes, I'd walk away from here and keep walking and not stop—ever. If it was God's will that I die, I'd rather die away from these migrant camps and these growers and crew leaders. I'll bet that if you get far enough from here, and walk into a town, you might meet someone friendly and helpful, and she'd give you a sandwich, and tell you where you might go get yourself a job. Then you'd be living a new life. Like the minister says, you'd be 'born again.' You can be 'born again' as a Christian, and 'born again' as a plain old person—a woman."

She adds to her sudden sexual qualification the other possible one: a man, too, can be "born again." She is thinking of "him." She never even thought to get his name! They were so close so fast; they seemed beyond the need for names. For that matter, she doesn't usually, in her mind, connect the crew leader to a name. The thought of the crew leader makes her feel even more upset and a touch wistful. Why hadn't she stayed longer at the Lounge? Why had she bolted, after getting so close to the man? Was that crew leader wiser than she had permitted herself to believe? Several years earlier he had called her, among other teasing names, a "bleeding heart." She had laughed, asked him what in the world he meant. He had told her that she worried about everyone else too much. The migrants, for example, who can take care of themselves, he kept insisting. She realized that there was one person she didn't worry about at all: him, the crew leader. He needed no compassionate concern from the likes of her; she knew that—and, in her heart, admired him for his independence and success, qualities she was at the moment in a mood to think about.

She began to look inward, more so than she ever had allowed herself to do: "Those two men are opposites. I don't mean that one has a lot of money, and the other has none. That's true, but there's something else that makes them so different. The crew leader keeps telling me he doesn't need anyone; all he needs is that his head works right. He says I'm like him, but he's wrong. I used to think he might be right, but in the Lounge I was beginning to lose myself, and I think I've still not found myself since holding that man. I've been praying for him. I've been wishing that God would take out some time from His busy schedule, and try to extend a hand to one of the most hurt people you'll find in the whole world. Of course, I know that God is very busy, so busy He can't mix into what we do here in this world. But the minister says we should pray, and maybe our prayers will be answered. I think if I'd stayed a little longer with the man, I wouldn't have ever left him. That's the difference between me and the crew leader. I'm not sure if I'm more upset because that man got to me the way he did, or because he's such a sad one and I feel sad for him. I think it's because he's made me worry about myself. It's selfish of me, but I have to be honest."

She caught herself, a day after the meeting in the Lounge, having a long fantasy—a daydream she then kept having for weeks, every morning upon rising. In her mind she returns to the Lounge. She looks for the man. He is nowhere to be found. She waits for minutes, which turn to hours. She asks after him. No one has the slightest idea who he is, where he might be. She decides to go find him. Perhaps she has mistaken the lounge where they met. She goes from bar to bar, but always the answer is the same: he is not there. She walks the street, rebuffs men strangers on foot or in cars. She sees a dog who looks at her knowingly. She bends down and talks to it. The dog begins to walk, and she follows. They cross the town, end up in the fields. They walk through rows of celery, cucumbers, peppers; reach the edge of a grower's land; approach his packing plant, where the produce is sorted, put into boxes, shipped off. Near a shed of corrugated metal the dog begins to bark, and suddenly the man appears—as if out of nowhere.

She asks him what he is doing there. He is silent for an unnerving length of time. Finally, the dog barks at him. She is grateful, and smiles. He starts talking. He tells her that he has decided to begin the new life he was sure she wanted for him—right there, as a worker on the conveyor belt, separating the good from the bad vegetables. Would she like to join him? She laughs, at first warmly, but then derisively. What gives him the idea that such a job will save him? He has no confident answer for her. All he can do is suggest that he will, at least, be standing up all day, rather than moving on his knees, and he will be under some shelter, and not beaten into a pulp by the demanding, exhausting sun. And he will be a long walk indeed from the bars. She is skeptical. Suddenly the crew leader, *her* crew leader, appears, orders the man back to work, asks her what she is doing there. She mocks him, calls him the big shot of the colored gypsies, sends him directly to Hell. At that point she is staring into his eyes, breaking the look occasionally to seek the man she'd met at the Lounge, but finding him, once again, nowhere in sight.

That is the end of her train of thought, her "story," she called it—a dream of sorts she kept experiencing, trying to forget, but for days found impossible to shake off. She also found herself thinking of the Lounge—not just the man she met there, but the place. Sometimes she would, in her thoughts, be standing at the bar alone, listening to music, sipping a beer. Other times there would be men nearby, though she was ignoring them. Still other times she would be sitting at a table talking to one of the "regular women." She put rather a lot of imaginative energy into those daydreams. Often they came upon her while she worked at picking; they were both visual and auditory in nature—and even, she pointed out, connected to the sensation of taste: "I'll be out in the field, doing my work, and I start with dryness of the mouth, and soon I can taste the beer. That worries me because it's something different. Before, I'd taste some Kool-Aid or orange pop or a Coke! But I go on to think about where I'm drinking the beer: at the Lounge. I'll be looking into the dark of the place, staring at the jukebox, most likely. If I had a lot of money, I'd buy one. I'd sit and play it all day long. Once the crew leader joked with me; he asked me what I wanted more than anything else. I told him a jukebox. He said he'd get me one—if. He never went further, because he didn't have to! I said O.K. I'm still waiting!

"When I'll be picturing myself looking at the jukebox, I'll hear my favorite music. I'll be hearing Nat King Cole. I love him. His voice is like a silk dress to your skin. His voice is the angels of God coming to you, telling you that you've made it and St. Peter is going to let you into Heaven, and no fooling. I like Elvis, too; he's different. He gets you going more. I believe he's not as relaxed as Nat King Cole. I'd rather go on a date with a man who's relaxed. But there's something to be said for the excited person, too; and Elvis just jumps at you and makes your blood get going, and you want to get yourself going and keep going. I think it's more than I know what to say—describing how music gets to you. But when I'm out there in the row of beans, filling up a hamper, I'll be listening to the music coming out of that jukebox in the Lounge, and I'll be seeing the place, and I'll be feeling the cold air on my skin. The only trouble is this: I'll see some beads of sweat roll down my arm, and I'll taste the dust, and that's not beer on your tongue! So I'm brought back to myself, and where I'm at."

A few weeks after she turned twenty-three she was brought even more forcibly back to herself, and to a consideration of where she was at. Her younger sister fell seriously ill, and within a few days died. The sister had kept saying that she wasn't feeling well, but had also kept working. It was the height of the harvesting season, and there were three children to feed and a fourth on the way. Suddenly, in the fields, she had a miscarriage and died. The entire crew stopped working, and refused to go back for two days. The crew leader had been told that the woman was not at all well, but had agreed all too willingly with her desire to work. It was not the memory of such an attitude that upset the migrants; it was a remark of his: "She died working; that's the best way to go."

Among the crew, Ruth James was least inclined to be angered by such a comment. She knew what to expect from the crew leader, knew him capable of only that line of reasoning. She angered already outraged relatives and friends by shrugging off the crew leader's statement: it was him and so what! She angered them all even more when she refused to take responsibility for her two nephews and one niece. She was angry herself: "I don't want to do it, and I won't be pushed. My mother has been caring for those kids anyway. She's the one who has been cooking for them because my sister would come back too tired. They're all trying to get me into a different life than the one I've been leading. They want me to work from sunup to sundown, then come back and be the mother of those kids and, pretty soon, marry their father. I know what's on their minds. I read their thoughts. I wish I could disappear. Since my sister died, I've spent more time than ever thinking about that lounge! But you can't live in a lounge. Even my daddy had to leave, and go meet the crops every day. I used to wonder if the wine in him ever stuck to the beans, so that the people who bought his hampers of beans got to eat them pickled. I could always smell where he'd been!

"I asked the crew leader what he thought about my sister's kids. He backed me up. He said that I have my one and only life, and I should be selfish, because if I'm not then I'll end up being a servant to everyone. As soon as he said that, I felt terrible. I wanted to go to my sister's grave and pray and beg her forgiveness. I wanted to go to her children and tell them I love them, and I'll always love them, and I'll never leave them. When I end up on the same side as the crew leader, I have to stop and think —well, I know I'm on the wrong, wrong side. But that's what a lot of the crew say; they say I'm a 'selfish woman.' They've been calling me that for a long time.

"The way not to be called 'selfish' is to let a man get you in his grip, and soon you're having his baby; and then you're having another one, and you're still picking the crops, and there are the babies to keep a watch on; and meanwhile the man is drinking away the money you make, or he's got a girl friend on the side, or he comes home and he sits there, and he's the biggest baby of them all: he wants to be waited on hand and foot, and if you remind him that you've been out in the fields and taking care of the babies, then he'll look at you and tell you that you're the mother and you're the wife, and you're supposed to do all these things, and that's what his mother did, and that's what your mother did, so no more talk. I know how I'm 'supposed' to live. I've heard my mother complaining that she must have forgotten to tell me my lessons when I was little because now I'm behaving like a rich white kid, and she doesn't know what to do. I told her the other day that there's a lot she can do. But she wouldn't want to hear from me what I think; she doesn't even want to hear from herself what *she* thinks. She long ago gave up having an idea for herself! The crew leader agreed with me when I told him that. It was another time when I felt I was becoming a bad person— and was on the wrong side, his side."

Her mother eventually eased at least some of Ruth's psychological burden. The three children remained very much with their grandmother. But in a way they would not stay with her completely; they began to haunt their Aunt Ruth, and she found herself walking away from home in order to be away from the sight of them. For a few days the adjoining fields were distance enough. But to walk the fields in the early evening, after having worked in them during the long, arduous days, was no joy at all. She took to walking along the sides of a road that leads into town. She would stand and watch the large trucks go by, taking the day's harvest north. She would look at the cars, observe their license plates, wonder what it is like to live in Wisconsin or Pennsylvania, New York or Massachusetts—and not be a migrant, coming and going, always just passing through and never feeling part of this or that town, county, city, state. She would go to a service station; buy a Coke; stand and observe the attendants filling up cars with gas, lifting their hoods, checking the oil, putting air in tires, water in batteries.

After a week or so she became a familiar figure, welcomed by the two black men who worked the evening shift—for a white owner. They asked her to come sit inside; offered her a cup of coffee; inquired about her place of residence, her work, her interests. She was talkative but discreet. She told them that there was "sickness" in her family, hence her need to "get away" for a brief spell each evening. They were sympathetic; each of them had learned what a serious illness can do to a home. They became attentive to her. They asked her if she wanted to hear any particular radio program. They tried to share their suppers with her. They offered her the use of the phone and, of course, the ladies' room. She would take nothing from them. For some reason—she herself found it "strange"—she would not even use the rest room. On her way home, if the need arose, she used the fields —no unusual alternative for her or other migrants. Perhaps she felt herself privileged—so she once speculated—at having a relatively luxurious, scented rest room to use when she knew her family up the road had at best a broken-down, foul-smelling outhouse. The point, after all, was to get away from her mother and father and nephews and nieces, not feel their presence all the more.

Within a month she was considered by the two service station employees a virtual necessity to their shift. They wondered what it was like before she started paying her visits. They would listen to the radio with her, talk about the sports news, discuss favorite music, pore over road maps, a favorite pastime of hers. She had never before seen a road map. The crew leader knew all the roads to everywhere, or so he said. She discovered some he hadn't mentioned; she discovered that there was an interstate highway system and a series of toll bridges which he carefully avoided. The two men told her why: to save money, to avoid highway patrols, to give gas or food business to trusted business friends who no doubt made various "arrangements" with him.

She stayed longer and longer at the station, and eventually expressed a desire to be of concrete help on a volunteer basis.

Why couldn't she help when it got busy? She had studied closely what the two men did and was quite able, she was sure, to make their peak work load lighter. They agreed. She started at the gas pump. She was quickly declared a "natural." She was fast, precise, methodical, polite, and certainly eager to please both the customers and her two friends. She referred to them as such— the first two adult friends she ever had. In no time she was familiar with the various kinds of latches that guarded the motors of cars and trucks. She was a virtuoso at plunging a metal object into an oil can so that its contents could be emptied into the hot, thirsty, somewhat threatened engines. She was agile with the batteries, able to unscrew and screw back the covers to the cells. As a matter of fact, she loved peering into those small dark wells, estimating how much (if any) water was needed. She was rather soon an adept professional at reading the various notches of the oil measurement rod, telling the customer what was or was not needed, and tending to the rest: the oil or the immediate, smooth closing of the hood.

The men wanted to pay her in recognition of her enthusiastic, competent help. She refused even the smallest sum. Yes, they could bring her a sandwich or two from home. Yes, they could get her Cokes, orange soda. Yes, they could feed money into the "snack" machine, and send her off with peanuts and cookies for her younger brothers and sisters. But she wanted to be known as a friend of theirs, who volunteered to take a burden off their shoulders. She liked the deference shown her by the men. She liked not being obligated to do anything. She liked being thanked, being complimented. She liked her independence. She liked the air of mystery about her involvement: the men were never sure she would show up or how long she would stay; her family knew where she probably was going, but they weren't certain either that she'd actually been to the service station when she came home—and they gained neither affirmation nor denial from her.

In order to make sure that no one—at home or at the station
—took her habits or commitments for granted, she skipped evenings, stayed home and collapsed in bed with exhaustion, or
walked in a direction that took her away from the gas station
rather than near it. She was especially anxious to keep everyone
guessing because she had known in her bones that the crew
leader would soon enough get word of her new activity. On the
day he did find out, he came looking for her in the fields; he
wanted to talk with her. She said no, not then. He said right then
and there. She turned her back on him, began picking beans with
a furious vengeance. He ordered her to stand up. She ignored
him. Her mother came over and urged her to relent. She ignored
her mother also. The crew leader stopped talking, looked
around, decided that he was not willing to force a confrontation
at that place and time. He left immediately. The migrants were
stunned; they had never seen the crew leader thus rebuffed,
challenged, ignored, frustrated. They began to assume that she
had something on him—an affair they were conducting. She
knew that would happen; she laughed and laughed when the
gossip got back to her—a matter of about an hour, under the hot,
harvesting sun.

Later that day she went for a walk, and was seen by no one the
rest of the evening: "I knew there would be trouble if I didn't
disappear. That crew leader doesn't back down without getting
mad. I think he knew he couldn't just hit me or fire me. I hadn't
realized, until that moment, that he really does have a soft spot
in his heart for me. He's been telling me that for a long time,
and I've been laughing and saying he's trying to trick me with
his phony compliments. I was sure he'd come to the house and
try to quiz me, so I decided to go away and stay away all night.
I was sure he'd speed to the station if I wasn't at home. My
mother told him the truth; I'd gone—to the station, she thought.
He left roaring his engine and making clouds of dust. When he
got to the station and was told I hadn't showed up, he didn't

believe the men. They promised to call him, but when they didn't, in about an hour, he showed up again.

"The men said no, no sign of me. He said he didn't believe them. They told him they would call him if I came there later. He got mean. He told them he was a friend of the sheriff's, and he could cause a lot of trouble for them. They thought he was kidding at first. They asked him what was the matter—with him. He told them they'd find out. He got in his car and was ready to leave, but suddenly he got out. He asked them which one was loving me up! They still thought he was kidding. They both said they were the ones—that I was in the ladies' room, hiding from him, and getting ready for some 'loving up!' He got out of his car, ran to the office, got the key to the ladies' room, went there. Of course, I was not inside. The men were laughing and laughing —they told me afterwards. They closed up at midnight, and were still laughing. They wondered what was going on. So did I— hiding in the woods, and thinking about the crew leader and the man I'd met in the Lounge and those two guys who have been so nice to me in the service station.

"I thought I should never go back. I thought I should start walking and never again lay my eyes on anyone I knew. I wouldn't miss my own family, I knew that. I wouldn't miss anyone. But I was afraid to go. I guess I didn't want to be *that* alone. I guess I knew I'd fall by the way and die. I didn't know how I'd die, but I knew I probably would. I'd be hit by a car. I'd be attacked and beaten and raped. I'd be arrested as a 'loose woman' by some sheriff and raped by him in his jail! That's what happens. The crew leader has told me many times what happens to women on the road, and he wasn't trying to be scary. He was telling me the truth. When I wasn't thinking those bad thoughts, I was fighting off the mosquitoes. In our cabin, the little kids attract the mosquitoes, so I get left alone. Out in the woods, I near went out of my mind. I used up my cigarettes. Then I tried to cover my face, but it was hot, and I couldn't stand it; I thought

I was going to suffocate. I kept dreaming I was in the Lounge. In my eyes I saw the sign: The Long Night Lounge. I dreamed and dreamed of being there, holding a bottle of beer in my hand —the cool air on my skin, instead of sweat and the ants and the mosquitoes buzzing and buzzing, and making me think I was going to scream and run toward Lake Okeechobee, and go swimming there. I'd have drowned because I don't really know how to stay afloat. Suddenly I was scratching my arms and my face and my legs—and I realized I'd been asleep and it was beginning to be morning."

She went home. It took her more time than would ordinarily have been the case. She kept thinking of *not* going home. She kept thinking of the Lounge. She kept wondering where the crew leader was. She kept asking herself if she dared go talk with one or both of the service station attendants. She knew where they lived, had heard them giving their addresses to customers who wanted daytime odd jobs done. By the time she arrived at the migrant camp it was virtually empty. She had dragged her feet and, in a way, achieved her purpose: more privacy. She was frightened, though. She had a sudden vision of the sheriff's car arriving; he would grab her, under threat of a drawn gun, and take her to his lousy, rotten, corrupt jail, where migrants get the hell scared out of them so that crew leaders and growers can, later on, talk about how "reliable" their "people" have become, and how nice that development is. For a second she thought she saw the sheriff's car approaching, but no, she was tired, and prone to "seeing things" when under a spell of terror.

But a moment or two later, as she was preparing herself a cup of coffee, another car approached her cabin, a large black sedan she knew rather well: "There it was. There he was. I knew he'd come. I think I'd dreamed in the woods that I'd gone home and his car was waiting. He was a little slower in real life! He came in without knocking. He is the boss-man all right! I didn't turn around. I was stirring the coffee, and I kept stirring. I decided to let him see my back for a while, let him see that I was not going to rush toward him and start begging, the way everyone else does. He sat down and didn't say a word. So I turned around. I didn't say a word either. Finally, he started talking. He asked me why I didn't offer him a cup of coffee. I started pouring some for him. Then he tried to be funny. He asked if I had some gas for his car. For a few seconds I didn't even catch the joke. Then I did; I said he could go over to the station, and the men would fill his tank up. He laughed. He said he wanted me filling up his tank. I said I won't—ever. He said I'm a stubborn mule, but I'm going to be broken by someone, so it might as well be him! I didn't even answer him. He went on with his smart talk. He told me I was headed for trouble. He said the owner of the gas station heard that the two men on the evening shift had a girl there, and they were taking turns with her. He's going to fire them both.

"I couldn't believe what I'd heard. I stared at him, and I said to myself: Kill him, that's what you should do, right now. I saw a machete of my father's—for cutting celery. I thought of picking it up and trying to stick it into the crew leader's chest. But I'm not a murderer. Nothing could get me to kill someone. I sat and said nothing. He told me I was going dumb on him, like I always do. He told me I'd better watch out because there were those two men and their jobs on my conscience. I went mad then. I wish I had killed him. Instead I threw the cup of coffee at him, and I got him in the face. I got in his car and locked all the doors. He came out and started trying to break in, but he couldn't. He screamed at me. He told me he'd kill me. He told me he was through putting up with me. He told me he'd rape the hell out of me, and then tell the sheriff to send me to jail for trying to steal his car—unless I got out. But I decided to take his car. I decided to try to run him over. That was a way to kill him, if he'd only oblige by standing in the middle of the road!"

She has tried to go on several times, but always stops talking at that point. She claims not to remember exactly what happened, though she does in fact know. She drove off. She turned around when she saw the crew leader in the middle of the road, shouting. She approached him slowly. He did not budge. She came nearer. Still, he stood fast. She swerved, avoiding him narrowly, stopped the car, got out, ran for her cabin, grabbed the machete, and stood near the door, sobbing. He came to the door, saw her. He did not push her. He moved back, hesitated, walked toward his car, drove off. The next day she was in the fields, working; he came up to her and she was friendly, and he decided to forget their nearly disastrous confrontation.

A week or so later he told her what had happened after she insisted that she didn't remember. He also told her that he was going to leave her two friends at the gas station alone. She thanked him, and found herself swearing that she would stop going there in the evenings. She was puzzled later on: why had she made that promise? Who was the crew leader to determine her evening activities? She decided that she feared him. He was the kind of person who would say that he intended to leave the two attendants alone, then secretly arrange for their arrest. He might even set up their murders. She believed him capable of anything. Best not to provoke him. Best not to jeopardize those two fine men. Best to keep working, keep teasing him, holding him off, yielding only slightly with a smile, an occasional friendly remark, a faintly suggestive joke, and, in the clutch, a firm no.

When she was midway between her twenty-fourth and twenty-fifth birthdays, she began to realize more fully how influential she was with the crew leader. He had stopped flirting with her. He had begun to talk to her about his business matters, ask her advice on what he ought do with his increasing reserves of money, confide in her his long-range plans for retirement. Almost every day he brought up something for discussion—to the point that she felt strangely let down when he abstained from such confidential business intimacies with her. He noticed her willingness to be friendly with him, supportive of him, during those exchanges. Occasionally he asked her why. She always denied any real sustained, explicit interest in his commercial affairs. She pretended naïveté, surprise, confusion: what *was* he trying to get at? But he knew that she knew that such was the case —that she was intrigued with his financial situation—and he knew that she knew that he knew.

One day he turned to her as they were driving north in his car, the crew behind them, all headed for the eastern part of the Carolinas: "I thought he was deep in thought and that he didn't want to talk. I'd put my head back on the seat, and was beginning to daydream, with my eyes closed. I was in the middle of remembering the gas station and my two friends there and the good times we used to have, when all of a sudden he started talking real loud. And what did he say? He said that he'd been thinking of taking a lot of cash he's hidden all over the place and buying a store, maybe, and a gas station—the one where I used to work. I opened my eyes and looked at him. I thought he'd read my mind. I wanted to say something, but I know him too well. The best thing to do when you're with him is to keep quiet and let him talk. He doesn't ever want to listen to me—or anyone else. He wants to go on talking and have me nod and say yes, yes, yes, every few minutes. But this time he was watching me, and I knew he wanted me to say something. I told him he would be making a big mistake. I told him he's got all the cash, so why take it and risk losing it! He smiled, and said I was 'real nice' to be thinking of him and his money. I said I didn't care what happened, either to him or his money. I was saying what I felt! He laughed. He started moving toward me. He always gets turned on when I get tough with him and tell him he means *nothing* to me. I moved away and told him to cut it out. He did.

"He shut up for a while. I got nervous. I never trust his silences. He's up to some mischief when he stares and stares and does that coughing of his. We pulled into a gas station, and he didn't fill up the tank himself. He went to the pump that the attendants use—for old people who don't know how to help themselves. I heard him talking. I heard him tell the man he'd bought a station in Florida. I heard him tell the man it was a Shell station, and it was in Palm Beach County, but to the west, near Belle Glade. I couldn't believe what I was hearing. I figured he was trying to play one of his games with me. Oh, he's the clever one, that crew leader! In my mind I had a terrible thought; I saw that machete of my father's, and I saw the crew leader driving and then stopping to relieve himself, like he does, in a deserted place, and me saying I had to go do the same—and then I could place the machete right inside him, between his shoulder blades. He'd fall to the ground, and I'd walk away and drive away, and that would be the end of him. No one would ever find out who he is or what happened to him. He's always so anxious to make sure that people don't see us drive off together. But everyone knows I drive with him, so I guess they would find out if I did anything. I guess I'd have to disappear."

She had those thoughts as he talked and talked with the gas-station owner. She decided that the crew leader was not "fooling around"—after observing his earnestness, his obvious familiarity with the business issues a gas-station owner must face. She was convinced that he had indeed purchased that gas station she had come to like so much. And he was up to something in that regard, so far as she was concerned—she knew that as she sat there, waiting for him to finish his increasingly self-important line of inquiry; waiting for him to come in and—she could visualize it —give her his sidelong, knowing, smug smile; waiting for him to edge closer and closer to the subject of her and what she might want to do; and, yes, waiting for her own reaction, which she could never really anticipate or take for granted.

She knew the futility of planning a conversational response in advance: "I will say something to myself, but then I won't follow my own advice. Sometimes I get scared of him and I want to cover up how I feel, so I talk a lot and he pays attention to what

I'm saying, and he overlooks *me*—my body. Sometimes I hate him so much, I don't say a word—because one word would lead to another, and I'd be in trouble with him. I don't want to have him an enemy of my family's. He wouldn't stop with me; he'd go after everyone I know. I guess by now I have to believe that he won't ever really turn on me. He's told me that I'm his cocaine. He used to snort it—lots of white stuff, lines of it. I don't see what I do for him! I just sit and listen; a lot of the time I tell him he's wrong; and I won't let him touch me! But he seems to get high on me!

"When he came back to the car he told me: 'I've bought that gas station you liked so much. It's a present for you.' That's what he said! I decided to ignore him. I'd heard him bragging. I figured he was setting me up; he likes to do that. But I know him and don't fall for his tricks. I was cool. I wasn't going to nibble on his bait. I wanted to make him sweat. I wanted to show him that he could buy the entire United States of America, and there I'd be, Ruth James, sitting in his big, fat, air-conditioned Cadillac, and listening to my Nat King Cole tape, and pouring salt over his every word, and not being in the *least* impressed. When he told me what he'd done, I just said to him: 'Is that so?' I didn't even look at him. I kept my eye on the road. I can remember that a big truck went by; I counted six Fords on the truck going to six lucky customers. He began to shout. He said I hadn't heard him—that he'd bought a gas station for me, and it was the one I liked and worked at. I decided to be a little funny; I said: 'That's a good start, but I'd like two or three more, and when you get them, I'll look them all over at once.' He didn't say anything after that for a minute or two. He stepped on the gas—was he *angry!*—and kept speeding down the road. He put off my music and put on his stupid station with the weather and the farm news. I sat back and closed my eyes and decided to pretend I was taking a nap.

"My eyes were closed tight, but I was dying to see his face.

I peeked without being caught. He was puffing on that cigar. He
was mad. If he was white, his face would have been as red as the
tomatoes we pick. Suddenly he pulled the car over to the side of
the road. He put off the motor. He stopped the radio. I was
scared. I decided not to open my eyes. That was the last straw.
He screamed and screamed at me. I only can remember some of
his shouting: 'The trouble with you is you're a damn fool. You
think you're so great. You're in the gutter with all the migrants,
but you're trying to act like an uppity nigger. Where did you get
such big ideas about yourself?' There was a lot more! Then he
started threatening me. He said he could throw me out of his car,
and let me try to find a place to live or work. I'd be arrested as
a 'traveling colored whore.' He said he could push me into some
irrigation ditch. He said he could talk to his friends, the sheriffs
he knows all over, and see that I get arrested and kept in jail. He
said that he could 'take' me on the spot. It was high time! Why
not? Who did I think I was, the Virgin Mary? Better now than
never! Oh, he went on and on—trying to scare me, and laughing
at me in between while he caught his breath and thought up new
bad things to say."

Meanwhile, she sat still; sat frightened; sat staring out the
window at the cloudy sky; sat wondering what would happen—
running the various possibilities through her mind. She decided
that she had only one weapon, only one chance of surviving this
worst wrath of the crew leader she had ever witnessed: a continuing show of calm and, yes, a studied indifference to his threats
and blandishments. So she kept still; conjured up in her head the
smooth, silky, sexy songs of Nat King Cole; and wondered what
it would be like, seeing him, hearing him sing, getting to know
him. Finally the tirade ended. The threats stopped. All words
ceased being spoken. The motor started; the Cadillac moved
forward slowly—no roar to the engine. The radio came alive
and, after a couple of buttons were punched, her kind of noise,
not his, filled the car.

She gave him a quick glance, meant to be seen by him, and he told her quietly, in a matter-of-fact conversational tone, what he had in mind: "He told me that he would like it, if I went to the station and worked for him—as the manager. He said he knew he'd make money on the deal because the station is located in a good place—a lot of tourists go by, and trucks and salesmen. I told him he already has a lot of money, so he shouldn't be worrying himself about making more—and more and more. He said that people who talk the way I do never make any money. He said you have to fight to get ahead, and then you have to fight to stay ahead. I told him I got tired, hearing him talk like that! He said I was a typical migrant, headed nowhere except for one thing. Well, I could see the vanity written all over his face. I beat him to the punch. I said he thought he was Mister Big, but he had a lot of sins on his record, and God was keeping track of them. He laughed, and said that anyone who listens to those preachers is a damn fool. I asked him why. He said he slips a lot of preachers a ten-dollar bill and tells them to get his crew drunk on God; it's cheaper for the crew and better for them than wine, and they work harder the next day.

"I stopped talking then. I thought to myself: he thinks *he's* God, that's the trouble. But I don't have to kneel down and pray to him. He's just a two-bit, conniving crew leader, trying to bleed a hundred people dry and thinking he's Jesus Christ Almighty. So long as I can see the difference between a crew leader like him and the Lord, I'm in the running to be saved. So long as I think it's those ten-dollar bills that I'm after and I'll do anything to get them, then I'm headed for Hell, I know it. I kept thinking like that, and he kept talking about money and the United States, and how the only way you get respect from people is through your wallet, and how he wanted to give me a chance to fill my pocketbook and get some first-class clothes and be important. I didn't answer him. I didn't say a single word for a long time, and I began to wonder if my tongue was tied. He kept asking me questions, and I just stared at the trees or the sky. Then, all of a sudden, he switched his talk. He *begged* me! I couldn't believe it! I thought: This man has gone and lost his mind, and he may never find it! I told him to stop talking like he was talking. I told him he couldn't win me over to his wishes that way. I only wish my family could have heard him! They wouldn't have believed he was that crew leader! He sounded like a whining dog, crying because its supper wasn't around.

"Well, he stopped talking, finally. I was ready to ask him to put the brakes on and let me out. I told him that I thought his nerves were in a real bad way, and he needed some good tonic. He said I was right, and he was sure the gas station was just what he needed. I couldn't see how the gas station was going to get him any better; I asked him how. He said he'd have fun, just knowing he was collecting money from all the traffic in the Lake Okeechobee part of Florida; and he'd have fun thinking of me behind the cash register. I told him to forget the whole idea and go get himself a good doctor. He could take some pills, and they'd make him feel good again. He said he'd go see a doctor when we're back in Florida. Then he stopped talking. I put that radio back on, fast."

Several days later she simply assumed that she would eventually work in the Florida service station. She had never said yes. She would never say yes. That was how things worked between her and him; they drifted into agreements, ended up living by them, unstated though they were. She had never agreed to ride with him all the time, as the crew moved from state to state. She had never agreed to let him buy lunches or Cokes or cigarettes. For a while, when they were traveling together, she carefully kept her fingers away from the radio push buttons. Who was *she* to presume to use them? But he would casually ask her to change stations, and soon she was doing so on her own. He would casually ask her to go have a cup of coffee, and soon she was eating with him regularly. He would casually ask her to ride with him between place X and place Y, and soon she had forgotten what it was like to sit in a hot, crowded, bumpy bus, or be herded into a truck like an animal and driven for hours and hours with no stop so that the smell of gas fumes and road dust and sweat and urine and feces was all one smell—"the migrant people's smell," she called it once when comparing the Cadillac she took for granted with the other vehicles she had come to know over the years.

In fact, she would one day acknowledge, as soon as the subject of the gas station was mentioned, she knew deep inside that the crew leader had indeed bought the place with her in mind; and she knew, too, that she would end up working there: one more casual adjustment of sorts between the two of them. Yet there was something rather special about this particular moment in her life—in their life together: the enormity of his deed, of the opportunity she realized full well was being extended her. Not for the first time in her life she became introspective, ethically concerned, philosophically alert: "I couldn't eat a thing. We stopped at one of those favorite spots of his, where they know him and pile on the toast and eggs and grits and ham and coffee. I just had a Coke. He couldn't understand what was the matter with me. He told me *I* was the one who had a bad case of the nerves, and *I* was the one who should go see a doctor. I told him he was right; but I would be my own doctor. That's the best way: talk to yourself, and find out what's the matter with you! I left him to his piles of food; I went for a walk. I saw two birds, sparrows, I guess. One would fly to the branch of a tree, then the other one would. But they never got too close. And sometimes one would go off, but the other wouldn't follow. I thought of the crew leader and myself. I guess we're a pretty strange couple!

"A lot of people just assume I'm with him; I mean, they assume I'm his girl friend. I don't care. They can think what they like. It's what *I* know that counts! And what God knows! The smarter people can see that we're not just a pair of lovers—him the boss-man and me his young favorite in the crew. They probably think I'm a little strange. I guess I *am* strange. So is he! Why does he put up with me? What does he see in me? I don't understand him! Up until now I thought I could read him as clear as could be: He was trying to break me down, step by step. But when he bought that station, I got all shook up. He knows by now that he isn't going to get anyplace with me. He's waited and tried and tried. Maybe he thought I would give in—because of the size of the 'present.' But he could tell by my reaction that I won't. And I won't! He could offer me the sun and the moon and all the stars on a big plate of solid gold, and he could buy me a Cadillac with everything in it and give me a man to drive me around, a chauffeur, and I'd still say no to him if he tried to approach me with his wiles. Those wiles of his—they turn me off. I don't like him. He's a bad person. Why do I spend so much time with him then?

"I kept asking myself that until I thought I'd lose my mind. I decided that I like my 'creature comforts,' the preachers call them. I decided that I like his attentions. I like him to be nice to me, even though I get angry at him and show him my disgust for the way he tries to win me over. I'm selfish, that's the explanation. My mother says I don't want to get married and have children because I'm always thinking of myself. She may be right. I think I'm like the crew leader. He's always thinking of himself. But my father is the same way—with all the drinking he does. And my mother used to tell me that she wished a lot of the time that she never was born, or that she never agreed to be my father's wife. She wished that she never married anyone! She said she used to have dreams that she was a singer in some lounge someplace. That's a selfish dream!

"I'd like to be a singer myself. If only I could sing! But who can figure out what life is all about! I try, but I fail. I just don't know what the best thing is for me to do—the *right* thing. I pray to God and ask Him, but He hasn't the time for me. I don't hold it against Him! But I keep on asking. I tried and tried to figure out whether I'd go along with the crew leader, and leave the migrant life, and manage the gas station of his. I asked myself so many questions that I began to wish I could drink a lot of wine, like my father does. That was a bad sign, and I knew it. So I stopped. I decided that too many questions leave you with too many doubts. The only thing you can do is pray to God and go and try to be true to your own nature. I think each person has a *nature,* and it's up to you to find out what kind of nature you have and then go and follow your nature—let it be, I guess I mean to say. When the crew leader offered me that job, he was testing my nature; I'm sure of it. He didn't know what he was doing. I'm sure of that, too. But my nature was aroused, and I did what I had to do."

Her psychological determinism was the prelude to a dramatic material shift in her life. She allowed herself to be driven to the gas station. She allowed herself to be shown around—as if she needed to be! She allowed herself to be told what had to be done and what the business details were of a rather profitable "operation," as the crew leader called it. She allowed herself to begin showing up for work—to take charge, actually, of the gas station. After a while any other life was, for her, unthinkable. She moved her two friends to the day shift, so that they could spend more time with their families. She gave them substantial pay increases. She paid the evening employees well, too. She took little for herself, however, thereby confusing and angering her crew leader boss or friend or benefactor or would-be suitor.

She knew the various possible ways to think of him—and herself. When she had turned twenty-five, she was reflective enough to think about every facet of her involvement with a man she referred to as "the him" of her life: "I have my place to live. I feel like I'm rich, having an apartment and knowing I won't be leaving it in a few weeks or months. My back is feeling good— no stooping all day out in the fields. I use the repair truck to drive around; it's my car! I guess I could go buy a fancy automobile.

He would have bought me one, if I'd asked. But I don't want his presents. I don't even want to buy myself any presents! I love the work, and I like sitting in between the time the cars show up —sitting and talking with my friends. They asked me about him; they did right away. I don't know what to say—he's the him of my life, I guess. I used to think I had him around my pinky finger. But I'm beginning to realize that he's got me in the palm of his hand—like he says of everyone else!

"What if he decided to sell the station? What if he lost interest in me? What would I do then? My mother says the crew leader is an evil man, and he's put a spell of evil on me. She doesn't believe that I've never had anything to do with him; but because I say I haven't, she thinks my head is all mixed up, and it's because of the bad spell he's caused me. My father wants money each day for his wine. I give him nothing. I tell him the truth— that I don't make a lot of money. I don't want a big salary. I just want a bed to sleep on and Cokes and a hamburg—and air conditioning. I love to be cool. I have a unit in my apartment, and he put one in the station, where we sit. He said it makes 'good business sense' because we're rested and feeling good when the cars drive up, and we do better with the customers.

"To be honest with myself, I think he wanted me to like the work—that's why he put the air conditioner in the station. He's afraid I might walk out on him. His daughter did. She ran away, and no one has heard of her. She wrote a letter a year afterwards to her mother, and told her she was working in some bar near Miami, but not to come because she'd be leaving soon with a man, and she'd be in New Orleans, and they'd both be 'working.' Well, that's his blood she's got in her! The daughter probably has high-class customers, and she makes a lot of money, and that's all that counts—to him! There is another daughter, a little one they adopted; and she's got an injury to her brain. She keeps the wife company. I guess I keep him company! He says he has no family; but I know in his mind he thinks of me as his family.

I've lost my family. They go on the road a lot; and when they're nearby they stay in the camp or they're out in the fields, picking and picking. And I'm here, living my life that's so different from theirs.

"I guess he's my family. He's still a crew leader, though. He goes 'on the road.' I was glad the first time he left—after I started at the gas station for him. But then I got to missing him. Even the two guys, my friends—even they didn't make up for losing the crew leader. That's when I knew he'd come to mean a lot to me—a strange thing it is. I don't think he even wants to touch me anymore; though, if I gave him the idea that I wouldn't mind, he'd be at me in a second and on top of me in two seconds. That's him! He's just a crooked crew leader, like all the rest. But with me he becomes like a bad little boy sometimes. He told me the other day that he wished I would go on the road with him, and let my two friends run the station while he's away. I told him I *am* on the road; I'm living on the road, just like before—working on cars instead of the crops! I'll never leave the road. It's my life."

She had made an accurate prophesy. Years later, in the middle 1970s, she would still be, in many respects, the person she had become a decade earlier. She would be a "success" as migrant people go—the one person in her family to live a settled, reasonably prosperous life. Not that she ever sought luxuries. There has always been a puritanical side to her—as if the suffering of her kin, never far removed from her sight, exerts its continuing hold on her. The crew leader, on the other hand, has influenced her enormously in ways neither he nor she acknowledges easily. She has never "given in" to him; yet she has never stopped being the person he most likes and trusts. Perhaps, as she well knows, there is a connection between those two existential and emotional facts. Even as she has rebuffed him, she has become, like him, a careful manager of a relatively flourishing enterprise. She watches the cash; supervises the daily rhythm of things; proves herself a competent, energetic, strong-willed person. And, over the years, she has become, like him, a loner. Her friends are her employees. She has shunned any and all would-be suitors. Occasionally she has gone to various lounges, only to leave in a mixture of nostalgia, aroused romantic emotion, and disgust—all of which she finds, later on, hard to contemplate, never mind talk about with someone else.

On her thirty-fifth birthday, in 1976, she looked back and forward: "I've had a lot nicer life than I ever thought I would. Some of my cousins, my age, are becoming grandmothers. They're also sick, and it looks like they might not last. I've already seen too many people of my age buried: the bad, bad migrant life. I get up and I say to myself: Ruth James, it could be a lot worse! I like my work, and I'm grateful to him, very grateful. He knows it—that I thank him a lot in my thoughts— but he doesn't really want me to say it. He told me the other day that he was signing over the station to me—that it's mine. I told him I didn't want it. He said that was why he was signing it over to me! I guess that settles it—my life. I'm glad, mostly."

part

TWO

MOUNTAIN DREAMS

"I believe that on my deathbed, when my soul is leaving my body and preparing to meet God, I will be having one of those dreams I've had, on and off, all my life. I do believe that." She always added that shorter, four-word affirmation—as if a long one, in and of itself, won't quite do. As for the particular dream she was referring to then, she did not hesitate to report it in full—as she had been doing for years, long before anyone appeared claiming to know the various meanings dreams may have: "A long time ago, about the time I was bearing my first daughter, I had a dream like the one I had last night. I told my husband what the dream was, and he said it must be the baby inside me, causing the dream. But I don't have a baby inside me now, and I'm still having the same dream. I guess it's my mind repeating some message, over and over again. Last night I had the dream; then I woke up and I sat on the side of my bed, and I could see the whole dream a second time.

"I was walking up a path, one of the ways to get to the top of the hollow. I heard a noise; it was my dog, chasing a fox, probably. Then I looked up a tree because I heard a woodpecker, working away. It was dark. I saw the moon, but clouds came and covered it over. I got scared; I don't know why. I wished I wasn't alone. I wished my sister Pauline was with me. But she died a long time ago; she was fifteen and I was sixteen. She had something wrong with her heart, and she had more and more trouble breathing, and they didn't know what to do; and one morning I got up, and she seemed cold, and I looked at her face, and I realized she wasn't breathing; and I knew it right at that moment that my sister had left me. We were like twins. We'd always slept in the same bed. I felt as if I'd died, too. She comes to my mind a lot during the day—when I'll be sewing or cooking or washing clothes. We used to do so much together. But I don't usually see her at night in a dream. In this dream, when I was standing there, looking at the sky, and wishing that the moon would show up again, and feeling a little scared, my sister Pauline's voice came to me. She said I'd be all right. Then I saw her face in the sky. It was strange. I think I began to run up the hollow, and I fell in a ditch, and there were dead bodies there—people and animals both. That was when I woke up."

She named her first daughter Pauline, and became quite attached to her. Sometimes her daughter figured in a dream. The worst one has never been forgotten. Five years after it took place the dreamer seemed able to recall every detail: "I can't shake off that dream; it is like a devil, hunting me down. When I'll be tired, and sitting and holding my head in my hand, all of a sudden it'll come upon me, the terrible time I had that night. I woke up, and my husband was holding on to me and shouting my name, loud as he could: Hannah Morgan, Hannah Morgan. I kept saying no, no, no—that's what I remember on my tongue when I woke up. The more he called my name, the more I said no. I'd just taken his name, of course. Maybe that was the reason for all my no's. I suppose I still thought I was Hannah Cable. But I've never been able to forget the way he was so nice to me, Tim— the best husband a woman could have. He quieted me down, and he told me I'd be all right, and he got me some milk that he'd warmed up, and he gave me a biscuit, and I began to think I was *alive*.

"Sometimes I'll not be feeling too good and I'll want to go to bed, but I'll sit there on the edge; I'll be tarrying along, keeping my head from touching the pillow, and Tim will know what's in my thoughts; he'll tell me not to worry in the least, because if God should send me a message in the middle of the night and it turns out to be a bad message, then there's no need to feel alone. And I don't; I know Tim is a good man, and he loves me, and he would die to keep me and the kids safe; and he works so hard, and when he comes home and his face has the coal dust on it, and I remind myself what he's done all day and where he's done it, then I want to cry. I want to cry for him and not myself. The trouble with me is this: I cry too much for myself, and that's no good. I should stop worrying about *me*. I should stop having those dreams.

"The one that was the worst took place up the side of the mountain over yonder. I was trying to cook supper—a nice dream: the potatoes boiling, and I had the bowl before me, and my masher. I was looking at the milk I was to add, and then I left the house; I don't know why. My sister Pauline came toward me, my dead sister, and she was holding my baby, Pauline. I couldn't see them too clearly; the morning fog was on them, I thought. I had to leave, anyway. I don't know why; I just had to keep moving. Maybe I was running from them. Then the trouble started, bad trouble. Some hawks kept following me. I'd look up, and they were circling, circling. I thought: so what! But they came closer and closer, and then I felt I was a field mouse, maybe a chipmunk, and they wanted me real bad—and they were going to get me. I saw them right above me, and I kept running and screaming, and I got away.

"I wish I'd woken up then. Instead I ran and ran, forever it seemed, into another dream, I guess. I was nearer that mountain, and I was tired, and I stopped, and I sat down near a tree, and it suddenly fell over—away from me. But I was scared. I felt as if nothing was working out in my favor. I felt as if I was headed for more trouble whatever way I turned. I tried to head for a road I could see, but it was too hard to get through the bushes. I turned back. I started to pray to God to come and take me. It's better to die than suffer and suffer. That's what my mother used to tell me. While I was praying, I looked up, and I saw smoke coming from the mountain, and then it happened: the trees started falling, all of them, and a river began to pour down from the mountain toward me. I could see the water headed my way. And in the water were pigs, hundreds of them. They'd fallen in, I guess. They were snorting and bumping into each other. The river was full of them—a river of pigs! I thought I was going to drown. I saw the pigs drowning. Then I saw one pig, and its face began to look like my own! And another pig—its face began to look like my sister Pauline's face! I think I saw her lying on her bed, dead. I began to scream. That's when I woke up, and Tim was holding me. I was crying. I was shaking. I was afraid. I don't know what I was afraid would happen. I was just afraid. I think I'm afraid a lot during the day, even when I'm not having a bad dream, or any bad thoughts either. I start shaking; that's how I know that I'm afraid. But I can't find for myself what it is that has me sweating and feeling so jittery. It's a mystery. But my mother always told us: 'Life is a mystery, and if you think you've solved the mystery,' she said, 'you're in real trouble.' "

She doesn't usually describe her everyday life as mysterious. Rather, she seems all too aware of what each day holds in store —and why. She is a woman who was born in Harlan County in eastern Kentucky, of Scotch-Irish yeomen stock. Her roots in Appalachia go back many generations, "a long time," she says, or "over a hundred years, for sure." She was born in a cabin halfway up a hill, lived there almost exclusively, save for bus trips to a one-room schoolhouse located "beyond the hollow, some."

When she turned ten she stopped going to school; too much needed doing at home. She was her mother's first daughter and had become, in a decade, an exceedingly important person in the household. She remembers the day her mother told her there would be no more bus rides: "I used to like the trips; it was a chance to see the outside world. Until I rode to school, I'd never stepped foot outside our hollow. I was born here, and I will die here, but it's nice to go and see a few other places in the county. (I've never been outside Harlan County; I don't expect to travel that far, ever.) One morning, early, my mother took me to her and told me she needed me to stay home and be at her side. I was happy. I said I was glad to do anything she wanted. She held me close and said thanks. I remember feeling real good the rest of the day.

"But at night, in bed, I felt sad, and my eyes became all filled up, and I didn't know why. My sister Pauline saw my face, and she wiped my tears away. We went to bed holding each other close. I think she knew me better than I knew myself. When she died I was afraid I'd never know myself at all, because only she had the answers to what I'm like! That night, while she held me and cleared my cheeks of tears, she told me I'd see more of the world later on—when I got married. I guess she knew I was just feeling sorry for myself at losing those two bus rides every day, Monday through Friday, in the early morning and the middle of the afternoon. I think I didn't want to admit to myself how keen I'd been on riding off. My father wasn't one of those people who had a car."

Mention of her father prompts an abrupt halt to her reminiscences. She stares outside; a strong wind hurries through the woods, pushes branches aside, shakes the cabin a bit, as if to let it know that a bit more force and there would be trouble indeed. Her mind goes from the temporarily distracting wind back to her father, who had his own problems with the air: "He died fighting to fill his lungs up, but they wouldn't work, I guess. He had a sickness in his heart. My mother would tell me that when she married she knew he was in trouble. He worked the land hard, but he'd get pale, and he panted and panted. He laughed it all off, though. He said he had enough strength to live until a hundred, but not much more. He was thirty-seven when he died, and it wasn't too far after Pauline died, and we've never stopped missing either of them.

"The last day was terrible for my daddy. We had him sitting up, and we wished we could grab air, like you do water, and feed it to him, one scoop after another of something to breathe. He was fighting to talk to us as well as catch his breath. He wanted to be heard, I guess, for the last time. When he couldn't find the air to speak, he got red in the face, and we feared he'd go. So we tried to talk for him. My three older brothers knew what he wanted to tell them, anyway. He wanted them to go work in the coal mines. He knew they all couldn't stay up the hollow and try to scrabble off the land. There's not enough land to feed a large family. We were getting poorer and poorer. You have to make some money and around here there's less and less to do. My father was supposed to go down the mines, but the company said his lungs were already bad because of the illness he caught when he was a boy, so he'd better stay away. He always told us, before he got worse and worse, that God had been kind to him—getting him sick with the illness that made his heart skip and keeping him out of the coal mines. His older brother got killed in an accident down a mine. His younger brother got hurt bad, the same way. But they made good money while they could, and Daddy tried the best he could to make us a living out of the land we had. And it was very hard on him and on my mother, too."

She remembers hunger vividly as a child. She remembers chronic, widespread unemployment. She remembers a hand-to-mouth existence even after the Second World War, when the rest of the country seemed headed for lasting good times. She remembers, as a matter of fact, the first time she tried to make sense of all that—a region's continuing sadness and suffering: "I think I was born to accept trouble; but I've never liked it, and I've always wondered why some people live such tough lives and others have it easy. I was about five when I asked my mother that question. I think the war had just ended. I had an uncle who came back; he was shot up. He wanted a job, and there was none. He said he was leaving to go live in Cincinnati. Everyone was upset. They said he should stay. I recall my grandmother crying. I asked my mother why. She said it was because everyone believed that if you leave the hollow, leave the mountains of Kentucky, then you become lost. We've found out different since then."

She has been one of the many who made that discovery. She and her husband Tim and their five children have gone back and forth for years, from Harlan County to Dayton, Ohio. They tried living in Chicago, too. For three years, they attempted to stay put there, in the north side of the city at the edge of Evanston. It was a time she still describes with an intensity of emotion that indicates, as she well knows, how difficult it is to put aside certain experiences, even when one tries with all one's might: "I tell myself never, never to think of Chicago again. But each time I say that, I end up shaking, and I get choked up. I start crying. It's stupid. I try to stop myself, but I can't. We had a terrible time in Chicago, and I think it hurt my children for life. We were away from all our kin. We were afraid of the streets there. And I had to work, along with my husband. We came there to make as much money as we could. We hoped that we could save some, and then go back to Kentucky, and maybe work some land that belongs to Tim's daddy. Tim said he hated the mines, and he'd rather go to the city and work in a factory than go underground. Of course, when we left for Chicago, there was no work in the mines, anyway. On the way up to Chicago, we were full of hope. We thought we'd done the right thing. We thought we'd found courage, and that we'd be rewarded. All we had was ourselves.

We didn't have a car. We took the bus. We'd saved and borrowed for the tickets. Tim was sick; he had a fever. He'd been
working and working for everyone up the hollow just to get our
fares. We thought that in Chicago we'd do right well.

"We were foolish. We hadn't given thought to the future.
We'd become upset by our life up the hollow, and we'd heard
there were jobs in the city, and Tim had a cousin in Chicago, so
we decided to go there. We had his address, and we were sure
he'd help us get settled and started. Neither of us is a writing
person. If we'd been smart, we would have gone to the schoolteacher who taught us, and asked her to send a letter for us to
Tim's cousin, asking him if we really should come. We wouldn't
have got any reply. He disappeared, and no one heard from him
—until the sheriff in Harlan County got word to Tim that his
poor cousin had been killed in a car accident. That was a long
time after we'd left Chicago, though. The cousin had left there
before we did, I guess. He died in Detroit. Thank God we never
got *there*. I hear it said that Detroit is the capital city of Hell."

She wants to go back to her remarks about Chicago. She wants
to tell how the family got there, became utterly confused, turned
to Traveler's Aid, had some help finding a boardinghouse
through that organization, eventually found work—and encoun-
tered one terrible problem after another. But she needs some
coffee, and she wants to go look at a few spring flowers, which
have shown themselves at last. Best to work her way toward
Chicago indirectly, she seems to feel. Not that anyone is coaxing
her to talk about the place at all. She will find herself, upon
occasion, having a conversation with herself and no one else—
the subject matter: Chicago and the miracle that took place there.
The miracle, quite simply, was the survival of a family. The
spring flowers prompted her to come at her experience in the city
through that angle—endurance against terribly grim odds: "The
flowers in a city try hard to be brave; it's their big chance. They
don't have much room; they're penned in—the sidewalks, the

houses—and the dirty air doesn't do them any good. A lot of
times the winter comes back and kills them. We missed so much
we love about the hollow when we came North to Chicago. We
never saw the mountains, the woods, the animals. We were like
the spring flowers—and Chicago was a long winter that near
killed us. I will be in Dayton, working, or home in Kentucky
with our kin, and I think of Chicago and I get cold, and there's
sweat on my forehead and I want to sit down for fear of fainting.
When I do sit down, I'll let my mind wander back to that city;
it's the second biggest in America—that's what the teacher kept
telling my oldest son. He told her that it's too big for him. The
teacher asked him why he didn't go back to the place he came
from. Her words were hard for young Timmie to take: 'Well, if
you don't like it here, why don't you turn around and go live in
your mountains?' *Your* mountains! They don't belong to us;
they're everyone's mountains—well, the parks there are. The
coal companies own a lot of that land, and they're tearing it to
shreds. The greedy coal companies!

"I shouldn't bear a special grudge against the coal companies
—not after working in a factory myself. It was just outside Chicago, and they made light bulbs, and I showed up at eight in the
morning and got out at five, and it took an hour by bus each way;
and let me tell you, months would go by and I didn't know what
part of the year it was or much of anything else, except that I'd
get up, and I'd have my coffee, and I'd wake up my oldest son
and my oldest daughter, and while they were yawning and half-
crying and fighting to stay awake, I was getting dressed and
thinking of what was coming: another factory day, worse than a
bad dream. If it wasn't for one friend I made at work, I believe
I would have given up all hope and probably died."

She is not being melodramatic or self-pitying. She knows that
she lost a lot of weight, began coughing blood, was feverish, yet
kept coming to work. Her friend told her that she had to stop,
had to consult a doctor. But Hannah Morgan had never con-

sulted a doctor in her life. Her children were delivered by a midwife. She had regarded illness as part of life, as something like the weather or the economy: one does the best possible to endure the various changes or crises that come up. And always and often, one prays. Then, midway through a winter morning, she collapsed while at work. She was brought to, gradually, by her friend, who wanted to take her to the company doctor.

But the drowsy, confused, ailing woman refused the advice stubbornly; and finished the day at her job; and went home, at her insistence, by herself; and the next day was up at five-thirty, as usual: "I said to myself that I was living a death, so if I died, it wouldn't be so bad! I was ready to leave this earth. I hated the thought of not being with Tim and the children, but I was sure they would go back to Harlan County. I spent the night tossing, and dreaming scary dreams. One was that I was on the assembly line, with a bulb before me and a bulb after me, and I tried to get off, but the bulbs got bigger and bigger, and they broke, and there was sharp glass all around me, and it started moving toward me, and it came up my body toward my face. Oh, my God, that was bad! I had a fever. I was coughing real bad. Then I dreamed I was at a funeral, and I asked people who had died, because I didn't know. It turned out to be me! and the people who were there didn't know me—I mean the me who was standing, not the me in the casket. They weren't our kinfolk from Harlan County. They were from Chicago, I realized—by their dress and the way they talked. There were one or two of my friends from the factory."

She decides to interrupt herself with a medical reflection or two. Perhaps death had been about to win her, and she knew it in some way, asleep though she was. Perhaps she had been upset by Chicago's life, and her "bad cold" made her even more upset at night. Even as a girl she was given to vivid, confusing, unnerving dreams. And Chicago was certainly no city to encourage restful, dreamless nights. Moreover, she was indeed afraid at work—handling all that glass. When she was in apparent good health, she nevertheless wondered whether, one day, she would squeeze a bulb too tight while testing it; crush the glass; end up with splinters in her veins, blood all over the place, and a foreman shouting at her that she was fired.

It was the last possibility that truly frightened her. She desperately needed the money she earned. Her husband had found a job as a packer in a warehouse, and between the two of them they barely managed to get by—and send some dollars home to their respective families: "We didn't come to Chicago to walk on sidewalks and run out of the way of crazy drivers and inhale smoke and ride on buses so crowded that you stand for an hour —before you get to the factory, where you stand all day long. We came to Chicago because we wanted to make some money, and come back with it to our home, and live in Harlan County, and work on the land. We thought that if we could just save a few hundred dollars, then we wouldn't be so close to the poorhouse; that means having zero dollars, and it's winter; and you've run out of the food you put up, and you're hungry; and the chickens have stopped laying, and you can't build up more of a debt at the store; and your family isn't in good shape either; and so all you can do is hold your stomach and wait until the hunger pains go away, and then you're tired, and you feel weak, but you don't desire food—it's strange.

"Every day in that factory I would think to myself, I would talk to myself. I would remind myself—freedom, later on. So would my husband, when he was breaking his back in that cold, dark warehouse; he would tell himself that it would be worth all the pain, in the end. Half the day I wasn't in Chicago; I was in my thoughts. In Dayton it's the same thing—a little less. In Chicago they would come and pinch me and ask me if I'm all right. I was doing the work, but my eyes were in a daze, they said. I was in Kentucky; that's where I was! I was in my dreams, my mountain dreams.

"I was running down a path with my dog and telling him he was getting lazy, and stopping all of a sudden because I saw some good mushrooms, and there was a soup I was working on. I was out with my tomatoes and my beans, coaxing them along. I was talking real strict to my hens: Better keep going, or you'll join that soup, too! I was sitting and telling that pig that he's having a great time now, but we'd be licking our fingers later on. I was collecting leaves, fallen leaves. All my life I've done that. When I was a little girl, my grandmother took me aside and said she wanted to tell me something important, and I must never forget what she would say. She practically whispered her story to me —that I was a girl and not a boy, and a girl should pay attention to the colors of leaves in the autumn, while boys just ran all over them and didn't see what was there on the ground before them: yellow and red and green and orange brown, a rainbow of colors, God's love spread out before us to have a feast on."

She is not entirely happy with her grandmother's observation, but she would not want to contradict her directly. She stops talking. When she has resumed the conversation, it is about her oldest daughter, Pauline, and what her life will be like. Worked into various predictions, statements of apprehension, expressions of hope, avowals of concern are an Appalachian woman's sense of social change—and her conclusion that old cautions or explanations don't quite work: "I've stood there in Chicago testing those bulbs, and I've stood here in Dayton checking food out, punching numbers on the cash register all day until I see numbers when I come home and not my family; and while I do the work I wonder about my sister Pauline and my daughter Pauline. It's a terrible sin, but I get discouraged, and I think to myself that there's little to hold on to, and we're in such trouble, and it's so bad being in Chicago and now Dayton, and back home our people don't have much success fighting for themselves against the coal operators or just fighting to stay alive up the hollows, come a bad winter. And when I'm thinking like that, I wonder whether God wasn't good to my sister, by calling her back to Him so young.

"The ministers will tell you—some of them are too smart for their own good—that it's God's decision, and we shouldn't try to second-guess Him, or try to say what we want from Him or what we wished He'd done for us. I know, I know: He doesn't make sure that everyone gets treated equal, and we have no right to complain or to pout. My grandmother used to say that so long as you can find something beautiful to look at, you're rich, even if there are only a few potatoes left to eat and no money to buy a single thing at the store and no more credit there either. My mother would nod, but I could read her face. She was trying to be respectful, even if she thought otherwise. I don't talk to my children like my grandmother used to talk to me. I tell my daughter Pauline about her Aunt Pauline, how she died; and that's not talking about pretty leaves, and the sun doing its tricks with the water, and the shadows coming and going.

"I remember two winters ago; it was my sister's birthday—dead twenty years. I reminded my daughter that her namesake had been gone that long. Then we got to talking; it was a long heart-to-heart. My daughter was twelve, and she was already a woman, and she was asking me all these questions—I near went mad. I told her to stop. But she said if she stopped, she'd still ask them of herself, and I knew she was right. So I listened, and I tried to give answers, if I could think of some. The main thing on her mind was where she would be living when she was older, and whether she would have a job, and what kind. She told me she didn't want to have five children because it's hard to make enough money. She's been listening to Tim and me talk! I tried to tell her that you don't think of life that way—of having children that way. You don't sit down and say you can *afford* to have a certain number of boys and girls; you *have* your children and try to do the best you can to be a good parent. If my mother and daddy had thought the way my daughter was talking, she wouldn't be there talking. I came along after five brothers. I told her that. She near floored me with what she said in reply; she said that didn't make any difference, because what's right is right, and you mustn't be selfish. I had to stop and think about things for a while before I could continue.

"I made an excuse that I wanted to get rid of the garbage because it was smelling up the house. In Dayton, the first apartment we had was old, and even without garbage there was a bad smell! My daughter said she'd help—and, of course, she saw there really wasn't much garbage to take out! She also saw that she'd got me upset! It was then that I realized full well that I had a grown-up woman on my hands, and I'd better be careful of what I say! She's very smart, and she looks at people, and she seems to know what they're all about. I don't know how she does it! I think she's seen so much—what with all the traveling we've done—that she can't just sit back and accept God's will, the way all of us were told we should do by my mother, and she by her mother, going way back in time."

The daughter Pauline increasingly confused, alarmed, and intrigued her mother. Even at the age of nine the girl had suggested that she get her friends together, and they agree to pledge themselves to support, in the future, one of them for a political office, the higher the better. The mother had shrugged off the notion as mere child's play—only to be asked all sorts of bluntly political and economic questions by her not-so-old child. The answers were usually brief, hesitant, unsatisfactory, as even the one who supplied them knew: "I didn't know why she was asking those questions. I don't recall having thoughts on my mind like she has when I was her age—or even much older. I talked with my husband, and he said it was the city living; in the schools she was probably hearing talk like that and repeating it to us. I think he had a point. But I think it was *Pauline,* too. She's a sensitive child, and she's smart. She saw me feeling low and working hard, and she wanted to know why, and then she wanted to do something. So she turned to her friends, and they said yes, they'll help —later on, when they're old enough to vote!

"When she was a little older, eleven or twelve I'd say, we had good talks. I'd be tired in the evening, but she wouldn't be even near sleep, I could see, and I'd sit at the edge of her bed and mostly just ask her what happened during the day, and she'd tell me all right. She's never been one to hold her tongue. She'd say she hoped to make enough money to feed her children. She'd say, even then, that she hoped never to have children until she could be sure they'd be fed and have the clothes they need. I told her what I'd tell her over and over again later—that you don't think that way in life. You do the best you can, of course; but if everyone sat and tried to figure out if they've got the right amount of money to go get married or have some children, pretty soon there wouldn't be but a few people in the country, and that wouldn't be so good. Once I asked Pauline: How much is 'enough'? Of course, she was still young, and she couldn't give me an exact number, and I knew it. I guess I was upset by all her questions, and I was beginning to see that she wasn't going to be satisfied with a pat on the head from me. My husband has blamed it all on television. The children sit and hear all these people saying all these things, and they're bound to pick up strange ideas."

On the other hand, her daughter's early rebelliousness brought back surprising memories of her own. She began to recall some of her private childhood reveries, usually stimulated by walks up the various paths that branched off the hollow. Once, when she wasn't "much more than ten," there was "bad trouble" at home. The family was having difficulty with its bills. Back from a walk outside, full of her various thoughts, she asked her mother and father why it was that the county officials and the coal company foremen lived better than the hollow people did. They told her that such is life—the world's various circumstances. When she persisted, and characterized the social distinctions she had perceived as "unfair," her father became visibly upset, spoke bluntly: "He told me I'd better learn to be a good girl, then later on, a good woman. He said if I started stepping out of my proper shoes, I'd get in trouble—I'd fall down and get hurt bad. He said the county officials and the coal-mine owners and the foremen run things, and that's how it is. He said no matter where you go in the world, you'll always find the ones who own a lot and the ones who don't have much of anything. My sister Pauline didn't like what she was hearing: I could tell. She started lifting up one foot, then the other, and finally she turned to me and told me that she had a pain in her stomach, and she wanted to go lie down on her bed. I told our father. He said no; he said she had to learn to listen to bad news and pay attention to her elders. She was always trying to run off; that was her way, and you can't run away from your life.

"Tim has told all our children the same thing—that we don't ask to be born, we get born, and we shouldn't try to change the world; because if you do, you'll end up in more trouble than you had in the first place. But our daughter Pauline didn't believe that when she was a little girl, and now that she's growing up into a woman, she believes it even less. Since she was thirteen, she's been telling me that she wants to stay in Dayton and stay in school and become a nurse and not go back to Harlan County, except on visits. I've told her that she doesn't know a good life from a bad life, but she won't let me get away with saying that. She asks me what we've been doing in Dayton (and before it, Chicago) if it was so good living in Kentucky. I try to talk reason with her, but she argues. I'm not like her father; I let her have her say, and I can see her side of things."

She can do so to such an extraordinary extent that she begins to wish, at times, she were far less empathic. She will be listening to her daughter Pauline talk to the other children or to a friend, and suddenly the words inspire in a mid-thirtyish woman a mixture of sadness and alarm. Is the daughter correct? If so, what might be done? Why has this "child" of hers suddenly turned against her own origins—and, yes, the cherished values of her people? And what is a mother to do—tolerate such a rising inclination in her offspring? For Hannah Morgan there were no satisfactory answers to such questions. She did have, though, at least one unassailable advantage from her mountain background: an ability to live with contradictions, ambiguities, confusions. If she could for years regard Harlan County as a fine, fine place to live, even though she knew how much her family lacked, she could certainly manage to put up with the realization that cities like Chicago and Dayton manage to provide not only money, but a fresh outlook—for all the dreary side of life in such places. On balance, she decided, it was better that Pauline have her rather strong-minded and even caustic views than that she be living "up a hollow," with no prospects whatever and, maybe, a somewhat undernourished body.

And how fine that the "girl" should want to be a nurse. Others would be healed by her, even as she has claimed to find in Ohio a certain redemptive experience: "My daughter thinks that she was 'saved' by our decision to try living in the city. As Tim and I see it, we've made a few dollars, and we've had better food, and we've sent home some money. But she says she's seen how the rest of the country behaves, and she's been 'saved,' and she doesn't want to go back to Kentucky, except on holidays. She would really like to work in a hospital and take care of very sick people. I ask her why. She says she is sure the life would be interesting—doctors and their operations, and people fighting to stay alive and needing a nurse real bad to lend a hand. She was taken to a hospital by a schoolteacher—the whole class was. Pauline couldn't stop talking about all she saw. I guess that's the difference; in Harlan County she'd have long since stopped school, and there's no hospital there like the medical centers in the cities of Ohio or Illinois. It changes you when you move and you see another place different from your own. Even if Pauline came back with us and stayed in Kentucky, I believe she'd be a different woman."

The mother had become rather different herself, for all her insistence that it was her daughter who had changed so tellingly in the cities of the North. The mother occasionally found herself thinking of some of the high-rise apartments near Chicago's Loop: what was life like inside them? The mother found herself thinking, too, of the life lived by some of the people she saw in Dayton. If they intended to stay where they were, why ought she think of leaving, eventually, for the rather more harsh and mean world of the Appalachian hollow? When her daughter turned fourteen they had occasion to ask each other, out loud, those questions and others. In school Pauline met a young man who was not by any means of wealthy background, but whose father, an accountant, was on the rise. The family was planning to move to another part of Dayton. Pauline wished her family would at least be aspiring to move there—rather than always talking about the eventual return "home."

Pauline wished many other things, her mother realized after one long, strained conversation: "I began to realize that there are mountains between us—as high as the mountains back home. My daughter will never be part of Harlan County the way I am. She has dreams of her own. We told each other of our dreams. I told her that when I stand in the supermarket, punching numbers, my mind is up the hollow. I'll be thinking of the chickens, walking toward the woods, but hurrying back if there's a stir. I'll be thinking of the creek, so full in the spring that we worry. I'll be wishing we had four or five acres here and a garden and a few good, sturdy trees. The trees in the city look so sad; they droop out of loneliness and because the air is so heavy and dirty, and they don't get the nourishment they need out of cement. Sometimes I'll be packing grocery bags and a lady will say to me that I'm 'gone,' and where was I. I'll say I have a headache. I do— living here.

"With Pauline it's different. She notices too many people; she asks for too many answers. She said the teacher wants to correct her accent, and I told her to ignore the teacher; but Pauline gave me a long lecture on America—how people keep moving to build up their lives, and how good it is. She wants us at least to move nearer to the neighborhood where her boyfriend will be living. We can't move *into* that neighborhood; we don't have the money. But we could get ourselves a few miles closer. We'd be exchanging one place for another—both about the same. I talked with my husband; he said no. Pauline talked with him; he said no again. He got real angry with her. He said she was turning on her own people, just for some boyfriend. He said she was losing her self-respect, and when that happens, you're in real trouble. My daughter fought him back, real hard. I'm glad I was working that night in the supermarket!

"I guess Tim was in a sour mood, anyway. Pauline hadn't cooked the biscuits right, and she'd burned his pork chop, and he told her she was spoiled because she should be a grade A, number one cook by now. He went and opened a can of beans and cooked them himself. She should have waited for another day to talk about moving, but she didn't. She tried to be nice. She served him a plate of ice cream. She cleaned away the table. She scrubbed the dishes. Then she went and sat down and watched television with him and the other kids. During an advertisement, she brought up the subject, and he exploded on her. He took her into the kitchen and said she should be practicing there—how to cook—and not having big dreams for herself of becoming a millionaire, or marrying one. He said the Lord Himself would look down on her because He chose to walk among the poor, and that was meant to be a lesson for the rest of us. I guess Pauline said something that she shouldn't. She said that ministers always seem to live pretty well, and the one in Dayton we know drives a big new car, a Buick, so why shouldn't everyone try to get the best deal possible? And Pauline reminded her daddy about the ministers back home in Kentucky. A lot of them have nice cars, too—and they have the finest homes you'd want. Tim told her she was headed for Hell if she didn't watch her every step. She ran out of the house, I guess."

It was shortly afterwards that the mother and daughter had an especially long talk. Nothing dramatic took place, but Hannah Morgan began to realize that she had, in a way, "lost" her daughter, and that such an outcome was not altogether a tragedy. And the more she thought about her daughter's words, assertions, arguments, the more she recovered for her own reflection certain past moments of her life—certain spells of confusion and wonder, certain reveries banished from awareness years ago: "I'm not the kind to do a lot of thinking. If you have a home to keep, and a job, then there's little time for your own ideas. I used to have some strong ideas, though. People forget what they believed when they were young. No wonder children get impatient with their parents. But when the children become grownups and have their own children, it makes a difference. I guess there's always some disagreement between parents and their young ones. Right now I can feel the blood in my own kin changing. I know my daughter is going to stay North and live her life in Dayton or some other city. If she'd grown up back home, she'd have different ambitions. I'll bet she'd still take issue with her dad and me, though.

"Once in a while I'll be sitting on the bus, going to work or coming home from work, and I'll remember some of my dreams when I was a kid growing up. I remember the time my mother told me I was getting 'big and strange ideas.' I didn't know what she meant. I didn't understand why she was talking like that, so strict and upset. All I'd said was that the teacher dressed real smart, and she showed us a picture of her sister; and she lives in Louisville, and she works in an office, typing and answering the phone, and she draws a very good wage; and her clothes are just beautiful, and her hair—she wears it so that she looks real fine, and she goes to a place, and they work on her with soaps and perfumes and machines. I guess I thought I wouldn't mind going to Louisville myself. I didn't want to live there, and I didn't want to be like the teacher's sister. I just wanted to go see, and then I thought I could come back and in the dark, I could tell my sisters, and they'd be excited. We had no electricity then, and we'd tell each other stories. But my mother thought I was getting 'stuck-up'; that's what she would call me a lot, when I was about ten or eleven."

After she has said that, used that expression "stuck-up," she finds herself even more tired than is usually the case; and she is strangely restless, even a touch agitated. She wants to deny an old accusation, however distant the time of its utterance. She protects herself and her mother's memory by pointing out that years ago a woman like her mother had to contend with frustrations, obstacles, hardships almost unimaginable today (lack of electricity, for instance), and so was apt to be irritable almost all the time. She has, over the years, tried to evoke her mother's reality, that of her grandmother, for young Pauline, but to no good effect. But the mother does finally acknowledge quite explicitly that she still feels like defending herself against the charge of being "stuck-up," rather than trying to understand the reasons why such a description was used: "I guess I wanted a different life, too—just like my daughter does. My mother was wrong not to see what was on my mind. I would never admit it to anyone at the time, but I told Tim once, before we got married, that I wished we could just get a ride from someone to Louisville, and he and I could get some jobs—anything, anything at all—and try to begin a city life there. He said he'd had thoughts like mine, but they were silly because the chances are we'd get nowhere and end up lost as can be. I argued with him. I said we're willing to work, and my daddy told me all the time that if people want to work, they'll stay alive. They may hurt; they may hurt real bad; but they'll stay alive.

"Tim kept telling me no; he was sure that in Louisville it's not the same as up the hollow—no land to work, if you're a visitor, and no kin to help out. But they have factories there, I answered; or we could wash dishes in a restaurant. I used to dream of going down the hollow and getting a job in a store up the road outside of Harlan. It seemed like a chance to look at the world. But I've gone a long road from the county I knew when I was a girl, and there's no fun for me anymore in imagining all the things to do —up the road in Harlan County or in Louisville or in the big cities of our country. That's what my daughter is doing, dreaming and wishing and hoping and praying—for *her own* life. I tell her no one's life is his own. She always corrects me: No one's life is *her* own, but someone can at least try. Well, she'll find out."

From still smoldering resentment at unfair charges long ago made, she has moved rather briskly to a working mother's resignation. She herself supplies the latter psychological characterization. She refers to the burdens of her job, of her home life, of her advancing age. At thirty-seven she viewed herself as at best "getting old"; sometimes she deemed herself arrived—quite simply, "old." She remembers her grandmother telling the grandchildren that she became "old" the day her first grandchild, a boy, was born, when she was thirty-six. Hannah Morgan knows that she married later than her mother or her grandmother did, and that her daughter has made remarks which cast doubt on the desirability of early marriage—and on other customs or beliefs once simply a part of mountain life. Now and then she is able to make connections between her values, even those of her mother or grandmother, and the avowals made by her teen-age daughter: "I was a little one, maybe six or seven, when my grandmother took me into the woods to collect berries. She knew so much, I thought—where to go, what to pick, how to pick, what to shun. She'd see me grabbing at something because I wanted to imitate her, and she'd say no. I remember her words: 'Shun that, child.' While we filled up the baskets, she'd talk and talk. I couldn't follow a lot of her words. I thought she was a bit 'daffy'; that's what I'd hear someone talking to himself called. But she'd look at me, off and on, and try to make sure I caught her meaning. And I did; I understood her when she said that it was no fun being a woman, and I'd find that out sooner or later, and better sooner.

"I'd ask her hows and whys, but I knew what she *meant*, even if I didn't understand what she said, trying to explain herself. I'm no better with words now than I was then, but I still do know what she meant. She'd suffered a lot; she'd lost children, and stood by the stove, trying to feed those she still had. Often she consoled her husband when he came home sick and ready to go shoot himself. He drank a lot; and she stood by him. He'd get mean and nasty, but she still stood by him. She said it was her job to be like that—a woman's job. I once asked her after she scratched her hands trying to get as many berries as she could, why Grandpa didn't come and help us, because he had tough hands, and he could go into bushes we stayed clear of. She said for me to hush and not be silly. If Grandpa heard me say that, I'd get my mouth washed with soap. I don't believe I'd have got my mouth washed with soap by my father, if he heard me suggest that he help my mother and me pick berries. He'd just shake his head and say no. I think Tim wouldn't mind going berrying with Pauline—if we were back there, up the hollow. But I don't know for sure. When we go back, he becomes different. And up here, he sends her on errands to the store and asks her to sew, but the boys don't get asked to do either. So it's always the same— women keeping their eyes on the menfolk, and not getting the fair treatment they deserve, and being afraid, maybe, to say so."

Mostly, she apologizes after such remarks. She has not been fair to her husband. He does not in any way have "favorites." He loves all his children equally. He wants them to have a better life than the one he has had. He would gladly let them go anywhere, live anyplace, do whatever they wished—provided they continued to respect their parents, harmed no one, maintained their faith in God. She recites those mandates not as pieties but as strongly held convictions. She prays for her children every evening upon retiring. So does her husband. Sometimes at work she prays for herself, rather than anyone else—to be able to last the day. Then, ashamed of her self-indulgence ("feeling sorry for myself"), she turns her mind to her boys and girls: may Jesus Christ, Almighty God, Father of us all, have mercy upon her family, and show each and every one of her children "the right way." And that is what Pauline may be in danger of doing, her mother believes—falling away from a path, a course of travel that is set by the Lord, and deserves no manmade alterations, however earnestly upheld or well set forth.

When Pauline turned fifteen, she entered high school, and became even more difficult and vexing a "child" (as she was still called) to her parents. Now the mother showed less patience with the daughter than the father did. He shrugged his shoulders and called her "a girl becoming a woman." What else should one expect? Don't "all women" become "temperamental" some of the time? And especially young women? Pauline needed a man, he kept insisting—though, of course, he was the first to point out that she was much too young for her requirement to be realized. Soon enough, though, she would be "old enough," and then "everything" would somehow turn out well, or so he believed.

For Hannah Morgan, it was quite another matter. She found herself becoming angry at her daughter for no apparent reason. She took to chastising her: sloppy attire, poor posture, laziness in the kitchen, a dour or grim expression on the face. The daughter decided that her mother was becoming "too strict" because she was tired and needed to stay home and rest. She had a bad cold; perhaps she really had pneumonia. Best to talk with her father, Pauline decided one day; and she did so. The mother heard about the substance of the talk, started crying as her husband finished his account of what had transpired, and a few days later was still tearful as she asked herself what was making her, by her own admission, a somewhat overbearing person for Pauline and no one else, it appeared: "I think I was too close by far to Pauline. She was my first child, my first daughter, and I couldn't stop myself from telling her what was on my mind. I don't know if a mother should do that with her child. I'll be looking at Pauline now, and I'll want to run away from her. She gets me angry. She's so sure of herself, it seems to me. Then I'll leave the room, and I'll miss seeing her, and I'll wish it could be like in the old days, when we'd sit and talk.

"I can't share my thoughts with my other daughters, the way I do with her. But now I can't talk with her either. I think I miss the old days—but I also keep wishing she was a little older, and could leave the house and go start her own life apart from us. She's always talking about being 'a free person.' She hears that in school—those words. Let her go and see how 'free' a 'person' can become. If you have a million dollars, you're plenty 'free.' If you have zero dollars or maybe a ten-dollar bill tucked away someplace, you're not so 'free'—I don't care what the teachers tell you about the law and the Constitution. But there's a certain age children reach when they have to learn for themselves and not from anyone else, especially a parent. That's what they say up here, at least—in the papers and on television. It wasn't that way with me. Back home, we never stopped paying regard to what our parents or our grandparents or our uncles and aunts had to tell us. But that's why I have trouble with Pauline; she's not in a mood to admit that she's got a certain kind of *blood* in her, and because of that, she's going to end up being a certain kind of person. She's fighting her own kin. Can there be anything worse than that? Won't she get into the worst trouble for being so sassy?"

She expects no answers to such questions. She has second thoughts about the desirability of asking them. She turns upon herself with other questions. Does she envy her daughter the chances or possibilities that northern cities offer? Is she more unhappy with her own fate than she ordinarily acknowledges even to herself, never mind other people? And if so, why pick on a young lady who is trying her best to stay in school and plan ahead for a career and build a friendship with a decent, thoughtful, attentive young man? There are no answers, either, to those self-directed inquiries. She sits on the bus, or stands at the counter, and looks at people intently, wonders long and hard whether they, too, might have the worries, apprehensions, conflicts of attitude and feeling she experiences, sometimes to the point of exasperation. She finds it hard, though, to arrive at conclusions about others. Who knows what masks they are wearing? Who can get around the various illusions or self-deceptions they may have constructed as sanctuaries for their hard-driving, vulnerable lives? She can't even figure out what she herself believes, wants out of life—or wants from her daughter—so why turn to the enigmatic faces of others (so automatically smiling, so stubbornly impassive) for assistance?

Once, wrapped up in such thoughts, she missed her bus stop and found herself in a rather pleasant neighborhood; she became alarmed and was about to pull the cord and run up to the driver to plead for help, when something came over her, starting with her body and only gradually reaching her mind: "I thought I was sick. I couldn't move. I couldn't lift my arm to pull that cord. I couldn't get up to go talk with that driver. I couldn't open my mouth and talk, even though I was only four or five seats back. I thought I was going to pass out. But I didn't. I just sat there and looked out of the window. I felt as if I was no longer me! I felt as if I was watching myself and watching the others on the bus and watching the world go by through the window.

"I had a strange idea—a *crazy* idea; I wondered if it was like that to die—your soul leaving your body behind, like they tell you in church. I wasn't even nervous at the thought of dying. I remember thinking to myself that I'd had enough of life, and I would just as soon find out what was ahead of me in the next world. Of course, I wasn't going to meet St. Peter; I was riding a bus in a nice part of Dayton, the kind of place my daughter's boyfriend lives in. I wondered if he did live there. I wondered who those people were. They had nice homes, big lawns, nice cars, and I saw some swimming pools. They all had money—to afford such living. I tried to picture myself in their shoes. What would I look like? What kind of clothes would I buy for my children and myself? Would I be happy there? I didn't know what to think. The bus stopped, and I saw a woman coming out of one of the houses. I thought she was going to get on the bus, but no, she was walking to her car. She had a nice dress on. Her hair was all done up. She looked like a movie star. The car was beautiful, a convertible. I wondered where she was going so early, fixed up so nice. Maybe she was going shopping. But she didn't look like the women I wait on—buying their groceries, and carrying them home or hauling them on the bus. I couldn't picture her in a supermarket, ever. Maybe she has a maid, I thought. Maybe she is going to visit some kin. Maybe she has an appointment with a doctor. Maybe she has to go on a trip, and she had already packed her car before I came along on the bus.

"I forgot about her for a minute. I saw a woman walking down the aisle of the bus, and she got out. She walked toward a house, and suddenly I realized that she was a maid, and she was working for someone like that lady I'd just seen getting into her fancy car. I felt like running after the woman who'd left the bus, and asking her if she thought there was any point in my changing jobs. Would it be better for me—better pay and less pressure on you every minute? I'd rather sell people their food than clean up after them. At least you can keep some privacy for yourself, working in a store. When you're in someone's house, you are a servant, and that's below being a clerk; and you can be ordered around, and your every move can be watched by the woman of the house or her kids or her husband.

"The bus didn't stop too long; it kept moving. Each time it did stop, I thought I should get off, and wait for a bus to take me in the opposite direction. But I didn't; I stayed right where I was. I couldn't seem to find the energy I needed to lift myself up! I'd get lost looking; I was looking at the toys all over the place—so many bikes!—and at the new cars and at the houses. I was so lost, I didn't realize that I was alone and the bus had stopped and the driver was talking to *me* and saying 'last stop, last stop.' I don't know how many times he repeated himself before I came to my senses and realized I was the only one listening to him."

She got back to her job without being late. She was always quite early; for once she came, like others, barely on time. The foreman who supervised her work, a blunt, outspoken man, was surprised, teased her: she was becoming 'like all the others,' meaning those who aren't troubled, as she had been, by the moral compulsions of a mountaineer's conscience. She nodded, with a smile. She knew what he meant. She knew how demanding her conscience is, how sternly she had been brought up, how anxious she became when it came to work. She knew how angry she felt when she saw others loafing, avoiding their responsibilities, doing only the least amount necessary to get by. But this time she had, without realizing it, wandered far from her usual urban path, and her mind would not quite let the experience be forgotten. All that day she saw pictures—the woman getting into the car, or a particular house on the street she had watched from the bus, or the maid getting off that bus and walking up the street toward a home. All that day she saw herself sitting in the bus, looking and wondering what she was seeing, and finally getting her body from one bus to another, from a strange world to the familiar one of work. The question she put to herself, frightening indeed, was this: "What am I doing here?"

She did not mean by that to assert a newfound superiority; nor did she have in mind some large-scale existentialist inquiry. She had all along felt torn, confused, split in her affections, loyalties, commitments. She yearned for a return to the hollow she considered her home, yet knew (*especially* when there on a holiday visit) that she not only had to go back to Chicago or Dayton (out of economic necessity) but actually wanted to. The *desire* to return north to a city struck her (when she allowed herself to be introspective) as unseemly—a betrayal of her family's values. Until recently, however, she had been able rather easily to avoid examining the implications of such a mental shift. It is not that she lacked a meditative side; quite simply, there was always so much for her to do that she had to put tight reins on what it is she lets herself think deeply about. ("I don't have the minutes to ponder God's reasons," she once said, not too ponderously.) How could she possibly acknowledge that, like one of Christ's disciples, she had been bribed—persuaded by steam heating and an electric stove and, most of all, a job, that it is best to live among the heathen, the noisy materialistic city people, each one of them more desperate (by her observation) than the others?

It was Pauline's explicit apostasy from the dream of a "return" that first prompted Hannah Morgan to wonder about her own attitudes; but it was also the long bus ride, the trip across town, across the tracks, so to speak, that caused a significant and, for a time, terribly unsettling change in her sense of what she was about—what, even, she wanted to be about: "I keep thinking of that woman in the nice dress, with her hair so pretty, getting into the car. I'll wonder what she does inside besides drive. Does she smoke, like a lot of women do up here? Does she listen to the radio while driving? Is she a good driver? Does she own the car, or is it her husband's? Does she drive it every day, or only every once in a while? My husband says women don't make good drivers, and I've always agreed with him. I don't know how to drive, and I don't really want to know. But maybe there are some women who can do a pretty good job at the wheel. It's not fair to say that *all* women are *this* or *that* or *something else.* I can see why my daughter would object when her father makes some of his remarks—though I don't think she looks at it from his side.

He saw a woman smash a car up right before his eyes, and all she had needed to do was turn the wheel a little to the left. Of course, men get into accidents. But there's no reason to argue the matter.

"Since that day I stayed too long on the bus, I've been finding myself irritable; I'll be irritable at work, and in the kitchen at home, and even in church I'll get upset. I'll think that no one's listening to *me* or to *Pauline.* Everyone has his ideas, and we're supposed to follow, obey. I can't have a coffee break when I want a cup of coffee; I have to take the break when the manager remembers to *tell* me to do it. He never asks; he calls out. He says, 'Hannah, time for you to get some coffee.' Of course, I never call him Warren; I say, 'Yes, Mr. Patterson, thank you for thinking of me'—something polite like that. I don't feel polite! Even my husband falls into the same kind of habit. He'll ask me if supper is ready, and I say no, not yet, but soon. He goes back to watching the television. But when the program is over, he doesn't ask anymore. He gets up and comes into the kitchen and sits down at the table and watches me, while I try finishing up the cooking and setting the table. I know something then: I know that I'd better get that meal on the table, *fast.* I always do.

"There used to be a time I thanked Tim to myself, for speeding me up by coming in and plunking himself down on a chair and keeping his eyes glued on the stove. But lately, I've been ready to cry when he comes in. And the other night I did; I just sobbed away. I didn't know what I was sobbing about. If I'd had to save my family with the right answer, I'd have failed the test. But I couldn't stop myself. And when Tim finally noticed—much longer than it would have taken me to catch on if he'd been sobbing—I couldn't stop myself. I cried harder and harder, until he came over and asked me where the pain was. I told him I didn't know; that was the trouble. He said I shouldn't be crying, then, if I couldn't tell where there was pain, or whether any part of my body was in trouble. I felt like shouting, not crying, but I kept mashing those potatoes and adding more butter, and I talked myself into stopping the tears. By the time we were all sitting at the table, I felt bad, as bad as I've ever felt. I'd made my husband worry, and my children, all because I'd spoiled myself by feeling sorry for myself. I swore I'd never again behave like that. But no sooner did I tell my husband I was sorry for the tears, than I thought to myself that I'd been away from home as long as he was, that day and every day, working as hard as I knew how. So I deserve a little respect, too."

She immediately pulls back, upon making that assertion. She has no right, she insists, to compare her situation with that of her husband. He is, after all, just that—an extremely hardworking *man*. And *men* shoulder responsibilities, if not strenuous burdens, that women can only guess at. Or so she'd been told all her life. Her daughter Pauline wasn't by any means convinced by that truism; and for some reason, Hannah Morgan began to believe that the woman she saw leave the house and get into a car and drive off early one morning also might have some reservations about such a well-worn proposition. Maybe that woman had a daughter like Pauline, Hannah Morgan began to speculate. Maybe the daughter was the one who suggested that her mother get out of the house more, use the family car—buy one for herself. Pauline had taken to making a few suggestions of her own. Why shouldn't the family go get a pizza or two once a week —so that her mother would have at least one day's vacation from cooking supper? Why doesn't everyone in the family help with the cleaning, the cooking? Why should there always be one and only one place to go, come holidays or vacations—especially when she and her mother do so much when they get "home": even more cooking than before and the same chores that they have always done, such as collecting eggs, feeding various animals, trying to find some edible roots? But such questions were asked only of the mother by her eldest daughter—as if there were no reason for the two of them to share their ideas with anyone else in the family, never mind risk an argument.

One day, the mother asked Pauline where her boyfriend lived.
Pauline had told her parents the address several times, but they
were indifferent—one street being like any other to people who
knew very little about neighborhoods outside of those where
they worked and lived. The mother told her daughter what had
happened weeks earlier, asked her whether she knew the neighborhood, heard rather a lot from her surprisingly knowing
daughter, and days afterwards, found herself hard put to know
what she believed or wanted for her daughter or herself: "I wish
I hadn't encouraged Tim to stay here a few years ago. He wanted
to return to Harlan County and live there; but I said no, let's stay
a little longer, then we'll be that better off when we do go home
for good. Now I'm confused. I sit on that stool, hitting the
register with my finger, seeing those numbers, and I wonder why
I was put here in the first place. Did God mean for me to be
doing that work all day? I know somebody has to do it, but I
wasn't born to this city life. I wasn't born to be watched all day,
and spoken to as if I'm a dog who isn't trained well enough.

"Yesterday I took my coffee break, and I went outside, instead
of sitting in that back room, watching the hands of the clock go
round and round and drinking their weak brew—weaker with
each price rise of coffee—and feeling their doughnuts sink into
the bottom of my stomach and stay there all day, no matter how
much water I send down. I took a walk. I guess I forgot myself;
I walked and walked. In my mind, I wasn't even in Dayton. I was
back home, up the hollow. I was looking at the pines. I was
hearing the wind coming at them, and hearing them say 'yes,
we're here,' and singing and singing. I was hearing my great-
grandmother just before she died, telling me about those pines
—how brave they are, and proud, and full of hope: evergreens.
I guess I was about seven when she took that last walk with me.
She had me sit down under a pine in a bed of soft needles, and
she told me all about her life, and her memories. She remembered *her* great-grandmother taking a walk with *her*—and that's

going back a long time, I'll tell you. That's going back to an America that was different. I'm not sure there was a Dayton then; but there were our people up those hollows, trying to live the way God wants us to, and failing every day, like the minister says, but still trying.

"I guess I was thinking like that, and so I forgot myself. I'm no clock watcher. I don't try to measure my life by the seconds and the minutes and the hours. I worry for Pauline. She got a job in a laundromat; she sits there, taking money, like I do. She helps people with their laundry. She bought herself a watch, first thing. She's so proud of that watch. She wears it like the Queen of England must wear her crown. I made the mistake the other day of saying something bad—telling her she was more worried about that watch than anything else in the world. I knew I was wrong right after I spoke. I bit my lip. After I heard my words, I said to myself: You are a fool. The worst of it was this: she said nothing to me. She even smiled! I knew she didn't like what she'd heard come out of me, but she wasn't going to have an argument. She's got her own world. I've never felt so far away from a child of my own."

Ironically, she had never felt closer to her daughter. She was beginning to wish at times that she had another life to live—a chance to try it out Pauline's way. On her walk during the coffee break, Hannah Morgan had, in fact, thought of her daughter, wondered what kind of life she would eventually live. And the mother had been late in returning to work because her mind became entranced by one of its flights of fancy: "I pictured Pauline opening the door of a very nice home, like one of those I saw on that bus ride I took by accident. She was going somewhere, I guess. She looked beautiful—all grown up, but still herself, as she is now. She had on a nice dress, like one I've seen advertised in the paper. She had a big pocketbook, I remember. It was slung over her left shoulder. She had keys in her hand— for the car. There it was—a nice two-door Oldsmobile. I've always dreamed of owning an Oldsmobile. My older brother used to be able to spot every make of car. He'd see them coming, and he'd call their names; he'd be on the bus, going to school. He called them Oldsies, and he said they were the best looking of all the automobiles. If Pauline ever has one, she'll have to take me for a ride at least once a week. That's what I imagined *her* doing—going for a ride. She was like that woman I saw—off to work, maybe. I guess I wanted to have fun; I was in the car, waiting for Pauline. I wasn't in the driver's seat, though! It was her car, not mine.

"I suddenly realized I'd been daydreaming in broad daylight, and I was late, and I'd better get back fast to that market; so I ran all the way, came in panting, *way* out of breath—and was told that the next time I'd be fired. It was only five minutes over the time limit. They have no heart in these companies. It's dog eat dog—except that back home our dogs never behave so mean. They don't try to break each other's spirits. They run together, and help each other. I saw one dog, my uncle's, share food with my daddy's dog. It's wrong the way people bad-mouth animals. It ought to go in the other direction: dogs should tell all they know about us! My grandmother used to say: Don't worry about the animals in the woods; it's the people you have to worry about —and the further away they are from here, the more reason there is to worry."

She was indeed worried about her work situation, but she was less and less worried that her daughter would get into personal trouble. Somehow, her daughter would know how to build a reasonably strong and useful life. It was her husband who developed increasingly grave doubts, who kept saying that for Pauline's sake alone the family should go back to Kentucky and stay there. He didn't worry about the daughter's more explicitly urban way of looking at the world; he was afraid she would get hurt by Dayton's "strangers"—a word he used more and more to describe just about everyone in the city except the members of his family. The parents began arguing the matter. They agreed in principle that no one in his or her right mind would voluntarily want to stay in Dayton if he or she had lived up one of Appalachia's hollows. But the father wondered aloud about the fate of an attractive but rather "innocent" person—"a girl," he called his nearly sixteen-year-old daughter—in a northern industrial city. The mother, in contrast, declared Pauline wise, observant, even "sharp-eyed," meaning well able to take stock of the world, to figure out whether to stand firm or take up and move away, maybe run.

A week before Pauline's sixteenth birthday her mother came home from work (as usual a half an hour after her husband did) and began to prepare supper. Tim was watching television and half dozing. The other children were downstairs, playing in the street. As she waited for the boiled potatoes to be ready, she went to get some aspirin for an especially bad headache. She happened to look in the children's room—they shared the master bedroom in the four-room apartment; she and her husband used the smaller bedroom. She noticed that Pauline's bed was not made, unusual in itself, and that on it lay her watch, upside down: "I stopped and stared at that watch. I felt cold. I was scared. I walked away toward the kitchen. I tried to forget what I'd seen. I took the potatoes off the burner. I cut the ham and started heating it up. I got the bread out. I began work on the gravy. Suddenly, I started to cry. I didn't even know why I was crying. I was afraid Tim would notice, but he was lost to himself—the way I am, a lot of the time, when I come home from work. I'm not really in touch with what I'm doing. I'm in a daze. I end up getting my work finished, but I'll be going to bed, and I'll think back, and I'll wonder if I did one thing or another. I'm ashamed to say that sometimes a whole day will go like that for me. I'll leave work, and I don't even remember if I've been at work; I mean, I've been there, but I can't see in my head a single person I've waited on. I don't really look at people. I look at their packages. I'm always being surprised when they try to talk with me. I try to look so busy they don't want to bother me!

"I tried to keep cooking. I kept saying to myself that I was being foolish, real foolish. What difference does it make—that watch on her bed? But I knew it made a lot of difference; I knew that child of mine, that grown daughter of mine—she'll be both to my last breath—was in some kind of trouble. I knew if I told Tim, he'd think *I'm* in trouble. He'd ask me why Pauline's watch there on her bed was a clue to anything—except the fact that she'd been in a rush that morning, as she is every morning, only this time a little more in a rush. I would then feel myself getting upset; I'd flush up. But what would I say in reply? I'd be searching for the right words, but they wouldn't come to me. So I didn't even say a word. I kept my worries to myself. I guess I kept crying—until he did notice. I must have blown my nose, and he could tell it wasn't just a little cold coming on. He got up and came over and asked me what the trouble was. I said that I didn't know. I said that I was worried, but I knew I didn't have anything to worry about. I said I just had this funny feeling inside of me —that Pauline wasn't doing so well. I was surprised, really surprised, when he agreed with me. He told me that he'd heard her crying one night when he woke up. He didn't know what time it was, but he guessed around midnight. That happened a week earlier.

"I was real upset after he told me what he'd heard. I tried hard to finish the supper, and I did. I went to the window and called the kids. They came in, one after the other—except Pauline. I was ready to cry again. Of course, I realized that it wasn't unusual for Pauline to come home late; she stayed in school and did her homework, and she went to the library and did some more. She had a part-time job, three afternoons a week, at a soda fountain. Was this one of the days, I asked myself? And I didn't know the answer. But I remembered that she never came home later than six o'clock. I ran into her room and looked at that watch: a quarter until six. I decided to keep the watch near me. We only have the alarm clock near our bed. I told everyone to sit down, and I put the watch near my plate. The children wondered why. I told them I wanted to watch the time pass by! They thought I was getting a bit daffy, but Tim told them to eat up, and they soon forgot about their mother and their sister's watch. We got through at nearly half past six, and we all scattered, as usual; *they* scattered, of course. I stayed with the dishes—and that watch. I was in a bad, bad way. I *knew* that daughter of mine was upset, and I wished I could run downstairs and run and run, until I found her. I imagined myself holding her in my arms and trying to comfort her. But I didn't know where to go—and even if I did have a clue, I'm not sure I would have decided to go find Pauline and try to talk with her. She's a grown lady, I kept reminding myself!

"By seven o'clock, I had to keep the children moving toward bed, but I felt like a child myself. Worse, I was crazy with worry. Tim was upset, too. He told me he was going to go out and look for Pauline; but I told him no, it was useless. What do you do in a city? This isn't our hollow. When he heard me say that, he stopped putting on his jacket. He calmed down. He sat down. He turned on the television! How could he do that! I wanted to scream! I ran and turned it off. He got up and put it right back on. That's when I ran into the children's room, and threw myself down on Pauline's bed, and started to cry. I had the watch in my right hand, and while I was crying, I looked at the time passing, one second after another, one minute after another. I must have fallen asleep, because the next thing I knew it was eight o'clock and Pauline was standing over me. I'd looked at the time, on her watch, right after seeing her face. The first thing I did was hand the watch back to her."

The mother was almost afraid to begin a conversation with her daughter. She was glad that there were other children still not tidily in bed. Ordinarily she would have lectured them on the

singular virtue of promptness; but that evening she almost encouraged their seemingly endless, occasionally rather original,
and always quite spirited delaying maneuvers. It was their father
who finally became annoyed. For the first time ever, he took part
in their evening retirement rituals. Usually, they came to him just
before retiring to say good-night and be kissed on the forehead.
He would always say to them: "Good-night, I'll see you tomorrow morning." Each of them would say, in reply: "Good-night,
I'll see you tomorrow morning." In fact, he never saw them in
the morning, except on Sundays, because he left the house for
work well before they awoke. That evening, he prodded them
into their pajamas, made sure they had scrubbed their faces, and
told them to hurry to bed. They were more than confused; they
sped to bed as if a military inspection was afoot, and omitted
saying their customary evening farewells to him. Their faces
indicated curiosity as well as surprise—so he told them something: their mother wasn't well, and neither was their older
sister, who often lent an assist at bedtime.

Meanwhile, the mother had motioned to her daughter with a
finger, and the message was received without spoken acknowledgment: let's go outside. The two went for an early evening
walk. Within no time at all Pauline was pouring out her sorrow
and despair to her mother. They kept moving, kept talking, lost
all sense of where they were going; eventually they found themselves utterly lost, shrugged off the discovery, and continued—
until they saw a sign telling them that they were no longer in
Dayton; whereupon they stopped talking, entered the world
once again, began to worry about time and space: it was late,
indeed, and it would be quite difficult to get home. They went
into a roadside coffee shop on the highway; noticed it was midnight; became frightened—the family, they knew, was also conscious of the time—and explained their situation.

They would never forget the response of the woman at the
counter: "She looked at Pauline and me, and said she could tell

by my way of speaking that I was one of her people. It turned out she was from Leslie County, near Hyden, and had been up in Ohio fifteen years, but always went back, of course, on her holidays and vacations. I guess her husband died five years ago, and she had him brought home, and she was going to stay, but she couldn't make any money in Leslie County, so she came back to Ohio. She has four children, and her second oldest is Pauline's age. She's my age. She's been working that night shift at the coffee house for five years. She comes home and gets her younger kids off to school, and her two older ones go to work, and then she sleeps; but it's hard, turning day into night and night into day, even after five years. She has a car, and it bleeds her bad, she says, but she's hooked on it, like some people up the hollows are on the rotgut they make for themselves. They'll drink it as if they have a glass of water from a mountain spring.

"We forgot what time it was again, Pauline and me, talking with her: Sara Means is her name. I felt as if God had given us to one of our own kin, to help us out. The only other person there was a man at the end of the counter, and he was drunk and trying to sober up with coffee. He drank so much of it, I thought he'd explode. He'd get up and put quarters in the jukebox. We couldn't stop him. We had to talk over the music—that rock music the young folks like so much. I don't know how it came about that we started telling Sara Means about Pauline and her trouble, but we did. I think it was after she said that we both looked worried, and to have an extra cup of coffee on the house. We told her we *were* worried—that we had to get back home, and it would sure be a long haul. We asked her if she knew of a bus that would start us off. She laughed, and said we could sooner take a bus to California than get where we wanted to go at that hour. I remember thinking to myself: I don't even have money on me, not a penny; and Pauline doesn't either. We had no pocketbooks, no wallets, not even the keys to the apartment. Sara Means brought us the coffee, and she brought an order of toast that we didn't even ask for, and she said our worries were over, because *she'd* take us home!

"We said no, she shouldn't. Then I thought to myself: how can she? She's supposed to work until six or seven in the morning. I told her I was grateful, but I knew she couldn't leave her job. She said yes, she could. She has someone come work with her from two o'clock on. I wouldn't have believed it, but it gets busy for a while then—the truck drivers beginning their day. And an hour or two afterwards, the traffic slows down, and she could drive us, and the other person would take care of the place. But we'd have to stay until then, about four or four-thirty. I was really happy! I told her if she wouldn't mind, we wouldn't mind! She said she knew where we live; she used to live in that neighborhood herself.

"Pauline and I were tired of talking, but we both began all over again. I guess we wanted a third person to help us figure out what we should do. It wasn't my idea to tell a stranger about our troubles. It was Pauline's idea. She just started asking Sara Means what she would do *if*, and another what she would do *if*, and *another* what she would do *if*, and finally we stopped pretending, and dropped the ifs and we talked about Pauline and what was happening to her, and about our life as a family, and about Sara Means and her kids—but mostly about Pauline. She and her boyfriend had got into a real jam, and they were both scared. They'd been getting closer and closer. I knew it, but I didn't want to think about it. Sometimes you know, but you don't want to know. Sometimes you're glad to be busy, busy—because if you had the time that you complain you don't have, then you'd be in even worse shape: you'd have to *find* reasons to be busy! For weeks I'd think of Pauline as soon as I got up. I'd wonder what's happening between her and that boyfriend of hers. I'd keep forgetting his name: Henry Boynton—a funny last name I've never known how to remember. But I'd jump out of bed and run to put on the coffee. As I was putting the machine on, I'd think to myself: good-bye Pauline and your troubles for another day!

"I told the lady in the coffee shop about my sins; they *are* sins. A mother owes it to her daughter to pay attention to her when she's slipping into trouble. And Pauline was slipping into something, I knew. She seemed in a daze a lot of the time. She didn't hear me when I talked. She forgot to wash her clothes; she forgot to do her chores; she left her books home, or left them in school. The one thing she held on to for dear life was that watch of hers. I would joke with her; I'd say that so long as she had the watch on, she was still doing all right. She would say *yes;* she once told me to keep an eye on the watch, because it was her 'good-luck charm.' When she thought everything was falling to pieces, she would even talk to the watch! She'd say: I have four more hours of school, or I have until nine o'clock to finish my homework. •he used to stare at that watch, sometimes, at the table. She never really seemed hungry, and I'd watch her out of the corner of my eye—her face bent toward her left wrist, following that hand that went around and around and around. I'd want to go tear the watch away and hide it or lose it for good. But she loved the watch, I knew that. I think it is our family's most precious possession. I don't own anything worth more than five or ten dollars! That's why it meant trouble, lots of trouble, when I saw the watch on the bed."

She can't bring herself easily to mention the details of her daughter's entanglement with a persistent, strong-minded boyfriend. Even when her daughter and she walked the long evening, sat out the early morning, she had trouble hearing various psychological or physical specifics. She kept saying "What?" Her daughter wasn't whispering, nor was she, Hannah, hard of hearing. The issue was a woman's modesty up against a much younger woman's almost desperate candor. The two women kept open to one another; but there were moments, and longer, when they had to make their accommodations. The daughter spoke and spoke; told her mother that her boyfriend wanted to have an affair with her; did not want even to talk about eventual marriage; would be going East to college in a couple of years; told her repeatedly that she was "slow," that she had "a lot to learn," that he would be a "good teacher," but that she had to be a willing "student." The mother would look half away, but obviously paid close attention. Even under cover of the night, even with the protective diversions of street life, even with the distraction that the momentum of walking offers, the older woman found herself shaking as she listened, and hard put to ask questions or say much of anything.

When she was especially upset or embarrassed, she made a point of noticing something—a passing car, a light in a building, a sign promoting a commodity. It was as if, thereby, she was not directly confronted with the words she was hearing, and with the sadness, the sense of vulnerability, the fear that both she and her daughter experienced as they plodded on so relentlessly: "We just kept moving for a while; and she kept telling me stories, and I didn't want to look right at her. I was grateful every time I saw a person walking toward us. I felt better; I felt I wasn't *just* with my daughter, being told by her so much that was upsetting. That boyfriend of hers is no friend at all. He's a bad, bad person. He's a young man who likes to brag and boast about himself. He's all stuck on himself; that's how we'd describe him in Harlan County, Kentucky. A lot of good-looking young men are like that. A lot of men who aren't so young and aren't so good-looking are like that, too!

"He was telling her he wanted to use her, then throw her away; that's what he was letting her know. But she didn't want to face up to the truth; that's what I figured out. When I began to tell her what I thought, she started to cry, and then she turned sour on me and told me I should try to be 'fair,' and understand *him!* Well, I told her I *did* understand him, and I wanted *her* to understand him. She said she did. She said she loved him. She said she wanted to stand by him, and take her chances. I think she would have done that and not spoken a word to me, and been very happy with him, if it weren't that he wanted so much from her. He wanted her to come and sleep with him, but he didn't want to go steady with her, and he didn't want to take her out to the parties his friends gave. He wanted her to be a secret love of his. She wasn't good enough to come meet his parents and his sister, who is a year younger than Pauline. She wasn't even good enough to go out on double dates with his best friend and the friend's girl. And my daughter was ready to say, Yes, I'll do anything, just to be with you, Henry Boynton, or whatever his name is.

"The only thing that stopped her was the drugs. He wanted her to use marijuana. He wanted her to get high on strong marijuana; and he used another drug. He inhaled a powder, cocaine. He bragged: it takes a lot of money to get the stuff he uses. His father gave him a big allowance—more money than I make in a week, for all I know. His father gave him other money —a savings bank-account. The boy just drew out the money and used it to buy drugs. He kept pushing them on Pauline. He told her that if she was going to get serious with him, she'd have to smoke the pot, and she'd have to do better than beer when he was drinking his scotch. She tried, poor lamb of mine. She tried inhaling the drugs; but she just couldn't do it in the right way. He wanted her dizzy and funny and silly and giddy and half out of it. He wanted her drunk. He wanted her a puppet, to play with. He was a coward; he was afraid to try anything so long as she was sober, even if she was showing him all the time that she had fallen for him lock, stock, and barrel, and was ready to oblige him—mostly. She even tried everything he wanted her to try. She just couldn't become successful enough with drugs to satisfy his demands.

"The day she left the watch on her bed was the day he was going to try something else with her; he was starting to use something that he put into himself with a needle. My daughter almost said yes to him that day. They used to go to a friend's house because that boy Henry didn't want her in his own house. She went there with him, and he had some powder, and he was mixing it, and he was going to inject it into her, and she ran away. She wasn't crying when she told me; she was sad. I think she loved that boy. I don't know why. I wonder what that kind of love is all about. I wonder why a daughter of mine liked that kind of person so much. What did Tim and I do to cause her to be like that?

"That woman in the coffee shop ended up understanding Pauline and me and the rest of our family better than I did. She was so smart, and so quick to spot our troubles. I was shamed afterwards when I came home and lay there in bed, knowing I couldn't sleep for that hour or two before I had to get up and start another day. Tim had gone to bed and fallen right to sleep; he'd figured I had to talk with Pauline about sex. Like I said, he knew she was in trouble; but neither of us ever wanted to talk about it. When I came home, I asked him if he wanted to hear what I'd heard. He said no, he just wanted that extra hour of sleep, or else he'd risk losing his job. They keep after him every second. I said we could talk the coming Sunday, and he said 'yes,' but I didn't bring up the subject then—not after he told me a day or so before that there are some things that mothers and daughters should keep between themselves, and he didn't want to get himself into Pauline's troubles; he'd leave them to me.

"I told him maybe he's right. I asked Pauline if she wants to talk with her daddy about all that happened, and she said no, never. She's always looked up to him. She's always said to me that I'm lucky to have someone like him. I reminded her of what she's said when we walked that night. I asked her why she chose such a boy when she had such respect for her daddy. She said she didn't know why. I don't know why either. But that Sara Means told us one thing I don't intend to forget; she said that all our trouble is due to coming up here to Dayton, and staying here too long. I'm not sure that *all* our trouble comes from that, but a good bit does, I believe."

The mother would never be the same after that long, sleepless night. She went to work the next day, determined to overcome the hazards of fatigue, and did so remarkably well. She was proud of herself in the late afternoon as she punched her card, left work: no one had remarked upon her slowness or lack of attention to the requirements of the job. Sitting in the bus, headed home for an evening of spaghetti, beans, and Texas toast, as she called the big pieces she cut from unsliced white bread (in order to make the fare seem more appetizing to her children), she imagined herself—for the first time in her life—collapsing, not doing what ought to be done, needed to be done, *was* done, day after day in the course of a particular lifetime. She had strange, unsettling thoughts—of getting off the bus, walking toward nowhere, sleeping on the sides of the various roads she came upon. She pictured herself working the night shift with Sara Means, coming home *after* her husband and children had left for work and school, seeing them only briefly in the evening, *after* they had prepared supper for themselves, because she would still be sleeping. She wondered what it would be like to stay home and drink coffee and watch television and go outside and browse through stores—and maybe make a friend or two: some woman of her age and background who had also decided to stop giving her life to a supermarket chain or a factory.

As the bus plunged on, stop after stop, she also found herself staring at various women. What were their lives like? Were they reasonably content, satisfied, at peace with themselves and members of their families; or were they vaguely or not so vaguely upset, anxious, bewildered? She especially noticed one woman standing in front of a tenement building not unlike the one she lived in; the woman looked somewhat like Sara Means, and for Hannah Morgan was a stimulus to a long series of speculations.

Perhaps she was downstairs in the street at that hour because she needed to get away from an apartment full of noise, friction, obligations. Perhaps she had decided to let her family manage for themselves, just that one afternoon and evening. Perhaps she had argued openly with her husband or with one of her children or, indeed, with all of them—and had walked out, slamming the door. The image of a door slamming came to her mind continually until she got off the bus and began to walk to her own apartment house. When she got there, she hesitated for a moment. Might someone drive by, see her standing there, and wonder about *her* life, even as she just did, upon seeing the woman a few miles away? She was not able to think much more; she had to go upstairs and get to work. But as she approached the third floor, where she lived, and saw the door of her flat, she had a momentary vision again of the door opening, then slamming closed.

This poor, hard-pressed, working-class woman, who had about the equivalent of a sixth-grade education, and who had never heard of the name Henrik Ibsen or the play *A Doll's House,* nevertheless pointed out to us several days afterwards symbolic connections not unlike those made decades ago by a Norwegian writer of considerable subtlety and sophistication: "That door being shut—I've kept seeing it in my mind, and I've wondered what's happening to me. I think I know, a little. I think Pauline's trouble has made me different, and try as I do to get back to my old self, I don't succeed. I've talked to myself as strict as I know how. I've tried to imagine my mother or my grandmother talking to me. I've even thought of confessing to Tim and telling him to get real tough with me, and then I'd come to my senses. But I really don't want to go back to the old way of doing things— not since the trouble with Pauline. She tells me she'll never be the same again, and I've been telling myself that I'll never be the same either. It's strange, but since I heard her story, I've been talking a lot to myself—as if she's me and I'm her. And I've called

Sara Means up three times, from a pay station. She's become like a mother to me—and to Pauline as well. We both turn to her in our thoughts."

After her long night with her mother and their new friend, Pauline had said no to her boyfriend—no about drugs, no about sex, no even about conversation. The young man had not quite believed her; had become insistent and plaintive; but in no time, aware that she meant what she said, turned mean, scornful, abusive. She was a "stupid hillbilly girl"; she was a "yokel," and he had only hoped to teach her "manners." Pauline then felt foolish for what she had allowed to go on. She was not quite ready to follow the advice Sara Means had given her: forget about not only a particular person, but all that he was part of—swinging, middle-class, suburban, twentieth-century American life. The young lady still wanted to be a nurse. She would take a bus to a Dayton hospital and go inside, watch the nurses and imagine herself one of them. Several weeks after her evening, night, early morning with her mother, she told her mother of the three or four hospital trips, asked her to come along. The mother was quite willing. They found it hard, though, to agree upon a time. The mother worked five days a week, tried hard on weekends to "straighten out" the house and "look after" the children a little more circumspectly than it was possible to do during the week: haircuts, torn clothes, complaints expressed but not really attended to. She sewed. She cut hair. She dusted. She glued broken dishes. She applied iodine, bandages, "drawing out" ointment.

She wondered, after her daughter's proposal of a hospital visit, about another kind of life: "I began to think I didn't want to see that hospital! I kept stalling; I told Pauline that I had to think of her brothers and sisters, and her father. He works *six* days a week. I only have the two days to catch up, and on Sunday we try to give a half a day to thinking of God, and praying to Him. But I knew in my heart why I kept finding excuses for myself.

I didn't want to go and see something I might like too much. I didn't want to come back upset. I knew before I went that the visit would get into my mind, and it wouldn't be so easy to think, afterwards.

"Finally, Pauline and I made an excuse to go see the hospital. I couldn't tell Tim the real reason we were leaving, because he would have been upset that I was doing something like that on a Sunday afternoon. I said there was more trouble with Pauline, and I had to go talk with her alone. Tim got angry; he said Pauline was becoming spoiled as could be. When we were her age, he reminded me, no one spent the night or a Sunday afternoon taking walks with him or me, so we could 'talk.' We had our chores, and we carried them to bed with us; we dreamed of them in bed, and when we got up, we started doing them; and when we got ready to go to sleep, they were still on our minds. When I hear Tim talk about Harlan County these days, I want to sit down and have a long cry. I want to go back there and start doing my chores. I'm sure they could use me up the hollow— our kin there. Not all my people, the Cables, and Tim's, the Morgans, are going to leave that county. Some are the saved; I fear we're the damned! But if you're in a bad spot, my mother told me, all you can do is use your head and your muscles, and try to do the best you can. So that's what we've been doing up North. I told Tim that it's unfair of us not to remember that Pauline hasn't grown up the way we did. She's been up here, and it's a no-good life, like he and I always say to each other; and some of the no-good is bound to stick fast to her; and it's our job as her parents to do our best, our mightiest best, to help her wipe away the city from her face so she can see better—so she can see the right way, and not be all dazzled by the lights up here, and the loud, loud music, and everything going so fast."

The two women got on the bus and took their hospital trip. They said virtually nothing on the way, each lost in her thoughts. They approached the hospital in silence, a bit gingerly, too:

where to go, how to stand and watch without risking the criticism of busy people, or appearing to be a nuisance or even suspect? Then the sign caught their attention, sent warm, encouraging memories to each of them: *Coffee Shop.* They no longer felt aimless, adrift, confused. They had a destination. And they had hope: another Sara Means, for all anyone knew, might well be there, standing and smiling and serving and asking and telling. Once in the coffee shop, however, they were disenchanted. It was a crowded Sunday afternoon—more visitors than at any other time of the week. There were no seats. The people behind the counter were rushed, irritable, silent—and not, it certainly appeared, from Kentucky. Mother and daughter stood just inside the crowded room; watched the three waitresses try hard and vainly to keep up with the demands of the customers; and finally, after a few minutes, left for the hospital's corridors, which now seemed somehow friendlier, less crowded, and without the disturbing drama of insistent request and harassed compliance. They walked those corridors, slowly becoming less self-conscious, less concerned about what others might think or say.

In a while, the corridors became Dayton's streets. The midafternoon rush of visitors, patients, hospital personnel gave way in the minds of the two women to dark roads and the hush of a city putting itself to sleep after yet another day of hustle: "We forgot where we were; that's what happened. We forgot why we came there. We weren't looking at the hospital. We were taking a long walk somewhere. We were talking about the way we lived, and how we should live. Pauline said I've been 'hypnotized' by the ministers in Kentucky, and in Ohio. She thinks my mother has always bowed before my father, and so do I with Tim. I think she's got these strange ideas. She sits there at the table and watches me, and watches her father, and she finds wrong where there's just a day and all that happens in a day.

"If you put on a pair of dark glasses, you're going to see a dark day; if you close your eyes, you're going to say it's nighttime,

even if the sun is out. I kept telling her to give her father a chance
—an even break. She said she wasn't against him; she loves him.
It's just that he was reared to think he can talk to her and me one
way, and to his brothers the other way. Pauline thinks he's nicer
to her brothers. She's dead wrong on that score. He loves her.
He loves her two sisters. Sometimes, to be honest, I'll see him
looking at those girls, and I get a little jealous. I can see his eyes
moving up and down and all over, and I know what he's saying
to himself: they're *nice!* I've heard him say so out loud. Then he'll
flush up when I'll joke with him, and tell him to leave them
alone! A father has a right to notice how pretty his daughters are
becoming! It's a funny thing, though—I don't think mothers get
as worked up about their sons as fathers do about their daughters.

"I told Pauline she ought to think of others. She's too much
on her own mind! My mother spotted us when we were like that,
and gave us even more chores. I can't do that with Pauline. I'm
not my mother, and she isn't me, the way I was at her age, and
this isn't our hollow. How can I change my daughter, when she's
changing me so much? I get scared, thinking of what will happen
if we stay here another ten years."

A pause; it is absurd to talk about a decade in the future. Best
to take each day as it comes—and each problem: "When we left
the hospital, I told Pauline it would be fine for her to be a nurse,
if she wanted. I don't know about the money. We have none to
spare. I have $140 in a savings book, and it'll go, come Christ-
mas. But if she can work and work and save and save, and if she
does well in her studies, and if she's willing to keep her hopes
up high, then maybe she'll see the dream she has become true.
Isn't that what our people did when they came to Kentucky? It
was no mean job, making the paths through the woods. My
granddaddy used to take me to the top of a mountain, his favorite
one, and tell me the stories he heard about the first Cables who
came to Harlan County, and how they had nothing; and there

weren't the roads or the stores or cars or mines or bulldozers or schools or much pastureland either or the electric wires or the buses—just woods and more woods, some of them high up, covering hills, and the rest spread over the valleys, and water, lots of it, coming from the snow, or in lakes and ponds and streams.

"He'd say that our people claimed the land from Nature, and asked God if He'd smile on them, and went to work, and after a while, they got the hollows going and the towns, and that's more than they could have dreamed of having when they first came and started out. The same might go for Pauline. She might want to be a nurse, and she might give her all to her dream, and she might end up in a hospital like this, walking down the hall as if it's that path I used to take when I was her age—way up to the top of the hollow, where I believed God rested sometimes. My grandmother used to tell me that when she was tired and wanted to rest herself she went up the hollow and waited for the wind to come: God's voice, telling her to have courage. She had bad arthritis. I wonder if she'd have gone to a hospital here in Dayton if she ever had lived here. I guess Pauline will live here all her life. That's what her life will be like—a Dayton life, not a mountain life."

They came home later than anyone expected. Her husband was upset, demanded an explanation. She gave one: they lost track of time. He was not satisfied, pointed to Pauline's watch, which this time had not been left on the bed, but worn. For the first time in her marriage, Hannah Morgan cried when criticized. Before, she would have nodded, set about her work, told herself repeatedly that she would try harder to do better. She would also have told herself how *fine* her husband is, how thoughtful and loyal and hard-working and honorable. Instead, she found herself not only crying, but unable to start supper, and with a flood of thoughts: "I went into the bedroom. I knew I needed time to pull myself together. I was upset. So was Tim. I just sat on the bed and let my poor mind do its wandering and its wondering. I had a strange wish pass over me—that I was like that woman I'd seen on the bus, with a car of my own and some money, and I was going to the hospital to be a volunteer, to work just like the volunteers do—we saw a lot of them when we were there— and that Pauline was asking me for a little help. She was dressed in a nurse's uniform. She was a nurse, of course! She seemed so happy, so sure of herself. She was running a ward, maybe. I think I was proud of her, but I was also sad.

"I guess I was sorry she had already grown up. I feel more and more that time is going too fast! When I was younger, my mother would take me up the creek, and she'd try to pick up water with her hands, and the water would go through her fingers. Then I would try and the same thing would happen. Then she would show me how she cupped her hands and held the water, at least for a while. Then she taught me how to do it, too. Then she'd tell me this: 'Hannah, time slips right through your fingers, if you don't watch out.' When I got home and told my father what I'd learned, he'd say my mother talks too much, and she says what everyone knows. My mother never spoke back to him, though. She respected him a lot; she told us that a lot. I respect Tim— and that day I felt bad that I wasn't a better person."

She left the bedroom fairly soon, returned to the kitchen. She started the meal: "Sunday pickup," leftovers from previous meals. She apologized out loud to her husband for coming home late and for "taking so much time" before making a start on supper. She apologized to him again and again as she began her work. The longer she grated the potatoes, meant to be french fries, the more she acknowledged her failures as a wife and mother. Tim was annoyed with her, confused by her profuse self-criticism. Hannah Morgan found herself, as she dumped the shreds of potato into the deep fat, confronted by evidence of her own weaknesses, or so she believed.

She stood there watching the pieces of potato toss and turn, squirm, become a bit shriveled, take on a yellow and then brown coloring. They are cooking well, she observed. And then came her sudden vision: they were going to Hell, those pieces of potato, right before her eyes. She was sending them to Hell. She briskly took the frying pan off the burner. She turned off the gas. She sat down. What was the matter? Pauline wondered that immediately. It was unlike her mother to interrupt the preparation of a meal, especially when it was late, and when the family was hungry. The others were involved in their own rhythms—games, the television. What *was* the matter? Pauline looked and hesitated. She decided to say nothing, to pick up where her mother had left off. She opened up the soup cans, emptied them, put them on the burner. She placed the cold cuts on a dish, and put some pickles nearby. She took the milk from the refrigerator and filled up the glasses. Then she stopped and looked at her mother. Not a second's return glance. The woman seemed to be staring, but at nothing. Pauline followed the trajectory of her mother's gaze: the window. But the mother was seated, and the window was too high for anything to be visible—except the shadow of an apartment building across the street, interrupted occasionally by some lights from various flats. What could possibly be the matter?

That was the last time the young woman would have to ask the question about the older woman. The mother suddenly stood up, ran across the room to the counter next to the stove, stared at the french fries, and shouted: "Save them, save them. They're going to Hell fast! They're all going to Hell fast!" Pauline laughed, but stopped quickly when she saw her mother's face: serious to the bone. But the mother suddenly ended the emotional impasse. She told the daughter to sit down and wait to be served. She became fast, efficient, steely in her determination to finish the evening strong: the serving, the prodding of stubborn or coy or finicky appetites; the cleaning up of the table, the washing and drying of dishes; the prodding yet again, this time on behalf of teeth and hands and faces and arms and legs and ankles and clothes and the floors of rooms.

When everyone was in bed, Tim included, the two women looked at one another. The mother was sitting in her kitchen chair; the daughter was standing near the stove, wondering about the words uttered an hour or so ago, and other words that might be forthcoming. Hannah Morgan put an end to speculation, apprehension, uncertainty. She told her daughter that she ought not worry, that "a woman has moods sometimes." She told her daughter that for a moment "everything seemed about to fall apart," but that a self-imposed lecture of sorts had worked, as had been the case so many times before. She told her daughter that we are all lucky; that, as the ministers keep saying, we are human beings, not animals, not stones, not trees, not metal—not pieces of potato, cut up and burning up and soon enough eaten up. We have a will, a fate, a destiny. Heaven is a possibility; Hell is no one's inevitability—given a change of heart, an effort of the mind. Best for them to retire—but not before a final word: "You stay here and become a nurse. You be a proud woman of Harlan County who has learned to become a proud woman of Dayton. You bow to no one. In my dreams, the ones I have just before I wake up and have to go to work, I see myself on top of my grandmother's favorite mountain, standing as tall as I can on my tiptoes to see more; bowing to no one; taking big gulps of the thin air, the way you have to when you're up high, and you're tired, but feeling good, real good. When I do wake up, I say to myself what my grandmother used to say to me: Don't bow to anyone, not in your heart. A mountain dream like that will carry a person right through a day working at that supermarket."

THREE

SOMETIMES, UNA CHICANA

S an Antonio has been her home for a decade; Teresa Torres Cardenas came there at the age of twelve from the Rio Grande Valley, where she was born. Her parents were farm workers. Her father decided one day that enough is enough; he took his family to the city, managed to get a job collecting garbage. He intends to do that kind of work until he dies, and he is not at all displeased with such a prospect. In "the Valley" he was bossed interminably; treated with constant rudeness and meanness; denied all social, economic, and political rights. He was, by his own estimate, "a Mexican peon," used by the Anglo growers to harvest their crops, but paid very little for doing so, and given no respect for the hard work involved. He was never even allowed to vote. The Anglos, five percent of the particular community he belonged to, controlled all the political offices. And always there were the Texas Rangers, ready in an instant to wield brute force—if a given sheriff, also no stranger to the gun, needed a helping hand or two.

"My name is Antonio Torres," he often said, "and I am now in San Antonio, Texas, where I can breathe without worrying that some Anglo will decide that I should stop breathing for good —but first dig my own grave and buy a coffin for myself from an Anglo undertaker." It was like that for him in the Valley, and it was like that for his wife Maria, who defers to him almost always. If one tries to draw her out, she insists that she is "only" Antonio's wife, and that she has nothing to say that he hasn't already said. But she, too, can get sardonic and bitter about the Valley: "When we were there, the Anglo chains were on our hands and feet. When we were there, we went to bed in fear and woke up in fear. We were 'troublemakers.' The Anglos called us that name because my husband talked with the union organizers. They came to the Valley and tried to fight the growers, so that our wages would go up. The growers called in the sheriffs and the Texas Rangers, and we ended up beaten, again. That was when my husband said *basta;* enough is enough. We had nothing. We left with no hope of ever getting anything for ourselves. We thought we could at least try the big city. San Antonio would be better for our children. We knew that. My husband said we should leave, and we left. We have no reason to be sorry."

For Teresa such memories of the Valley are dim. She claims to remember only a few "bad times in the Valley." She was the youngest of four daughters and rather protected by her older sisters, who have always spoken more harshly of life near the Rio Grande. After her came one son, followed by another: six in all. Her mother told her, as she did all her children, that she was "a wish of God's." Her mother told her that she must say her prayers upon rising, before each meal, and upon retiring. Her mother also told her, she remembers, that San Antonio would turn out to be a good city because it would provide husbands for the four Torres daughters. At the age of twelve, in San Antonio a week, and having heard such a prophesy, Teresa wondered who her husband would be—by name, by occupation, by height, by personality. She especially dwelled on the name—the shift that she and her sisters, but not her brothers, would have to make.

The girl Teresa was told many times that there is no way to predict the future, that she must wait on God's decision and be grateful for whatever He decides. But it was hard for a child to accept that line of reasoning. She continued to speculate, have hope, fret, show apprehension—as with these observations made at the age of thirteen: "Your whole life depends on your husband. My aunt tells my cousins what kind of man to marry— someone who will take care of you and protect you. I have dreamt that I would someday meet a man who would have a lot of money, and he would have a big car, and we would drive away and live in a big house. Then I would have a happy life. But maybe I won't meet a man like that. Maybe I'll meet a poor man, and he'll not even have a car. My father is going to buy a car one day, now that he has a job. He works on a truck. He fills it with the things people throw away. He comes home tired. My mother is waiting for him. She tells us that he is the first person in the family, and we should bow to him. We have his name. I wonder what name I'll have. There is a man who has a store and he has a boy who is my age. I wouldn't mind joining his family. They have two cars, and they are big. The boy has asked one of my brothers to go on a ride; his father is a fast driver, my brother says. Maybe I'll get a ride, later on!

"I don't think the family would like our family. They are rich compared to us. My father says that they have a lot of influence. The priest talks with them before he writes his sermon! I told my mother once that I pray that our father gets rich one day. (He bought a raffle ticket, and maybe he will win!) But my mother was very upset with me. She said it's wrong to think of money so much. She does, though—a lot. She worries about having enough to buy food and get us clothes. She says that if my father lost his job, it would be the end of the world for us. He's the one who keeps us going. I hope I meet a man as good as him when I grow up."

When Teresa was fourteen she left school and got her first job, carrying out food at a drive-in. She worked conscientiously,

ended up turning over all but five dollars a week to her father.
At first she handed her father the check, expected little if anything back. She was, after all, living in his house, eating his food.
She had few desires of her own—or so she was taught to believe.
She was not convinced that such was the case, however. She had
her secret wishes—not so secret, actually; secret from her father,
but told to her mother. When her father decided to give her five
dollars a week, out of the checks she continued to hand over
every Saturday, she acknowledged even to him a few self-indulgent fantasies: "I'd like to save up and buy a new dress, mostly
red with some yellow in it. Red and yellow are my two favorite
colors. I don't like green or purple or blue. I like the blue sky,
but not a blue dress. My father said I shouldn't think of dresses
too much. They cost a lot, and you wear a good one only on
Sunday. When I'm older I might go out in the evening. I get
home late, though—seven o'clock—and I've been on my feet all
day. I don't think I'd be much good dancing!

"I just want to sit and watch television. I'd like a set of my own;
then I wouldn't have to fight with my sisters about the programs.
My father told them I should have the first choice over them
because I'm working now. But they've been working for a long
time. I think he wants me to be a little spoiled. That's what my
mother says. I'm his youngest daughter, and he calls me his
'baby.' He told me he wished I could have stayed in school and
finished; then I would have got a better job. He said it bothers
him that I'm working in that drive-in; but if we'd stayed in the
Rio Grande Valley, I'd have already been picking the crops for
a long time, five or six years, according to my father.

"I wish I had one of the new cars that come into the drive-in.
Mostly, the people are Mexicans, but they seem to have those
five- and ten-dollar bills to spend. I asked my father where they
get the money, and he said they work and save, and then they
buy and spend, and they take out loans and pay a lot of interest
—and they're trapped. My father has never borrowed a penny

in his life. He says he would stop eating before he borrowed money. He says he would kill himself rather than borrow money. He says that the Anglos have their Texas Rangers, but worse than the Rangers are the loan companies. And worse than the loan companies, he says, are the advertisements on television. When my little brothers see something and say they wish they had it, my father comes over and puts the television off. My brothers don't say anything; they want to keep watching the programs. But I'll bet they don't give up wishing. Even my father said once that he collects garbage from some very nice homes. If he likes them that much, he must wish he lived in one of them!

"I told him that maybe the man I marry will be able to buy a good home for himself and me. He said I shouldn't have such dreams. He said the Mexicans are poor, and only a few of us have much money, and you have to be a crook or be very lucky if you're going to be a Mexican with a lot of cash in your pocket. I told him I thought the man who owns the store isn't a crook, and he works hard. My father said no, he _is_ a crook; he is part of a gambling organization. People phone in bets to him, and he takes them, and he gets paid by some racketeers. I think they are Mexican-Americans. They have Cadillacs. We've seen some big Cadillacs parked in front of that store. My father says you can be sure that the people who drive those cars aren't coming to our little store down the street just to buy some bread and some Cokes."

For a year and a half Teresa worked faithfully at the food drive-in. At the age of fifteen, however—just under sixteen—she was fired. She had been increasingly "slow," the manager told her. She had shown herself, besides, to be a rather proud, independent girl—"high on herself" and "not willing to please the customers enough," she was told. Those sweeping generalizations were mere evasions, Teresa knew; but they were not without their hard core of truth. A week before she was told not to show up for work the next day or any day, two men in a light blue Cadillac asked Teresa for small Cokes. She obliged. They then decided they wanted hamburgers. She obliged. They told her the hamburgers didn't look "too good." She suggested they at least *try* them. If they still seemed unsatisfactory, she would be glad to take them back. The man at the wheel started asking her questions: how old was she, how long had she been working there, how long did she hope to be working there, and where would she like to be working, were she given the chance? She answered forthrightly at first. She would, any day, be sixteen. She had worked there for well over a year—going on two, actually. She hoped to stay there indefinitely, and she had no real idea where she might get a better job.

The driver told her that *he* had such an idea. She smiled and asked him where; he smiled, and said he'd tell her—but at some other time and in some other place. She thought he was trying to be funny—though she didn't think he *was* funny—and she left for another car, which had just pulled up. The man called her back in a loud, demanding voice. She told him to wait. He repeated his request that she come back, and come back immediately. She ignored him. She took the order of the driver in the nearby car, carried it to the kitchen, and on the way, walking on the hot, midday asphalt, she heard the roar of a motor, the sudden screech of brakes, the noise of doors being opened in a hurry, and the further noise of shoes moving quickly on a hard surface: the two men in the Cadillac, she realized, as she looked up and saw their backs, then the car they had left—its doors open, the motor still going, and some hard rock coming from a tape deck inside. A minute or two later she was approached by the manager, told off, told to stop working and collect the pay owed her, told to go away and never again show up, even as a customer.

Teresa had a hard time getting a new job. She went to stores, offices, factories, was told no, no, no. She began to say no to herself, call herself a failure, regard the future with increasing gloom. She took to sleeping late, helping her mother with the younger children, eating far too much for her own good. Her mother became worried, eventually suggested a visit to the priest. Teresa obliged. She told the priest what had happened. She told the priest, too, of the burden she had carried: it had seemed best not to tell her parents what had happened that afternoon in the parking lot. The priest applauded her dignity, her ethical stand. He suggested that she tell her parents what had gone on, and that she pray hard, and that she keep looking for a job. He promised, in that last regard, to do what he could to be of help. He also warned Teresa that all through her life there would be various "temptations."

The weeks went by; Teresa continued her search. She cried on her sixteenth birthday, wondered what she would be doing on later birthdays. She began to imagine for herself a return to the Valley, a job as a migrant farm worker. She knew that there were aunts and uncles of hers still in the Valley, and she was sure that they would welcome her, help her get a job. When she told her mother of the idea, the mother started crying. Had they left the Valley for this—a return, another generation around? The mother suggested patience and, like the priest, hard praying. Teresa began to oblige. She prayed in the early morning. She prayed midday. She prayed in the evening. In between, she looked at the newspapers, sought out work, received her rejections.

She learned on television that San Antonio, like other cities, had an unemployment problem, and that it was especially hard for young people to find work, and that Mexican-American youth were at even more of a disadvantage. But she continued to try—to keep her ears open, to hold up hope for herself, to apply and apply for jobs. And one day, while buying food at the local store, she heard of a possible job: door-to-door selling of greeting cards—in Spanish, for her people. She was told where to go, whom to see. She went immediately. It was a neighborhood drugstore, a couple of miles from her home. The druggist asked her where she lived, what kind of work her father did, what kind of job she had previously held, how much time she hoped to devote to the job of persuading essentially reluctant people to make essentially frivolous purchases. She declared herself a willing and enthusiastic worker. The druggist told her she was hired.

The next day, she reported to work and learned rather a lot about her future job: "The druggist said he didn't own the store; he just worked there. He told me to go in the back, and I did. There was a big room, and several men were there. They had about ten telephones. They were answering them and making calls and writing a lot down on pads of yellow paper. There were two women there, waiting like me; we started talking. I found out that they were a little older than me. One of the men finally paid a little attention to us. He told us to sit down. We did. Then he came over and asked us what we wanted. We told him: work. He looked at me first, and asked me what kind of work I wanted. I said I'd heard about a job selling holiday cards, and that's why I was there. He wanted to know where I heard about the job. I told him—at the store, from a woman. He wanted to know her name. But I didn't really know the woman; I just spoke with her a few minutes, and she told me to come to the drugstore and ask for work.

"He told me I should go home and get some pictures taken and bring them back. I didn't know why he wanted pictures; so I said I had a picture of myself in my wallet and could give it to him. He laughed. He said that I should take it out and give it to him. I did. It was taken a year earlier. He said I looked like a 'pretty girl,' but that this was a job for a 'grown-up woman.' He said I should go to a studio and tell the people I wanted a lot of pictures. I asked him why he wanted a lot. He said a group of people would be looking me over—the men there, and some others. Then he told me; he said I shouldn't be wearing *anything* when they take the pictures, and if I couldn't get a photographer to do what I wanted, then he would send me to 'his' photographer. I didn't know what to say then. I got scared. I began to shake—my legs. He told me to go. I went, fast as my legs would carry me."

When she came home she wanted very much to tell her parents what she had just experienced; but she found it impossible to say anything. Several times she came close to starting; she had the words in her head, in her mouth, it seemed, ready to go forth. Still, she remained silent. She was so upset by her inability to talk about the incident, and had so much trouble understanding it, that she fell altogether silent—as if she would say nothing, rather than waste her energy talking about matters she knew to be of distinctly secondary concern to her. By evening Teresa's mother and father had decided that she was in a sad mood, and that the best hope was that a night's sleep would work a change of disposition.

Their daughter went to bed at the extraordinarily early hour of seven-thirty without having taken any supper at all. She slept late—until nine in the morning. Her mother began to think she was sick. What was wrong? What had happened? When the girl heard the questions, she burst into tears. She said that she didn't know what was wrong—even as she did indeed know that a lot was wrong. She asked her mother to leave for a while. She hoped against hope that she could entirely forget the previous day and resume the life she was living—for all the pain of joblessness. But she was still quite nervous because of the time she spent in the back room of the drugstore; more than that, she felt as if she had taken part in something "wrong," "bad," "sinful." She thought of going to the priest and talking with him. She thought of going to confession. She thought of seeking out a nun who had taught two of her younger brothers. The last alternative was the most pleasing to her, but she could not carry through her wish. When she thought of telling the nun what had happened in the drugstore, Teresa quickly abandoned the plan. She abandoned every plan, as a matter of fact, because in each case she could not possibly imagine herself sharing with anyone the strange story she had in mind.

For three days she mostly slept, ate by herself, took brief walks, watched television. Her parents were convinced that she was disheartened by her continuing inability to find work; and that she had finally given up all hope of success. But suddenly she seemed much better. She was up early, helping her mother with the younger children, full of ambition and hope. She would continue her search for work. She would pray hard for God's kindness. Somehow, as the priest kept reminding her and others in her family every Sunday, God would show His smile to her. For several weeks she combed the papers; walked the streets; talked with people, who in turn suggested other people. She was waiting, waiting for that smile of God's. Sometimes she herself began to smile—the likelihood of a job. But no luck, she soon enough discovered. Gradually her courage ebbed; she began to sleep later and later. She began to lose her appetite. She began to stay at home, watch television, stare at the picture of the Virgin Mother and her blessed Son. And she began to have "bad dreams."

One morning she told her mother that she had gone through the worst night of her life. She had been restless; had awakened every hour, it seemed; and had experienced a frightening nightmare, which she could not shake off the next morning or for a long time thereafter: "I'll never really forget that dream. It wasn't like any dream I've ever had. I felt as if I'd really lived what I'd dreamed. I was walking through the streets of San Antonio and I wasn't sure where I was going. I stopped a woman; she was standing near a gas station. I asked her where I was going! She didn't seem surprised at my question. She said I was going to church, she was sure. I kept walking, and there it was, the church. I walked up the stairs, but the doors were closed. I tried to open them. I tried and tried. They were locked, though, and I couldn't move them at all. I saw some people walking, and I called to them for help. Maybe we could all together get the doors to open. But they ignored me. Then the priest came, and I asked him for help, but he said no, too!

"That was when I saw all those black cats. Hundreds of them were there, right in front of the church. I don't know how they got there. I didn't see them coming. They were just *there*. They screeched and cried and howled, and they fought with each other. I was afraid they'd all get together and turn on me and scratch me. I just stood there, still as I could be. I wanted to run, but I was afraid that the first move I'd make—they'd stop their fighting with each other, and I'd become their big enemy. Then one of them caught my eyes. I stared and the cat stared, and then the cat leaped, and the eyes came closer and closer—and that's when I woke up. I was shouting, I know. My mouth was open. I could hear myself shouting as I woke up. My mother was standing there, holding my hand in hers. I started to cry and I couldn't stop, not for a few minutes, anyway."

She had not been happy, it turned out, with her mother's middle-of-the-night presence at the bedside. For Teresa, the mother's affectionate reassurance was an occasion for further sadness, and even shame that her dreams could interrupt her tired, burdened mother's sleep. Later in the night Teresa had another dream, less frightening, but by no means idyllic and reassuring. This time her mother was at her side; they were in a field, picking beans. A truck approached them, driven by an Anglo man—a foreman, perhaps, who managed a large Rio Grande ranch. The truck came so close that the two women had to scatter. The Anglo driver stopped his vehicle, got out, stood over the women, who crouched at his feet. He wanted to know what they were doing. Teresa said, "Nothing." Her mother said, "Working." The man told them both to get up, fast. They obliged. He started criticizing them. He didn't like the dresses they had on or the shoes or the bandannas, meant to afford some protection from the sun. He demanded that they show him their hands. There was dirt under their fingernails! They were "no good." They were not "clean" enough to pick his crops. They belonged in a hot shower; then he would show them how to dress properly.

Abruptly Teresa's mother disappeared. The grower was moving toward the truck, but had a change of heart. He moved back toward the young woman, who suddenly found herself standing in a new and quite startling wardrobe: "I had on a red satin dress. I don't know how I got it on. I had on a nice pair of shoes with high heels. I just stood there. I felt funny. I didn't know what was happening to me. Then I began to realize that I was sinking! I mean, my shoes were going into the muddy land, and the next thing I knew, I was in the mud up to my ankles. I was afraid I'd sink and sink. I looked for my mother, but I knew she was gone. I looked up at the sky, but I knew God wouldn't save me. I looked at the Anglo man, and he was just standing there, real close. I grabbed hold of his boots, I remember. That was when the dream was over. I think I was looking at his face; I don't know. He could have been smiling. I don't know."

She did not, a second time, wake up screaming. She was afraid, confused, a bit ashamed upon becoming aware that she was no longer asleep and had yet again, in that long night, experienced a vivid, hard-to-forget dream. The next morning she felt under the spell of the two dreams. She thought of them, tried in vain to understand them, thought of telling her mother about them, even thought of asking for the priest's help. Instead she left the house and took a walk: anything to be away from herself and her memories of that preceding evening's middle-of-the-night terror and humiliation. She looked at the people on the street almost gratefully—so long as they were there, she was not likely to slip back into the dreams. But after a few blocks, she found herself having quick flashes of memory: the church, the cats, the Anglo foreman, the dress, the mud moving upon her, claiming her.

Suddenly, she saw a jet airplane above, its exhaust visible—lengthening streaks of clouds. She wished she were on the plane. She wished she were flying somewhere—the further away, the better. She wished she were going to the Holy Land. A priest had talked one Sunday—a priest who had gone on a pilgrimage to the Holy Land. He had come back "closer to Jesus Christ," or so he had told the people of that *barrio* of San Antonio. Now, in her extended daydream, Teresa pictured herself on the plane, holding her rosary beads lest there be a crash; and then walking into the several churches the priest had mentioned—she forgot their names; and then feeling Christ's near presence. At one point, as she walked and had such thoughts, she felt herself getting a bit warm and sweaty. Maybe His presence was upon her right then and there. But no, she realized, it was a warm, humid day—no exceptional phenomenon for San Antonio—and she had been walking rather fast, lost in her own world of travel.

She decided to turn around and go home. She was, for a change, hungry. She wanted a salami sandwich, her favorite kind —lots of thin meat, mayonnaise, and nice, spongy bread. As she crossed the street she heard a car's horn. She ignored it—not for her. But she soon realized, after a few more sounds of the same horn, that a voice was also making some noise, and that she was the most likely object being hailed: "I saw a big car, and it was going slow. I realized it was the one honking the horn, and I began to wonder if the driver was trying to get my attention. There didn't seem anyone else around, and there wasn't a traffic jam. Then the car stopped beside me, and I saw there were two people inside, two men. The car looked familiar; it was a Cadillac, and it reminded me of the Cadillac at the drive-in place where I'd worked. Then the car stopped. One of the men got out, the man beside the driver, and came up to me. He asked if I remembered him and his friend. Of course I did! I just stood there, silent. He got annoyed with me. He said I was acting 'pretty high-class,' and where did I get the idea to be like that. I still didn't say anything, and he looked as if he was ready to punch me in the face. I got scared, and I thought I'd better get away.

"I started walking. He got back in the car, and I was glad. But the car didn't drive away. It followed me. And then it stopped; this time the driver got out and he came up to me and told me that he liked me because I'm 'tough,' and he wanted to give me a job, and I should come see him in a few days, and he'd make me a 'good job offer.' Then he got back in his car, and it took off so fast I thought it would rise up in the sky and fly. After he left, I didn't move for a while. I thought to myself: Teresa, are you asleep, dreaming, or are you out in the street, standing and trying to figure out what that man was saying to you? I decided I wasn't asleep dreaming, but I still wondered if I'd really just talked with that man—and if he would really give me a job."

She walked home a little more briskly than would otherwise have been the case. On the way she looked over her shoulder occasionally: were they following her? By the time she came home she was more relaxed. She began to realize that the first man who approached her was doing so on behalf of the other man, who had an air of authority about him. She began to feel less threatened by them, less afraid of them. True, they had been responsible for the loss of her job—but there they were, on the street, trying to make amends of sorts and, in addition, complimenting her for being a rather independent and plucky person. She decided that maybe she would do as he suggested; look him up. But where, when, and with what in mind? And she didn't even know his name. And she didn't know whether to tell her parents about the street scene she had just been part of, or keep her silence.

She ended up delaying: a day, another day—until a week had passed. Her resolve to go see the people she had met and find out what they had to offer was tempered by her increasing shyness, mistrust, and, not least, a vague, hard-to-explain sense of shame—as if she had, by virtue of a chance meeting certainly not initiated by her, become involved in something cheap, illicit, wrong. By the end of a second week she had effectively banished the whole troublesome, confusing matter from her mind. She had also given up, for a while, seeking any employment. Her mother had told her that she would marry one day and then would have to know how to take care of a house, how to bring up children. Why not spend her time helping at home? She had always done that anyway; but had never until now been free to do so all the time, day after day. Meanwhile, the mother would talk with her friends, and they with their friends. Surely, in time, something in the way of a job would come up.

Among her responsibilities, Teresa most enjoyed marketing. She walked every day to the *barrio* store, made her purchases, brought them home. On the way to and from the store she met various friends or neighbors, and loved to talk with them casually. Sometimes she would imagine herself a little older, still going to and from the store, but with a somewhat different order of responsibilities in mind. She would even have imaginary conversations as she walked the streets: "If I meet someone I know, I talk with her about the best bargains in the store or the weather. It's so wet here in San Antonio. I always look at the sky before I go to the store; I try to figure out the best time to go shopping —and not get caught in the rain. Sometimes I don't meet anyone I can talk with—just a few people who say hello to me, and they're gone before I can say hello back.

"I'll talk to myself, though—not out loud! I'll think of myself as older, maybe twenty-five, and I have a couple of kids. Maybe I've left them home with my mother, because they're small and I want to make a fast trip for groceries. Then I meet some friends; we went to school together, and live near each other. We stand and talk about how our kids are doing. I am proud of my kids; I have two boys, and they are big for their age and strong, and they started walking early, and they will be tall and good-looking —like one of my brothers will be, I think. We also exchange recipes, and we talk about our husbands. I hear the women do *that* a lot—talk about their husbands. I wonder what kind of husband I'll have. I try to imagine him, but I can't. It's funny, I can imagine myself pushing a baby carriage and talking with my friends, but I can't imagine what my husband will look like.

"I like quiet boys; I always have. If they talk a lot, I get scared. If they smile at you, but don't know how to talk much, they're probably very nice. My mother says so, and my sisters agree. One of my sisters married a real smooth talker; he's a crook, my father says. They live in Corpus Christi. I think he's a gambler, or he works for a gambler. I wouldn't want to be married to a man who isn't honest. When a woman marries, she becomes what her husband is—that's my mother's warning. She's been telling me all my life that when I get married I'll be starting a new life— my husband's. Until then, I have my own life. I hope the man I meet and want to marry will want to marry me, and I hope he'll be a good man. If he's a bad man, I'll be in trouble all my life. A lot of women never know what their husbands are really like until they get married, and then it's too late; then, all that's left is for you to smile, and pray to God, and do the best you can."

She had such moments of resignation as she did the marketing. She would alternate, it seemed, between flights of fancy connected to her future housekeeping obligations as a wife and a mother, and moments of apprehension tied to the unpredictability, as she saw it, of married life. Sometimes she would remember the priest's advice, forget the future and concentrate on the present—getting those groceries, bringing them home, unpacking them. One day, a few weeks after the incident on the street with the two men, she was again walking quite unselfconsciously toward the store. It was one of those clear, cool spring days San Antonio cannot take for granted. She was thinking about the weather as she walked—the pleasure of moderate warmth without humidity. She felt lively, hopeful. Her father had told her that a friend thought she might get a job in a restaurant. She would wash dishes. For Teresa, it would be an opportunity. She pictured in her mind not the drudgery, the dreary, boring, messy work, but rather the money she would get each week, and yes, the satisfaction.

When she thought of work, she thought of applying herself long and hard to tasks others might well call "menial"; she thought of carrying trays, cleaning tables, washing dishes, picking crops, working in a factory. For her such activity was not only a means to an end—money—but part of a person's life. One works because one is thirteen or fourteen or fifteen, and one is proud to have a job. If one is without work, that is an occasion for sadness. Teresa did not in her mind associate work with humiliation, exhaustion, indignity—even though others, relatively well-off themselves, would no doubt summarize the jobs she dreamed of obtaining as, collectively, "marginal employment." Put differently, Teresa had been proud of her job in the drive-in, missed it a lot, and that day, on her way to buy food, felt some hope that soon she would again be pleased with her fate: "I was talking to myself. I was saying: Teresa, you'll go to that restaurant, they'll hire you, and they'll give you your lunch free. I felt good. I was ready to carry a heavy load of groceries home. My mother had run out of everything! I was trying to remember what I was supposed to buy when I heard that horn again, behind me. This time I knew who it was—*them*. I didn't know what to do. Should I stop and wave? Should I ignore them? Should I stop, but wait for them to say something? Should I start running?

"I decided to be nice to them. I knew who they were; there was no reason to pretend. There wasn't much time for me to do anything, actually. I smiled when they pulled up beside me, and they both got out right away. The driver, who seemed the boss, just like last time, asked me where I'd been. I kept smiling, but I didn't know what to answer. Then they asked me why I didn't talk. I smiled some more! The boss said I was shy. I kept smiling.

Then he asked me: would I want a ride? I didn't know what to say. Then he asked me where I was going. I said to the store. He said yes, he could tell: my shopping bag. He offered me a ride there. I was afraid to say yes and afraid to say no. Then I decided there was no reason to be afraid. I said I liked walking, but if they wanted to drive me there, I'd like to go with them. They got in the car, and they waited for me. I opened the back door and got in. But the driver decided he wanted me up front. He told his friend to go in the back, and he asked me to come sit where the friend was sitting. I couldn't say no; they were taking me to the store.

"I just sat there. He drove fast. He had his music on—loud rock. He showed me the air conditioner. He said it was too bad the weather was cool. If it had been a hot day, I would really have liked the cold air coming out from all directions. There was a clock. There was a mirror that moved with a button. He made the windows go up and down with buttons. The seats were leather, he told me. Before I knew it, we were in front of the store. He asked me if I wanted him to wait. I said no. He asked me if I was going home with a lot of packages. I said yes. He asked me why I didn't want him to wait. I didn't know what to answer. I smiled. He said I was 'one shy baby,' and he told me to hurry up, go buy what I was going to buy, then come back, and they'd take me home. I told him not to wait. He said for me to hurry up. Then the guy in the back got out, and opened up the door for me to leave.

"I felt funny going into the store. I wondered if anyone saw me. I was afraid I'd been spotted, but I didn't know why anyone would be upset with me. I had a feeling that I'd done wrong, but I couldn't explain to myself why I should be worrying like that. Inside, I told the owner what I wanted, and he got everything for me. As I was paying, he asked me where my twenty-dollar bills are. I said I've never seen a twenty-dollar bill in my life. He said I was playing dumb, because he knew I had a lot of them.

I thought he was joking. I told him yes, I did have some of those bills—a hundred of them. I'd just printed them at home! He didn't think I'd been very funny. He said he knew a rich person when he saw one. Then I saw him looking outside at the Cadillac car, and I knew what he was talking about. I was all ready to start explaining everything to him, but I realized I didn't know what to say! I decided to pick up my packages and leave.

"When I closed the door of the store, I was sure the owner and the other customers were staring outside—at me. I didn't know what to do. I thought of walking home and not paying any attention to the men in the Cadillac car. I thought of saying hello to them, but telling them I had to walk because I was going to meet someone. I thought of talking with them, but asking them to drive away because the people in the store thought I was as rich as them, just because they saw me get out of their car. But I just went to the car, and they opened the door, and they helped me with the packages, and we drove off. Then they asked me if I wanted to go on a ride. I said I wanted to go home. They said they'd take me home, but I had to go the long way around because they had some errands to do. That was when I learned what they did. They stopped at stores and picked up money. They told me they collected money from cigarette machines and pinball machines. They work for a guy who is even richer than they are. They drove all over, and the next thing I knew, they said they wanted a drink and a sandwich, and there we were, pulling into the drive-in—where I used to work! I couldn't believe my eyes."

She pretended not to take notice of, or care, where she was. She agreed to have a Coke. She refused a sandwich. She sat quietly while the men ate, drank, listened to the radio. They kept pressing food on her; she kept refusing their offers. Finally, they were done and were preparing to leave when one of the workers, a young woman, came to the car. She had recognized Teresa, wanted to say hello. The men watched, listened, as the two acquaintances talked. Teresa cut the conversation off, told the men they could leave, then seemed lost in thought. But they would not be deterred. Why had the waitress come over? Who was she? How come Teresa and she were acquainted? Teresa chose to be silent for a while; at last she said she "just" knew the girl.

As they came within a mile or so of her home, she asked to be let out. It suddenly occurred to Teresa that everyone would be stunned by the sight of her emerging from a Cadillac in which there were two men, each of whom appeared to be in his early twenties. The men laughed at her request to stop short of her house. They knew she was being evasive; she would not single out a building as her family's. They could read her mind. They told her they would gladly get out of the car and tell her mother that she is a "good girl," and that they had simply seen her carrying bundles and wanted to be of help. Reassured, Teresa decided to see what would happen—and do nothing to stop her arrival home in the car.

Once there, she got out immediately, looking anxiously for her mother and her younger brothers, but saw no one. They were inside, she knew. For some strange reason, she was disappointed. She knew there would be excitement as well as suspicion or fear at the sight of her emerging from such a grand automobile. She hesitated, waited for someone to look out the window or come around the corner from the backyard. Meanwhile, the men asked her whether she might not want to continue riding, since no one seemed to be at home. She was tempted to say yes, but could not say the word. She felt her head shaking, rather than nodding. The men got ready to leave—but first the driver gave her a card with his number: call tomorrow morning and ask for Pete. No kidding. *Tomorrow.* Before noon. He'd be waiting. And if she didn't, he'd drop by.

Teresa found her mother and her brothers gone. They were at her aunt's house, she was sure, a little down the street. If they had been outside, they could have seen everything—the car, her exit from it, her conversation with its owner and his friend, their departure. But they had been inside, she learned later. It would be up to her to initiate something—tell her mother what had, in fact, been going on in brief spurts for a few weeks. She tried to figure out, later that day, how to tell her mother what had happened. She wanted to know whether she should go to a phone booth the next morning and call a man who was, actually, a stranger—older, rich, quite full of his own importance, sophisticated, demanding, presumptuous. She did not use such words, but she knew the psychological score—and a few social and economic facts: "I knew they were big people. They had a lot of money, and they didn't have to work the way other people do. They could just ride around and listen to their radio and put on the air conditioner. They said they buy a new Cadillac car every year. Once you've been in a car like that, you think every other car is not so good. The driver, Pete, had a gold watch. I saw it. I wanted to ask him how much it cost, but I didn't. If you have a lot of money, you can make people be nice to you. They want some of your money. They'll put sugar in your ears; they'll say what you want to hear.

"I could tell that Pete won't let anyone argue with him. He's the boss. He gives orders, and you're supposed to run and obey. I'll bet he has a temper. My father has a temper with my mother. If she forgets what she's supposed to do, he shouts and he scares her, and she begs him please to stop and give her another chance. He always does, but it takes him time to decide to stop being mad, start smiling again. I don't think I'd want to be that Pete's wife, and make a mistake. I'll bet he goes wild, like a dog that has to be killed later, because it's been foaming, and it's bitten some people."

She called up Pete the next day. She went to the store, used the pay station. That morning the owner had already forgotten what happened in connection with Teresa the day before. But he did notice that she was making a telephone call. Why? She had never before done so. She told him: a friend had asked her to dial a number, and she was merely obliging. The store owner looked at her intently. She remembers noticing his face—the concentration on her, as if her next remark would tell a lot. She said nothing. She went to make the call. He could hear her asking for Peter Diaz, telling who she was, saying hello to him, waiting for him to carry the burden of the conversation. She said virtually nothing, except yes, yes, yes—in answer to questions that asked whether she was near home, whether she was free to take another ride, whether she would like to do that. He told her to wait where she was. Then he hung up. She stood there dazed. How had it happened, so quickly, that she was once again in the store, and the Cadillac would soon appear and drive her away? Wouldn't her family hear, that very day, about yesterday's scene, never mind today's? And what was happening to her? She did not, at the time, ask herself the question she later realized to be obvious and important: Who was this Peter Diaz, and what did he want of her, anyway?

In moments the large car pulled up. Peter was not there, only his friend. He got out, approached the store, then had second thoughts, went back to the car, sat and waited. He had seen her seeing him and that was enough. She was out of the building quickly, with a small bag: cooking oil and soap and a loaf of bread. She got in the car, said hello, heard hello back, did not initiate any further conversation, and heard not a word from Peter's friend, whose first name, she thought, was Carlos, though she was not sure. Finally she decided to ask. He said yes, his name was Carlos, and that ended that. The next thing she knew they were passing the drive-in where she had worked, and a block later were coming to a stop.

Why was it difficult for her to admit to herself that they, in fact, were the ones who ordered her fired? It was not possible, she had told herself at the time as she handed in her last receipts, her uniform, her key to the women's toilet, that a pair of customers, however annoyed and however big their car, could prompt a man to let go as conscientious and hard-working a person as she was. Hadn't he called her "the best girl" he'd ever hired? Hadn't he promised her better hours, an eventual raise in salary? But soon enough her various questions would be answered, and she would know more about the world than she ever dreamed to be possible: "As I got out of the car, Carlos told me that his friend Peter might not be there for an hour or so, but that I should come in and wait. I said I would. He took me upstairs, and there was an office, and two secretaries were there, and they stopped working and just stared at me. I didn't know what to say. I smiled. I was afraid to say hello because they didn't look too friendly. I thought I might get my head chopped off if I said anything! Carlos told me to come with him; he took me into Peter's office and told me to sit down—in a big red leather chair. I've never seen a chair like that—so comfortable. I could sleep in it and be happy, I thought; I sank in, and just looked out the window.

"I could see the sky—the clouds going by in a rush that morning: a wind, I guess. Carlos asked me if I wanted coffee. I said no. He asked me if I wanted a Coke. I said no. He asked me if I wanted anything, and I said no. Then he asked me what I did want, and I didn't know what to say to him. I told him all I wanted was to go home—my mother would need the bread for the boys for lunch. He told me I was wrong if I thought I'd be home by lunchtime. That was the first time I became scared. I saw a look on his face that made me feel like running out of the room, down the stairs, and out into the street. I really wanted to go home. I started wondering what I was doing there. I started asking myself what I *did* want—I mean, why I'd agreed to come to that office and just sit there. I didn't even know who this Peter Diaz was and what kind of work he did. That was what I tried figuring out—how he made a living.

"Then he came back. He walked in and said hello, and asked

me how I was doing. I said I was doing fine. He told me I was a 'nice chick.' I knew I should smile, and I did. He told me I could have a future. I didn't say anything. He asked me what kind of future I wanted. I didn't know how to say it—a job, I thought to myself, and then the right husband, a good man. He said it for me: 'You're a clean chick, and you want a man who will give you ten children and keep you in the *barrio* with fifty cents in the bank in case of trouble.' I never heard anyone talk like that. I wanted to walk out on him and never see him again. He was a wise guy; that's what I realized. But he was being nice to me at the same time. He saw me sitting there in that chair saying nothing. He stopped talking; I guess he decided to be nicer. He went out and told his secretary to get me a Coke. He had a radio on the table, and he put it on—nice music for dancing. He asked me if I wanted to dance. I didn't say yes and I didn't say no. I looked around the room: no space to move. He saw me looking. He told me I was too 'nice,' and he'd have to do something about that! He said the best dancing is standing and being close. I guess that was when I really got scared."

Her mind went a bit awry. She didn't quite remember every detail of what happened, but she knew the essentials. She got up, managed to spill her Coke on her dress, walked out of his office and down the stairs, came into the street somewhat dazed, headed for home. Within minutes he was right beside her, his arm on her shoulder, talking and talking: she was a "scared chick," and she was a "little girl," even though she had "the body of a woman"; and she was being "stupid" because he wanted to "help" her and she needed his "help" quite badly, but she was like "all the other Mexicans," that is, "dumb, dumb, dumb."

She would not easily forget that word, repeated three times, or the speech Peter Diaz gave as an explanation, a follow-up: "He kept telling me I was going nowhere, and it wouldn't be long before I was another *barrio* mother with ten kids shouting and crying and fighting. He said I didn't know any better, so he wasn't really mad at *me*. He told me about his sister. She is beautiful, and he likes her, and he tried to tell her not to marry someone; but she did, and the man can't find a job, and so they're going back to the Valley. They won't take money from Peter because they call him a crook, and they say he wants to make them crooks. He kept telling me he wasn't a crook, and I was stupid to think he's one. I tried to tell him I didn't know what he was talking about! He wouldn't listen to me! He kept shouting that the *barrio* is a dirty place, and everyone is living a dirty life, and then they have the nerve to call him a dirty man!

"Then he told me I'm pretty and he liked me, and if I would work for him I could have a lot of money. He said I look like his sister. He said that if he can't help her out, he could at least help me out. He said if I didn't take a job with him, there'd be no other work, he'd see to that. Then he told me he was the one who got me fired from the drive-in job! I couldn't believe it! I stopped walking, but he kept moving, so I caught up with him. He said I wasn't paying enough attention to him that day when he came there—and he owned the place. I couldn't believe him! That's when I shouted—that he *didn't* own the drive-in. I told him I know who owns it. But he said the man is the manager, and he works for Peter and a friend of his.

"I began to get upset. I thought of stopping and letting him go on walking. He didn't seem to care whether I was there beside him or not. He was talking and talking, and a lot of what he said I couldn't understand. I tried to keep up with him, but I couldn't. He switched from one subject to another. He was very angry! When I said something, he didn't really listen. He interrupted me. He started talking again. Finally, he turned around, and we walked back to his office. On the way back he stopped talking, and I didn't know what to say, so we didn't do much but walk and walk—except twice he stopped and asked me if I still wanted a job, and I said yes, I did, and that was why I came to his office in the first place!''

When they came back, he again offered her a job; this time it was formally done—he in his office chair, she on the red leather one she liked so much. She would work in a dance hall he owned. She would be at a table near the entrance and would collect the money from those who arrived. She would have to dress attractively—and he would buy clothes for her. She would have to be alert, responsive, cordial, welcoming—and he would coach her. She would, of course, have to work evenings, and he would have a car pick her up at home, bring her back. She would be well paid, a hundred fifty a week to start [in 1970], with a quick rise to two hundred a week. The sums of money he mentioned seemed vast to her. She had received fifty dollars a week working in the drive-in, and considered herself lucky. Still, she hesitated saying yes, after he had made his case.

She wanted the job badly; but she was afraid. She feared her parents' reaction. They would not want her going to work at night; nor would they want her at a dancing hall; nor would they like the idea of a Cadillac arriving for her in the early evening. What would her young brothers think? She also feared for herself—her inadequacy, her shyness, her innocence. What did she know of dance halls? She couldn't dance at all. She liked music, Mexican music, but she was even a bit reserved about that. Best to keep the radio low at home. Her mother got angry when there was too much "noise" in the house. Often the children had to whisper: her "nerves." And then there was the priest to reckon with—and one of her older sisters, who had wanted to be a nun and who was a strict Catholic indeed. She went with her two young children to Mass every morning. The children, both under five, had somehow learned to keep very quiet in the church. Teresa had guessed that they were intimidated. Teresa was now intimidated herself. Would she be called "bad"? Would her father, as he always does, heed that sister's advice, step in, demand that the dance-hall owner, Peter, be told in no uncertain terms to look elsewhere for a young lady to help take in the money of *barrio* "dancers"?

Teresa's hesitations surprised and angered Peter. He pressed her: Why did she not say an immediate yes? Did she want two hundred dollars a week to start? If so, that could be arranged. She was, with him, tantalizingly demure, reserved, and—most puzzling—virtually speechless. She was struggling for words. He was talking all the time. Every time she thought herself ready to tell him something of importance to her, he came up with a new remark, which upset her train of thought and prompted further quiet (and anxious) reflection. Finally, he exploded again—and she yielded: "I nodded my head when he talked. I didn't *want* to stare at him. I was trying to talk. I was just thinking. But he got the wrong impression. He thought that I was being 'smart' with him. That's what he said when he began screaming—worse than in the street. He called me a 'high-price whore.' He said I was holding out for more and more. He said everyone has a price! I didn't know what was the matter with him. I hadn't said a word. I was smiling when he talked. I wanted the job. I knew in my mind I did. Who wouldn't want to make all that money? I just knew that my family wouldn't be so happy. My father is very strict. My mother is afraid of him. She told me a woman has to be afraid of her husband. If she isn't, the husband isn't a man!

"I got so scared of Peter when he was shouting that I started crying. That was when he stopped, and came over, and told me I should trust him and he'd be good to me. He told me I'm pretty, and he likes me, and he wouldn't hurt me. I stopped crying, and I said I wanted the job, and I'd go home and ask my mother, and maybe she would talk with my father. She knows how to win him over. I've seen her do it. She becomes silent, and then she cries, and then he worries. She tells him she's all right and not to worry. He says he *is* worried. She tells him that she is tired, but she knows he is much more tired than she is, so she begs his forgiveness. Then he begs *her* forgiveness, and they are both happy together; and she asks for her favor, and he says yes, whatever she wants, because she is the best woman in the world.

I see one of my older sisters with her husband, and it is the same story. I'm not sure I could be such a good actress!"

She went home and did rather well in that regard. She told her mother that she had received an offer of a job; that it was a high-paying job, but involved work with people who go dancing, drink a lot of beer (mostly), and are hungry for "company"; that she wanted to say no and walk away proud and clean, but she also felt sorry for some of the people who go to bars or dance halls; that she did refuse the job, though with a sense of disappointment in herself, because she kept wondering whether she might not be able to make friends with a young woman or two like herself, and thereby prove herself worthy of communion on Sunday. The mother knew little of dance halls—only that they were where "people get into trouble." Teresa told her mother that many girls go dancing without getting into trouble, and yet it would indeed be a dangerous place to be night after night. The mother expressed unqualified confidence in her daughter: she would not get into any trouble at a dance hall—and perhaps would "save" a few young women from "trouble."

Soon the father was of the same firm opinion. His pride made him even more convinced that his daughter was in no jeopardy and, as a matter of fact, might end up being of considerable help to others who might not possess her strength of character. Why *shouldn't* she go work in a dance hall? She would not be there, after all, as a barmaid or a lonely visitor or an entertainer of one kind or another. She would be there as a clerk of sorts, and with the clear understanding that she was someone apart. And the money—who could overlook its significance? They would all be propelled into quite another way of life; they would have enough money to buy a car, to buy furniture, to buy clothes, and maybe even to find a house big enough for them—as opposed to the small four rooms they now occupied. Money is not an evil thing, the father kept reminding Teresa and her mother. Money is something that can bring happiness as well as danger. Money is the Anglo's weapon, but it can be a friend of the Mexican-American. There are some of the latter, admittedly a few, who live rather well. Perhaps yet another family, Teresa's, was destined for that fate.

Teresa accepted such a line of thought with pleasure. She seemed surprised to hear it, but not so surprised that she considered upholding a different set of propositions. She wanted to work for Peter Diaz—and really wanted to do so for the same reasons her parents had set down during their talks with her: "I thought I'd have an interesting time. I was afraid to tell my friends; I knew they'd all envy me the job. Then they'd start wondering how I got it. I was wondering myself how I ever had such luck! I began to think of the money, too—more than I'd ever dreamed I'd make. I thought I should go talk with the priest, but my father said no—there are some things it's best not to tell priests. I never heard him say that before!

"The day before I was to start, the Cadillac showed up! I'd never seen the man who drove. He said he was doing a 'dry run.' He said he wanted to make sure where I live, and see how long it takes from the dance hall to my house and back. I didn't like him; he looked like a real tough guy to me. He was dressed smart, too smart. That's what happens to our Mexican-American boys: they grow up, and they can't find work, and they wouldn't think of sitting home and cooking and cleaning the house; so they get together and they start gangs and they fight each other, and the Anglos are very happy to see the trouble in our *barrios.* The ones who meet Peter Diaz—people like him—get jobs, and they're all set. The only trouble is, they act as if they're the most important people in the world.

"That driver looked at our house as if it was a cave or a cabin on one of the grower's places in the Valley. It's no great *barrio* here, but it's not as bad as his eyes seemed to think! I was going to tell him I'd *walk* to work, but I knew I'd be getting him into trouble if I did that. Peter would fire him for getting me upset.

I knew, even before I started work, that I had a special friend in Peter. He'd told me so on the walk—when he got so mad at me. And I'd seen him with the men who hang around his office, and with the other driver. He treated them as if they are Mexican-Americans and he is an Anglo who has a lot of money and a lot of influence—like a lot of Anglos do have."

The next day she did not wait for the Cadillac alone. Her whole family attended her, though discreetly, shyly. Her parents worried about the neighbors: what would they think? Her brothers wanted to go with her; stay with her; get the two rides she would be having in that long, large, ever-so-impressive limousine. When it did finally arrive, she insisted that everyone retire from sight. She walked out casually, almost indifferent to the sight of the car. She got in the front on her own and sat there without a word to say. She had decided that there was no reason at all to have a conversation with a man whose face and manner she did not like. At one point, after catching a quick glance at him, she thought of asking him to stop so that she could move to the rear. He seemed so mean at the wheel. He was always passing cars, using his horn, refusing to give any pedestrian—even old people or children—the benefit of the doubt. She began to wonder whether she could stand it—being driven twice a day by such a person. She even had thoughts of speaking to Peter. She had already sensed that in some way *she* was doing *him* a favor by working for him, and so was in a position to make otherwise unthinkable requests of him.

When she came to the dance hall, Peter was there as he had promised, waiting to help explain to her the nature of the job. She had a desk, a phone, paper and pencil, and, not least, a cash register. All she had to do, really, was collect money and let "customers" go by—though she was also asked to use her judgment about them; if someone was drunk or seemed nasty or truculent, he should be refused admittance. If he persisted, there was a button under the desk for her to press. Two or three strong men would immediately appear. There was nothing for her to worry about, Peter kept telling her; she was quite safe, quite protected. And she was isolated from the dance hall inside, though she could hear the jukebox going. If she wanted her own music, she could have a radio on her desk; but she said no, she rather liked the slightly distant music coming from the large room to the rear. If her parents or friends had phones, she could, of course, call them and talk with them. But such was not the case.

She remembers quite well the teasing Peter gave her about the distractive possibilities of a telephone. For her, however, the issue was in a strange way philosophical and political rather than psychological: "He uses that phone of his to command people. He uses that phone of his to remind people that he's around. I told him no when he was telling me I should install a phone for my parents. I wouldn't want to be at home, helping my mother sew or cook, and suddenly hear his voice telling me something. My father wouldn't want a phone, not with my money. He is too proud. My mother wouldn't want a phone because she loves the middle of the day, when all the children are away, and she can be alone. She taught me to be alone. She taught me to talk to myself! I do that all the time. With a phone at home, there would be no telling what voice would come into the ear any time of the day or night.

"Peter kept on opening and closing the drawer of the table. He kept pressing the button and waiting for his men to show up. They always did, in a second or two; then he winked, and they went away. He picked up the phone and held it to my ear: the buzz. I was not as impressed as he wanted me to be! I told him I would sit there and try to do a good job. I didn't want to call up people, and I didn't think I'd need help from his friends, and I didn't want a gun, not on my life. He said I should have a pistol in the drawer, in case someone got fresh with me. I told him I'd never had a gun in my hands, and I never want to start learning how to shoot. It was then that he told me I had to practice pushing the button and making fast calls to some other friends of his. It was then he told me he'd take me to his house and give me lessons on how to shoot a pistol and hit targets, even those that move. I told him not to worry, and he left me, finally. I just sat down at the desk and made sure I had the right amount of money for change. I must have sat for a half an hour, and no one came, and I began to think no one ever would."

She soon enough learned otherwise. She was besieged with men, some young, some older, who were eager indeed to pay five dollars in order to go "dancing." She did not know, that evening, where the women were who would "dance" with the men. At first she wondered why the men came alone. Wasn't she working for people who ran a "dance hall" to which couples came in search of a large room, a smooth and even floor, some music, some beer or wine or soft drinks? Perhaps, she thought as she received money from one man after another, Peter and his friends were more straitlaced and conservative and like her parents than she had thought—and so were reluctant to let couples enter a "dance hall" together. But she knew otherwise; she knew in her bones before she admitted it to herself in her head that Peter was bringing together women he knew with the men who were paying her. For a dance or two. For an evening of music and light drinking and a relaxed good time. And (she thought) how good of that cynical, sometimes imperious, man to offer lonely or somewhat timid men and women a chance to meet and be happy in each other's company. She could tell, after an hour or so of collecting money, that the men she would be receiving money from were not boastful, fresh, surly, or vulgar. They seemed beaten, she observed—almost afraid to pay her, rather than quite full of themselves and ready to make a conquest of sorts.

She was wrong, though. As the evening grew longer, a different breed of man began to appear—already with beer or wine or even stronger drink inside the blood supplying their brains. She began to hear those men before she saw them—laughter, jeers hurled at each other, swear words she knew, and not a few she could not understand at all. She began to see bodies swaggering, even weaving, rather than approaching her slowly, guardedly, all too carefully—if not primly. She began to feel in herself not interest and sympathy, but apprehension, suspicion, and, with each minute, a gnawing distaste. She had started her work at five in the evening, was supposed to work until one in the morning. She had brought no food with her, and while there had not once thought of eating. At approximately nine o'clock she was approached by yet another of Peter's men friends and told she ought go to supper.

She was taken by surprise. The thought of getting up, of leaving her chair and venturing outside, bothered her quite a lot at that point: "I was becoming upset. I was ready to leave—to quit. I didn't like the men coming in. They had been drinking. The music was getting louder. I didn't know where to go for supper. A couple of men had just come in, and they kept staring at me, even after I took their money and gave them the tickets. I was almost ready to press that button, but one of Peter's men came out and told the two that they'd better go inside, or they'd be on the street before they could speak their own names. The men got angry and wanted their money back. Peter's man said no. They decided to leave.

"Maybe I was afraid they would be outside, waiting for me. I didn't think so at the time. I just didn't feel hungry. I didn't even feel thirsty. They brought me a Coke, and I didn't drink it. My stomach was hurting. I had a headache. I felt sick all over. Then Peter came and told me to go eat. I was afraid to say no. But I didn't move. He looked at his watch. He said it was after nine, and I'd better leave right away and be back in a half an hour, because the busy time was coming. I wanted to ask him where to go, but I didn't really feel like going anyplace. I couldn't talk. Then five men came in, and one of them knew me, and he got all upset, and he said, 'Teresa, what are you doing here?' Then I started crying. Then Peter started shouting. Then I guess I fainted, because when I woke up I wasn't in the room where I'd been sitting. I was in another room, and Peter was there. I remember waking up, but not opening my eyes. I heard someone walking back and forth, and I heard Peter swearing and saying he was a fool to hire me, and one of his friends was saying yes, yes to everything Peter said. When I did open my eyes, he got a lot worse with his swear words."

She said nothing. She stared at the ceiling. She enraged him with her silence. He turned from abstract anger at the *barrio's* hypocrites to a specific rage at her. Exactly who did she think she was? Why was she so fussy, critical, superior in her manner? What had she done to earn the right to her quite apparent disdain for the dance hall and those who came to it? Where did she think she was going—tomorrow, the next day, or, for that matter, in life? Amid such inquiries, he cursed people like her parents, the Mexican-Americans of the *barrio*, and especially the women who lived there.

Teresa would never forget the remarks he made about her neighbors: "I stopped being afraid. I felt sorry for him. He reminded me of my youngest brother—the way he got into fits sometimes when he was two years old. My mother said children grow out of those fits, and my brother did. Not Peter, though; he was in the worst fit I've ever seen anyone have. He kept punching the wall. I was afraid he'd turn to the window, but he didn't. He didn't want to hurt himself! He wanted to make me worry, I now realize. I just kept praying to God: Please silence him and help me get home. Finally, he stopped. He said every Mexican-American woman he's met is no good; and we deserve to be servants to the Anglos. He said he wished he was Anglo, then he would never step foot in the *barrio* again. He said I should leave and never come back.

"I got up and started to walk toward the door. He came and stopped me. He took my arm and said I should stay, and he'd pay me fifteen thousand dollars a year, and I could learn to dance, and the men would love to dance with me, and he'd get me an apartment and buy furniture for it, and it was my *last chance.* If I said no, my life would be over. I didn't say anything, not a word. I just stood there. I knew he could stop me from leaving. I couldn't just tell him to get out of the way. He didn't move an inch. I didn't either. He just stared at me. I couldn't keep looking at him. I looked at the floor, and I prayed to the Virgin Mary please to help me out. She must have heard me, because after another minute or so he moved away, and I started to walk out."

She met no resistance. She found her way to the street without trouble, began walking in the direction of home. She had a long walk ahead of her, but knew that in an hour or so she'd be home or near home. She started out, unconcerned about time or space; she was lost in questions, riddles, reveries. She began hearing in her mind the voice of Peter Diaz—the threats, the dire prophesies, the scornful, mocking descriptions of people and places. Now she spoke up, however; in her thoughts she told him off: "I wish I could have said to him out loud what I said to him while I walked. I told him he should come and see my little brother and learn how to behave from him. I said I wouldn't take all the money in the world if it meant being treated like a street dog. We have a dog in our house, and we treat him better than Peter treats the people who work for him. I wondered if he had a wife. The poor woman—she would suffer a lot. I told him I hope he never marries—or if he's already married, I hope his wife is strong, and she knows how to laugh at him.

"I was in the middle of telling him to learn how to be nice to people when the Cadillac pulled up beside me. The driver who picked me up was there, and he got out and opened the door and said I should get in. I asked him why. He said he was told to find me and take me home. I asked him who told him to do that. He

said Peter did. I said no, I would walk home. Then he got out
and I was scared for a minute. I thought he was going to come
and grab me and force me into that car and take me back to the
dance hall. I decided not to run, though. I figured he could catch
me, anyway. But he was a nice man, I found out. I guess he'd
been listening in while Peter shouted at me. I guess he knew
what happened. He told me he thought I deserved a million
dollars for saying no to Peter. He said I would be poor all my
life, but at least I'd be able to look at myself in the mirror and
not be ashamed. I thanked him. Then he asked me if I knew what
the dance hall was 'really like.' I told him I'd never been in the
hall; I'd only heard the music and heard the men and women
talking. He didn't say anything more. He just looked at me. I
didn't know what to do. Should I start walking, or just stand
there and wait for him to say good-bye?

"He started talking again. He asked me if I'd wondered where
the women come from. I said no. I'd only been there a few hours.
I figured the women were told to use another door. I thought
the men didn't have any girl friends, and they came to go dancing, and the women were willing to dance with them. I hadn't
even gone that far in my mind when I was sitting there taking
money from the men. I was trying to learn how to be good in
a new job. The driver told me I would have found out in a day
or two what was going on. I would have discovered that the
women 'belonged' to Peter, and that the men paid so they could
look them over and then choose one. Then they went upstairs.
I guess I saw some of the rooms—down the corridor from the
room where Peter shouted at me.

"I didn't ask Peter's man any questions. I wanted to ask him
about the women. I wanted to ask where they came from. The
barrio? Other barrios? The Valley? Mexico? I wanted to ask why
they came and why they stayed. But more than anything else, I
wanted to go home. I told the man I'd just keep walking. He said
I should get in the car and let him drive me—please. I trusted

him. I said O.K. I got in. He took me right home. On the way
he asked me if I wanted a cigarette. I said no. He said I was smart
not to smoke. He asked me if I was hungry; I said no. Then he
stopped talking. I guess I didn't want to talk with him, so he
decided not to say anything more to me. When he stopped in
front of my house, I got out, and he leaned over and said: 'Good
luck, Teresa; you deserve it.' I thanked him. I wished him good
luck, too. Then I went inside and went to bed. I was glad it was
late and everyone was asleep. I tried not to wake people up. I
could tell by the way she moved that my mother was awake, but
she could tell that I was tired and I wanted to get to bed as fast
as I could. If I'd wanted to talk with her, I would have been
slower, and she would have got up and put on a light in the
kitchen. I was glad she left me to myself. I wasn't really sleepy,
but I wanted to lie and think about what had happened to me
since the afternoon—since I'd met Peter, actually."

She had trouble falling asleep that night. And when she did,
she dreamed and dreamed. She said, days later, that she had
never dreamed so much during a night. Nor could she easily,
even months later, shake off the memory of those dreams: "I've
always had a lot of dreams, but most of them I forget by the end
of the next day. Usually I remember part of the dream when I
wake up, but once you're doing things you forget your dreams.
But that night I didn't really sleep—I just dreamed and dreamed.
The part that I'll never forget was the firing squad. I was in my
house, near the door, talking with my mother. Suddenly we
heard a noise outside, as if someone was shooting. We opened
the door, and we saw police cars, lots of them. The whole street
was full of those cars, with the red lights on top going around
and around. Then I saw a helicopter, and it landed, like on
television, near the police, and some men got out—maybe detec-
tives. I saw the police knocking on one door, then the next. They
pulled out people from each house, and took them to a spot in
the middle of the street. Some police stood nearby holding their

guns, ready to shoot. Other policemen were holding up some rope, a circle of rope. The police took the people to the rope and made them bend under it and stand there, inside.

"The helicopter took off, but it didn't go very far; it was just there above the people, not moving. I asked my mother why it didn't go away or fall down. She didn't know. The police kept going in and out of homes, and my mother told me we would soon be going. I said no. She said yes, very soon. I asked her why, and she got angry. She said I should know the answer to my question. I said I didn't. That's when I began to cry. She wasn't very nice to me. She told me I was all grown up, and I shouldn't be crying. Besides, the police would see me crying, and they would be even meaner than they usually are. I tried to stop crying. Just then, the police came to our door, and my mother said they could take us, because there wasn't anything we could do but go along with them. So she walked toward the street, and I followed her.

"We got to the place where the people were standing. They told us to go under the rope and be still. My mother went, and so did I. The police were staring at us; they had guns pointing right in our faces. I guess I decided to die. I wasn't going to stand there and be sent to jail. I didn't do anything wrong. I left the other people. I went under the rope and started to run away. One of the police ran after me. He told me I was going to be shot. He grabbed me and put me in a car—the Cadillac of Peter's! The driver turned out to be Peter! I asked him where he was taking me, and he said to his dance hall. I said I wanted to get out, but he said I couldn't. I tried to open the door of the car, even though it was moving. I couldn't. He laughed; he said his hand was on the buttons, and they kept the car doors locked.

"When he stopped, it wasn't the dance hall we'd come to. We were back where we started! All the people were there in a circle, with the police guarding them. Peter told me I had a chance to escape. I could stay with him. He'd hide me in the trunk of his Cadillac and drive away, and I could live in his office; otherwise, I'd have to get out of the car and be pushed into the crowd. I looked for my mother, but there were so many people, I couldn't find her. I think I heard her voice calling my name: Teresa. Peter asked me what my choice was. I said to stay—not go with him. He said all right, I would die, and he didn't care. I left the car, and he drove away. Just as I crawled under the rope, the police started shooting. I saw people falling. I was still looking for my mother when I saw someone lying on the ground near me. It was her. She had on her favorite apron. I realized she was dead. Everyone was pushing to get away, but no one could. There were too many police, and they were using pistols and rifles and machine guns.

"Then they opened up fire on us from above—the helicopter. I was sure we were all going to be killed, wiped out. I thought to myself that I was too young—that I shouldn't die. But I guess I did. I saw a policeman shooting, and he aimed his gun right at me, and just then I woke up. I think it was Peter who was shooting me—wearing a policeman's uniform! I think we were all women; I think I noticed that before I woke up, or maybe I discovered that when I woke up! Maybe I was looking to see if my father or any of my brothers were there; maybe that was how I noticed that there weren't any men at all there."

She felt like crying when she woke up, but she also felt angry that Peter was still with her, so to speak, still able to affect her life. She had gone to bed with one long statement of self-congratulation. She had been, finally, strong enough to resist the demands of a man who seemed able to frighten everyone else. She had done so without becoming talkative—without even trying to defend her views or values. In fact, she had no clear idea of what she would have said on her own behalf had Peter Diaz simply stopped screaming and politely asked her to make clear her side of things. All she knew was the relief of being home, being in bed—and being "free." She did think of money for a second or two before she slipped into sleep: how nice it would be to hand her mother lots of dollar bills every week, so that she would not ever again be in the position of pleading every week with her husband for a little more to feed the family.

Many times, Teresa had heard her father say no, and pound his fist on the table. Teresa pictured her *mother* giving her father some money—Peter's money—and the father thanking her humbly, quietly, repeatedly. The mother's graciousness thrilled her daughter, who, of course, had arranged the entire fantasy as a reward, perhaps, for missing supper and going through a rather rough time of it. It seemed ungrateful of Sleep, supposedly an angel of sorts (so Teresa had been taught as a young child), to reward a rather virtuous effort with such a dream. Had it been a grave mistake to walk out on a job before its nature was truly fathomed? Was that angel, Sleep, saying something like this: You will suffer long and hard for your decision and come to regret it sorely? Those were the questions Teresa put to herself when she woke up in the morning with a nightmare lingering in her thoughts, not to mention a picture of her short-lived, gun-wielding boss—and the vivid memories of a long evening's personal, decisive struggle.

She grew stronger as hours, then days separated her from the dance hall, Peter Diaz, his fleet of Cadillacs and army of chauffeurs, handymen, sentinels, and henchmen. In explanation of her sudden economic denouement, she told her parents, brothers, and sisters that she had inadvertently stumbled upon a rather suspicious, perhaps quite illegal or immoral, activity, and had decided to have nothing to do with it. They questioned her a bit, but not too insistently. After all, she had only worked at the job for an evening, and they had never really believed that anyone in their family would ever make the amount of money Teresa was told she would make. She pointed out that the men came *alone* to the dance hall—contrary to what she had been told was the case—and her parents wanted to hear no more.

She noticed, however, that there was a discrepancy in their responses. The mother wondered aloud about the women who waited at the dance hall for their "customers." What kind of girl becomes such a woman, and what happens to her, living such a life? The father spoke briefly of the men. How sad for them, that they had to find such companionship. They were, surely, decent but lonely. Teresa was especially surprised by her father's response. He always sounded so firm, even harsh, when anything even remotely connected to sex came up for discussion. He never would speak of sex directly, explicitly. And he was a great one for condemning people as "dirty"—meaning sensual. Teresa still wasn't sure what exactly took place in Peter Diaz' dance hall. Perhaps not the worst of activity—or else her father would be angrier, more contemptuous. Perhaps she had too quickly come to an only partially correct conclusion.

She had been essentially correct. The priest told her what he knew after she went to him with her confession. The priest had once approached Peter Diaz in an earnest and quiet effort to win him over—to no effect. Teresa was told at church that she had earned God's respect and affection. She had, most certainly, faced down the Devil himself. Surely her life would, as a consequence, begin to become favored, enriched. A year later she had ample cause to agree. She had fallen in love with a young man who was a cousin of one of her brothers-in-law. He worked as a busboy in a rather elegant San Antonio hotel. He had hopes of becoming, one day, a waiter. He managed to get her a job in the same hotel. She cleaned the rooms, changed the beds. Between the two of them, they were (by *barrio* standards) rather lucky: two reliable jobs—and in a completely air-conditioned building.

In the summer especially, Teresa counted her blessings: "I hate to come home. It is so hot and so sticky in San Antonio. Inside the hotel, we are all cool. I don't mind working, although some people leave their rooms so messy I could cry when I come in and see. Why are they like that? But I always look at the air conditioners, and remind myself what it would be like sitting at home. It takes me hours to relax at home; I'm used to being cool, and at night the sweat all over keeps me awake. It must be nice to have money, and live in a house with air conditioning. My boyfriend Ricardo and I have agreed to buy an air conditioner before we buy a lot of furniture, when we get married. I'd rather sleep on the floor and get by on Cokes and little else, but be cool at night. If we didn't work in the hotel, maybe we wouldn't know any better, and we'd be used to the heat. I never used to mind the summer weather until I started my job.

"We'll be getting married in a few months. Ricardo has one hundred and fifty dollars saved. We'll be able to buy a few things. We may have to live with his family. They have more room than my parents do. It will be crowded, but I won't mind. His mother is unhappy sometimes, but I will try to make her laugh. Ricardo laughs a lot! But he is serious, too. He really would like to wait on tables someday. One of the Anglo waiters likes him, and maybe he'll give Ricardo a break. As for me, I don't have any big ambitions at the hotel. I'll probably have children pretty soon —a year after we're married, my mother says! That will be the end of work for me—unless my mother or Ricardo's mother wants to take care of the baby while I work. It's hard to keep up with the prices. It's getting so that everyone will have to work just to pay for food. Who will care for the babies then? But there aren't enough jobs—even for men. So the babies won't be left alone!"

She has no wish to analyze any further the exceedingly complex and confusing American economy of the early 1970s. At seventeen she was full of hope, no matter the ups and downs of that economy. In 1973, at eighteen, the economy was no more stable but her life was more settled. She had married, moved into Ricardo's home, shared his bed, formerly jointly occupied by him and his younger brother. She continued to work at the hotel, but her days were numbered, she knew: "I'm growing a belly! The baby is small, and I have time to work. I wish the baby had waited a little. I would have liked to work longer before becoming a mother. But the priest says there are millions of souls waiting to be born, and one of them picked me! My mother said to be careful with Ricardo if I didn't want a lot of babies, but she said it's hard to stop a man. Men don't worry about babies when they are excited. They know it will be the wife who will take care of the babies. If we had a lot of money, like the people who come to the hotel, we could hire people to take care of our children, and we could both work, and we would be making more money. But I guess that in the families with a lot of money the mothers don't *need* to work. They work because they *want* to work.

"I hear them talking sometimes while I am cleaning the rooms. There will be a husband and wife, and they're calling their children and talking to them, and then they hang up, and the wife says she loves to talk to her children every day when she's away —but she's glad she's away. I heard one woman who was a lawyer, I think, say she didn't really like the maid who was caring for her children, but it would do them good to learn how to take care of themselves and to fight back if the maid wasn't good to them. Her husband said they should interview their servants more carefully, and investigate them before hiring them. He kept saying that, and his wife got angry, and she said he was accusing her. He said he didn't know what she was talking about. She said he was saying it was her fault that they'd hired the bad maid. They shouted a lot, and when the wife noticed me—I guess they'd forgot I was there—she told me to leave the room. I must have stayed too long; I was in the middle of making the bed. She shouted at me to 'get out,' and I dropped the pillows in my hands and left. I told Ricardo afterwards that there are some mean people who come to that hotel, even if they do leave big tips sometimes, and even if you hear them saying that they love the 'Mexican look' of San Antonio."

As she became more pregnant, she found the work harder. One day, while lifting a mattress which for some reason a couple had put on the floor, she began to bleed. She was afraid to tell her supervisor. She sat on the toilet, waiting and praying. The bleeding became worse. The couple returned to their room. She left, still bleeding; she told her supervisor, who called the hotel doctor. He told her she was probably having a miscarriage. They called Ricardo, who took her by cab to the emergency room of a nearby hospital. The cab driver, a Mexican-American, would not charge them a penny. He didn't start the meter. At the hospital, however, they were told that she could not be seen; she was not under the care of a doctor who was on the hospital's staff. She had best find a private doctor and let him tell her what to do.

Bleeding and frightened, she walked out of the hospital, Ricardo holding her arm. They were not angry at the Anglos; after all, they have their rules, and they weren't directed at anyone in particular. They took a bus home, and Ricardo's mother cared for Teresa. A Mexican-American woman came by —a midwife of sorts, who had delivered many children in the Valley and, more recently, in the *barrio*. She attended Teresa, told her she did require medical care, took her to a newly opened clinic which was meant to provide service to the poor. The doctor told her to go home and stay in bed; she might thereby save her baby. Teresa obliged, but with mixed feelings: "I didn't like staying home and staying in bed. I was crying a lot. Everyone thought I was sad because I might lose my baby; but they were wrong. I wished I was back at the hotel, working—instead of lying in bed, sweating and feeling so hot. The mosquitoes were always there, even during the day. I hated to move because you feel the heat more when you're not completely still. I hate being still, even when I'm not carrying a child. I love to walk; and I loved the work in the hotel—the cool air and the rich people and the fancy rooms.

"Sometimes I'd be in a room, and the people hadn't checked in yet, and I'd imagine myself checking in—with Ricardo, of course! I'd lie on the bed and watch the television. I'd use the bathroom, and pick up the phone and call room service—but hang up right away! I'd look out the window at all the poor people outside, way down there, walking in the hot sun. I'd sit in one of those chairs and have a glass of water in my hand, and I'd picture Ricardo in the other chair—with a beer in his hand! We could go call home and tell the maid we'd decided to stay a little longer, just a few days, and be sure to get the kids off to school on time, and don't forget to keep an eye on their rooms, because they let the messes build up when their parents go away!

"I once heard a mother say that, and the maid must have said something she shouldn't have because the mother said: '*I'm* the mother.' After she hung up, she told her husband that they should fire the maid as soon as they got back home. Then she turned to me and asked me if I want a job. I said yes, I'd like to help her out. She meant *at home;* and that was in Illinois, I believe. She was only kidding, I thought. But she said she *wasn't* kidding. She said that the maid she had came from France, and she and her husband brought her to this country, and now she wasn't behaving herself, and they wanted to fire her, but it wasn't easy to get rid of her. I guess France is farther away than San Antonio from Illinois. I believe her husband is a doctor in a hospital near Chicago.

"Maybe that would have been a good idea. Maybe her husband would have helped Ricardo and me out. The lady told me she'd hire both of us—there was plenty for a couple to do in her house and on her property. While I was in bed, hoping I'd stop bleeding and be able to go back to work for another couple of months, I wondered if I shouldn't have asked the lady to hire Ricardo and me. I am ashamed now to say it, but for a while I didn't want the bleeding to stop. I wanted to lose the baby and go back to work; I knew we'd miss the money if I didn't. I kept having a dream about Peter Diaz: he came to the hotel and checked into a room, and I was fixing it up when suddenly he opened the door. He didn't recognize me. He asked me for ice, and I smiled, but he looked the other way. He started making telephone calls. I felt bad, but I went to get him the ice. When I came back, he was gone. I started crying, and I sat on his bed and cried and cried. I woke up crying!

"Everyone thought I was crying because of the bleeding; because I might lose my first child; because I wanted to be a mother more than anything else in the world. Ricardo's mother kept saying to me: 'Teresa, I know you want to be a mother more than anything else in the world, and I am praying to Jesus Christ and to the Virgin Mary that you keep the baby. But remember, there will be another one next year, if you lose this baby.' I kept thanking her for her prayers. One night I had a dream, and *she* was in the hotel. She was on the phone in a room, and I was making her bed. She hung up, and told me she called a priest and asked him to say some prayers for her. She was going downstairs to eat, and Ricardo was going to serve her. It would be the first time he ever served. The waiter agreed to let him do it. His mother said she would leave a large tip, but she had no money. I gave her my money; I had just cashed my check. She paid the bill with my money, left Ricardo a big tip—and had no money left. My money from my check was all gone. I woke up sweating even more than usual—and it was a little cooler that evening!"

She kept the baby, a boy, given his father's name. A year and a half later she had another boy. She prayed hard for a girl that second time. She dreamed of making a daughter a friend. She had no friend, only brothers and sisters and brothers-in-law and sisters-in-law, and cousins and more cousins. Her childhood friends had become absorbed into their families, even as she had become absorbed into a growing family—two big families, really: Ricardo's and her own. In 1975 the hotel where Ricardo worked was confronted with a strike. The maids and busboys and janitors, virtually none of them Anglos, wanted a little more money (a modest ten percent pay increase), but were told that the hotel had to hold down its inflationary costs, and also deal with the threat posed by a serious recession, which had caused a drop in reservations. The workers were unorganized and also badly divided. Some wanted to fight to the end; others were against a strike, but willing to go along with the majority, which favored a protest in the belief that the management would be brought quickly to its knees. The strike did no such thing, however. One day after it started, the picket line was crushed by police, by men and women eager to cross it and get jobs, and by some of the picketing people themselves—who had second thoughts about their effectiveness as labor activists in view of the location of their protest and the prevailing economic climate.

Teresa was glad the strike collapsed. She worried about a long period of labor struggle: no work, no pay for Ricardo. She still was living with her husband's family—and by now had given up setting deadlines for a move away. Where? With what money? She had grown used to the noise of the two boys, who slept on a bed beside the one she occupied with Ricardo. Her greatest satisfaction was listening to him when he came home from work. He always had a funny story or an ironic one or an exciting one —the remarks, incidents, accidents that he shared with her faithfully. She knew all about the elegant dining room and its elegant people, not to mention its quite ordinary people, such as Ricardo, who never has become a waiter, but keeps hoping that somehow the future will touch him favorably.

One evening, however, Ricardo was in no mood to talk about his day. He had been removing some used dishes from a table and been told by the man sitting there to leave and only return when called. The man put out a foot and tripped Ricardo as he obliged and left. What to do? Report him? To whom? And how long would Ricardo, thereafter, hold his job? When he returned to the table to clean up, the man was leaving, and had told the waiter to have "the boy" come and take the dishes away. The man welcomed Ricardo: "Hello, boy; I'm glad some of you Mexican-Americans aren't lazy."

One more crude, stupid, mean remark from a drunken, arrogant, cheap Anglo man of money—not the first or the last one, Ricardo Cardenas well knew. But one too many for him. He was tired of an exceedingly tiring life; tired of being summoned, dispatched, ignored, insulted; treated as if he were Mexican mud to be stepped on; regarded as slimy, distasteful, beneath anyone's concern. The activist labor organizers who had tried and failed to promote a strong strike effort were right, at least that day, in Ricardo's mind: only a struggle by *Chicanos* would make the Anglos pay attention, and make the people of the *barrios* feel a little more respect for themselves.

But Ricardo did not want to be a *Chicano,* he told his wife when he finally felt able to talk about the day's events. He wanted to be a waiter. She listened and sympathized. But suddenly, she lost her usual self, as she put it: "I must have had too much *chile,* strong *chile;* or maybe I was tired of his mother nagging me. She makes me so upset sometimes I retire to my room, sit and listen to the boys cry and fight—and dream of working for Peter Diaz, collecting money from the men at the dance hall! I am ashamed of myself afterwards! I know what he would tell Ricardo when he comes home beaten down to the ground. He would tell him to strike, to be a *Chicano,* to fight until he wins: no fight, no victory.

"Sometimes I wish I could fight. Sometimes I wish I could leave my boys with one of their grandmothers and go picket that hotel. I'd be a good fighter, once I got my courage up—*una Chicana.* But the next day, Ricardo comes home happy. He got a nice tip from a drunken Anglo or two who doesn't stop with the headwaiter and the waiter but goes and slips a few dollars to the busboy. And when my husband is happy, I am happy—sometimes. There are days when nothing can make me happy, when the children are too much for me; and my husband's family, and even my husband, are also too much. Then for a minute here and there I will think of Peter Diaz, or of the pickets in front of the hotel. Then I am *una Chicana* again—but only for a while, I'm afraid."

part

FOUR

ESKIMO WOMEN SPIRITS

The Arctic wind takes possession of her, she claims. For brief spells she is no longer herself. She stands still, closes her eyes, lets her self rise, spread across the tundra, then fade away —the return to her body. She loves leaving, loves coming back. Her eyes see the wind approaching: the aroused waves; the grass bending; the birds tossing, riding their way on the currents, holding to a course. Her eyes contemplate the return of her "spirit": quiet water, a gentle flat land, a new stillness to the air. And always there are the sounds, which her ears crave—the whispers, whistles, strong voices: "The first memory I have is of my grandmother's hand. She was holding my hand. I remember feeling the squeeze. I remember seeing the lines on her hand, and noticing how smooth my hand was. I remember the pressure when she wanted me to stop or move or be silent and listen— listen to the wind. She would tell me she was about to leave us; she believed that one day a strong wind would come up—sent by the ice floes—and she would be standing near the water, and she would know that it was time; and the next thing, her spirit would say its last good-bye and speed across the land toward the mountains, far away. But she stayed with us a few years after she first told me that.

"I remember being old enough to go to school, and hearing her tell me to pay attention because the wind was coming. She always was a step or two ahead of the wind. She kept her eyes moving and her ears wide open. 'Listen to the wind today,' she would say. Then she might tell us about the wind: 'It is someone's spirit—a very strong one, full of messages. Best to be quiet and learn.' I wouldn't dare open my mouth. I would stand and feel the wind coming toward me, then past me. Sometimes it would hit me, and I would try to hide behind my grandmother. She would try to get me to stand my ground, and not use her for protection. If the wind was very noisy and strong, she would turn her back to it and tell me to do the same thing. Some winds belong to bad spirits; some to good spirits. Some winds belong to spirits that have been hurt, and they are crying because they want us to feel sorry for them. My grandmother wanted to be a strong wind, but she wanted to rest in the winter and in the spring sweep across the sea and the land and up the river—a friendly smile, not a warning of real trouble."

She got her name, Lorna, from the missionary's wife; her father helped keep the church intact with his considerable skills as a self-taught carpenter. She remembers being with him, too, as a young child. She remembers watching his hands, rather than holding them—the miracles they wrought. Later, when of school age, she would hear the minister or the teacher praise his work. Whenever any of the coastal Eskimo village's buildings needed repair, he was there with his tools and his considerable skill and his willingness to work, and his determination not only to correct a mishap, but prevent its repetition. Lorna was his only daughter, and far more interested in his work than her six brothers, who were devoted to their father's father and their father's two brothers, three of the village's bravest and most discerning hunters and fishermen. Her father was himself no fool as a hunter and

fisherman, but he lacked the ingenuity and initiative of some
other Eskimo men—who, nevertheless, admired him enormously for what he did better than anyone else in the village.
Without him, the men often said, there would be no village. The
wind, the winter's snow and ice, the heavy rain in warmer
weather would claim the cabins at a faster rate than they could
be repaired by men who had all they could do some years to keep
people fed or build up a reserve supply of food.

Gradually, informally, an agreement of sorts had been
reached: Lorna's father worked on the buildings year around,
and as a result did relatively less hunting and fishing. And as
Lorna became seven or eight, another casual, unstated, but fairly
consistent ritual came into being: Lorna accompanied her father
as he went from cabin to cabin, as he worked on the school, as
he helped with nets or with poles or with kayaks, as he even took
on stoves or wires, and, not least, as he covered spring mud with
carefully shaped and placed boards. All the dogs in the village
knew him and delighted in his coming; he was the one who
tended to spoil them with the pieces of meat or fish he brought
—a bonus in midday. When Lorna took to keeping him steadfast
company, she carried the food. He was delighted to see the eyes
of the dogs acknowledge their arrival. He realized with pleasure
that the dogs noticed the change—food in her hands, not his.

Lorna was also pleased: "The huskies used to wait for my
father, but then I became the one who fed them. I remember the
dogs coming to *me*. I remember my father saying that if I wasn't
his daughter, he'd be upset. The dogs used to wait for him as if
he was God Almighty; but when I started feeding them, they
didn't pay as much attention to him. He told me I was turning
into his white man! The dogs had decided I was the boss! But
it'll take a long time before I ever know as much as he knows.
He can fix anything. He seems to know how the world was made.
He would laugh when I used to tell him that the minister said
he'd leave if my father left. He would tell me that the minister

came without knowing anyone, and will only leave when God tells him to leave. I once asked my father if God was the one who taught him how to fix things. No, he said; it's a spirit inside him.

"He used to tell me that I'm like him—that I have inside me the same spirit he does. My brothers have never respected him as much as I do. When the first snowmobile came to this village, my brothers couldn't stop looking at it. They looked at it as if God had sent us a gift and they must have it. My father called the machine 'trouble,' and he kept away. I agreed with him. I told him the machine would have a short life, anyway. I was right, but new machines keep coming. They die after a year or two, but there are always others to take their place. Meanwhile, my father has walked; he will never ride a snowmobile. I have walked beside him; I've never had the same tastes my brothers have. My mother used to tell me, when I was younger, that I was meant to be my father's shadow. I would ask her why me, why not one of my brothers. She would laugh, and tell me I was talking like the white people from the Lower Forty-Eight. They are always saying boy, girl; man, woman. They have strange ways of separating people. They take a quick look and then separate one person from another; they don't listen and take time to watch. They are too busy to worry about making a mistake. They think they know how the world works. They have the answers. They know where to go, how to get there. There's no use arguing with them. Best to say yes, and go find your own path, and stay on it until the end."

She was, as a child, her own kind of person. At seven, eight, or nine she had among the villagers a secure reputation as an especially sturdy, independent, self-reliant, and imaginative child who stuck close to her father and helped him more and more in the course of his various duties. In school, however, she was regarded as "strange" by the Anglo teacher, a young man who had chosen to volunteer his Christian energy and sensibility to the settlement's missionary church, and had found teaching the

best way to do so. The church's missionary minister also regarded young Lorna as "strange." Once he told her father that
she was a "tomboy." The father smiled, asked for a clarification.
The minister observed that the girl spent most of her time with
the father, or with some younger boys in the village, whom she
seemed mostly to boss. The father continued to smile, but said
nothing. Later, he talked with his daughter about the company
she kept. The girl, then nine, had heard similar comments from
others. She had her explanation—that she liked her father and
wanted to stay with him as much as possible, and that a few boys
admired her father for his magical abilities as a repairman, and
admired her for being of so much help to him.

As a grown woman, she still remembered a speech of sorts she
gave at school when she was asked what she wanted to do later
in life: "I told the teacher that I didn't know what I'd be doing
when I'm bigger. I told the teacher that I might turn into a
caribou, and run away, and never come near the village. I might
become a polar bear, and watch our village from some ice out
in the harbor. The teacher didn't like the way I was talking! But
I didn't like the way the teacher was talking! The teachers who
come here usually stay for two or three years. They want us to
think just as they do. They tell our children to dream of airplanes
and submarines and snowmobiles and radios and hi-fi sets and
television. They tell our children to go to school in the cities or
down in the Lower Forty-Eight, and to live there because there's
nothing to do here but get through one season and then another.
My father used to squeeze my hand when a season was ending,
and say that we'd won a victory, and now we'd better get ready
for a new struggle. But the minister thought my father wasn't
enough of a Christian. The minister always gave God the credit
for what we, the Eskimos, did—but he boasted about all the
things the United States has done. If one of us took medicine,
it wasn't God's; it was from a doctor or a hospital: the white
man."

She was a "difficult" student in school—so described by one man and two women, all from the Lower Forty-Eight, church-connected "volunteers." She asked too many questions, impressed her educator elders as too skeptical by far, as peremptory, even insolent. In the early 1960s, before political activism of any kind had reached Alaska's native population, Lorna was called by one teacher a "troublemaker." The girl dared suggest that the Eskimos had been doing rather well for themselves until the American adventurers of various kinds had come upon the Alaskan land and its inhabitants. She had dared scoff at the pretensions of the white man. She had dared predict that one day an aroused landscape would expel all the "outside people," as she had described them. She was not only a "troublemaker"; after expressing it, she was also "troubled." That is what happens to some Eskimos, the minister and the teachers had pointed out to themselves: a person becomes immersed in the constant, difficult, exhausting struggle for survival—to the point that the mind begins to become grim, suspicious, worn down.

Lorna remembers hearing about the diagnosis and prognosis given her, at the age of eleven or twelve: "The minister came to our house when I was out with my father, and asked my mother if she was worried about me. She said no, she wasn't. He said he was beginning to think I was in some 'trouble.' My mother asked him what kind of 'trouble.' He said I seemed tired, and he thought I wasn't behaving in school. My mother became worried. She asked him what I'd done wrong. He said I was saying things that bothered the other children. My mother was surprised, because she hadn't heard anything from the other people in the village about my bad 'behavior.' The minister told her what was wrong with me: I spent too much time with my father! My mother smiled. She told the minister that she wished she could spend more time with my father, but if someone was spending time with him, she was glad it was me! Besides, my father never sat down and chose me; and I never sat down and chose him.

"My mother was going to tell the minister that some spirits in me were like some spirits in my father, but she knew that would get the minister upset. If we went to his church he was very happy. If we stayed away, he looked unhappy. It was only an hour a week for us—and we gave it gladly to the minister. He was kind to us, and in the winter he shared our troubles. He ate less than we did. He gave us his food. The least we could do was go to his church. He left when I was about thirteen or fourteen. He told me the last day he conducted the church services that I was becoming a woman *at last.* I laughed and told him not to worry, because soon we'd all be gone. He will leave for the Lower Forty-Eight, and then he'll leave there; some spirit will call him. I'll leave, too. He told me I should speak of *souls,* not spirits. I said I would.

"I don't mind using the white man's words. They have a lot of them, and they use them a lot. My father and I used to spend the whole day together, and we never spoke. I would want to leave school, when I was younger, because I didn't like the teachers trying to get me to talk. Once I told my father I never wanted to go back to school. I was ten, I think. He didn't say anything to me. We went on walking. I figured out what he meant: Don't leave school, but don't worry about the teachers and what they want, because they can't make you talk if you don't want to talk. Too many Eskimos try to please the white people who come here. That is our biggest fault—we always try to make visitors smile and like us. We're afraid they won't like us if we don't do everything they want us to do. When I sat and looked at the teachers, but didn't talk a lot, they decided I wasn't very happy. They were right. I wanted to be outside, working with my father. They didn't like me any better when I did talk—when I told them that."

She may have had no great desire to exercise her vocal chords at school, but she could talk at home, given the right conditions. Often it was the natural world that prompted reflections or observations from her: a change in the weather, such as a heightening of winter or summer; the appearance of spring; the ebbing of short-lived warmth. She did not need a listener. She was not given, even with a listener present, to extended conversation. She had things on her mind, from time to time, and she delivered herself of them—in the presence of a person, *or* in the presence of (she believed) attending spirits. Those spirits might respond —a gust of wind, an agitation of the ocean, a movement of animal life. But not necessarily; there were moments when she felt herself quite alone in the universe, and inclined to talk out of her own efforts to fathom things, rather than because she wanted to get a message across or because she had emotions in need of "expression." When she was clear in her own mind about a particular day's obligations or purposes, she was not likely to have any interest in talking. When she sensed the jeopardy of her situation—no rare occasion for Eskimo coastal villagers who live well above the Arctic Circle—she spoke and spoke in order to set straight her mind's confusions or apprehensions, both of which have to do with the real struggles she and others have to wage all year long.

Not that she lacked a capacity for daydreaming, for flights of fancy, for visions that had nothing to do with the everyday demands or opportunities of her life. She would glimpse caribou on the run or clouds moving rather fast or some fish darting in a lake, and would imagine herself similarly unbound. Once, at fifteen, she saw a goose land on the tundra all by itself. She heard the honks, looked for other geese, saw none. She decided the goose was saying hello. She smiled, moved a little closer to the goose, sat still for some minutes. She was astonished at how long the goose stood still on the tundra—with a careful eye out, no doubt, for any movement from any quarter. She was astonished at how long she, too, managed to stand still. Her joints hurt when she finally came to, moved a bit—not in order to approach the goose, but to give her legs a signal: she was quite alive.

A day later she remembered the interior landscape of her moods, reveries, as much as the stretch of tundra, the awkward gray goose. She had felt within herself a mixture of quiet curiosity and restlessness: "The goose knew that it wasn't lost. The goose decided to leave the others, but it knew how to find them. The goose was looking in every direction. Where to fly next? Where to get some more food? I moved, and the goose moved. What to do about that Eskimo—me? While I watched, I thought of the pictures they used to show us in school of geese. The pictures were funny; I laughed each time. The teacher didn't like that. She said I was rude. But some artist made the geese look as if they'd been hit and they are asleep with their eyes open. Once the teacher asked me why I was laughing, and I said I'd told myself a joke. She didn't believe me. She asked me to draw a picture of geese, since I didn't seem to like the ones she had. I said no. I don't like to draw; I like to look.

"I thought of those pictures while I watched the goose. I thought of the pictures the teacher showed us of Eskimos— pictures in books read in the Lower Forty-Eight. Then I looked at the goose. Then I imagined myself a goose, standing there, or flying and looking down at our village and the ocean and the ice beyond the harbor. I used to think I might become a goose one day. When I saw that goose, I decided it's still possible. I might not stick with the others; some geese are always together, but some wander off, then come back. I'd be the kind that wanders, but I'd have a friend or two. Once I was with my grandfather, and he saw me looking at three geese standing and looking at us. He knew what I was thinking, because he said he likes them, and he talks to them, and he thinks he might become one of them when he leaves us. I asked him how we know what will happen when we leave. He said that's the kind of question the white people ask. He said we don't know; we find out. That's when I heard him talk about the minister and the schoolteachers and all the others in the Lower Forty-Eight, and about our own people here in the village. I could hear him again, saying all he said, while I watched the goose stand and then fly across the land.

"I kept saying to myself—to the goose!—that I wouldn't go to

Fairbanks. But no goose is stupid enough to land in Fairbanks! Some Eskimos don't learn from the right visitors. They pay attention to the white people who come here, but not to the geese. They listen to the honk of the ministers and teachers who come here, and to the honk of the machines, but not to the geese. That goose was giving me the eye. That goose was resting and looking around and getting a little food. Maybe the goose liked the land there; it was soft, but not too soft. A goose won't go just anywhere. A goose chooses the right place, to suit it. The Eskimo sometimes does what the white people think is right; the Eskimo doesn't decide what is right—for the Eskimo. My father says that we should be ourselves and no one else.

"I don't even care what my brothers say, or my friends and cousins—not when I'm working with my father. He and I have been building a house, and my cousins have asked why I'm doing it with him. I'm a girl, they tell me. They are girls, and they are reminding me that I'm a girl! I thank them! I tell them that it's a good thing they told me I'm a girl, because if they hadn't I wouldn't know. Finally, I asked them where they got their idea of what I should do and what I shouldn't do. They went to school, they remind me. They listened to the teachers. They go to church; they listen to the minister. I am supposed to be grateful that they know so much. They sure know what to tell me! They think I should sit and smile and wait for one of their brothers to come and ask me for a ride in the snowmobile. They think I should be dreaming of the five or ten children I'll have one day. They think that I should be cooking with my mother, not telling her good-bye, and going out to stand beside my father and try to help him. I'm too 'restless,' a teacher once told them, when she saw I wasn't near enough to hear. But I did—from them. At least they don't obey every word they hear from the teachers. That teacher told them not to tell me what she said."

A year later, two years later, she was still the same person— quite willing to pursue her own course, quite willing to leave the flock, place herself apart, try to make do in a way others found uncongenial if not incomprehensible. She was not, at sixteen or seventeen, especially "restless." In fact, she had never been one to talk a lot, play many games—or when a bit older, smile her way from one snowmobile ride to another. Nor was she one to play hi-fi, dance, run to watch the plane land every week with mail and provisions. She preferred a solitary goose to a prop-jet plane. She preferred the wind or the ocean's turmoil to the rock music of the late 1960s, imported (like so much else) from the Lower Forty-Eight. She was a steady, calm worker, close to her father, and increasingly almost indispensable to his work. When he went to tidy up a battered house, or help keep the landing strip accessible, or repair a fence meant to protect dogs from the worst of a sea-wind, she was there, quietly assisting.

Her brothers began to wonder whether she would ever show interest in a man. Her cousins also began to ask themselves that. Her mother heard such speculations, and decided to speak to the father. He agreed to talk with Lorna. At the age of seventeen, quite content with her life, the young woman heard her future questioned. Would she try to go to Fairbanks? Would she consider "having" one of the village's young men and, if so, which one struck her as desirable? How did she plan to spend her time later, when she was (presumably) married and a mother—and by the way, was she not worried that she was not quite as prepared as others of her age to become a woman with a husband and children?

Lorna would never forget that brief talk with her father; or, rather, the questions he put to her. She walked and heard him speak, but she had no answers to offer him back. He realized that she did not welcome his initiatives, and he was not, as a matter of fact, comfortable. The two arrived at an impasse: his hesitant, shy inquiries and her attentive but confusing silence. Eventually, he stopped talking, and she stopped looking at him closely. They were working on a sled in need of repair, and it was best to finish the job. When that had happened, they walked toward home in silence. Just before they entered their house, Lorna gave her father one word: yes. He understood what she meant—that she understood his concerns and would heed them.

A week or so later, however, she was wishing she could go south, as birds do, and return, perhaps, to another village—or to no village: "I kept thinking of the birds. They know when the weather tells them to leave. The weather in the village is not good—for me, anyway. The village is becoming the property of the oil people and the minister and the teachers who come here. The more they explore for oil, the more our people fall into their arms: money. I don't want to be in their arms! Some of our women rush to their arms. I have heard of the hotels in Fairbanks. But when the oil people come to our villages, they find their women friends there, too. All of us are becoming 'friends' of the outsiders. The men play with their snowmobile machines; the women wait for their rides on the machines. I have never taken a ride, so I am a 'strange bird.' That is what a teacher called me. I hope I am strange! If I stop being 'strange,' I'll stop being myself.

"I think of the dogs, and their new life here. What must they think? They used to have work to do. Now they lie around, waiting for food. And what food! They get pizzas, as our children do. My father wonders about children: will I have them? Yes— but I am waiting to meet the man who will stand up and be a strong Eskimo wind. He will blow away that store, with its bribes from the Lower Forty-Eight. I remember when we learned the word 'bribe' in school. We were being 'prepared,' like the teachers say, for 'the new Alaska.' If you're going to be bribed, you should know what's happening to you! When a bird is bribed, it can fly away and forget what happened. Not us; we stay, and wait and wait for more bribes. I've fed birds, but they leave right away. I suppose I could keep feeding them, and they'd stay. Would they be the birds we know? My father says the wind would take over—send them south, get them away from our bribes. Where is the wind to rescue us?"

A wind came to rescue her when she was eighteen—a cousin of hers. She had paid him little heed all her life. He was two years younger, and known as a somewhat selfish and lazy one. He distinguished himself in school by learning virtually nothing. He preferred to fight with his friends, gaze out the window, and, as he grew older, sport whatever loud and extravagant clothes he could persuade his parents to buy for him. He also took a fancy to airplanes. He waited for the plane to arrive on the landing strip as if the arrival was the Second Coming. Once, poor pagan, he asked the minister if Jesus Christ (as the One who rose on Easter, as Lord of the higher realm—the skies, where Heaven must be) had given His approval to airplanes, which after all were constantly invading His territory. The minister was stunned by the presumptuousness, and convinced that a normally fresh, even insolent youth had now crossed the line into sacrilege and mortal sin. The youth's parents were approached: what did they intend to do? No specific answer was forthcoming. The young man was their last child, an Eskimo Benjamin who had often perplexed them. He was, they once told Lorna's parents, a last wind of winter; 'Fred of the early spring wind,' they took to calling him when there was a suitable occasion for playfulness.

Lorna first began to think of him as an individual, distinguish him in her mind from a small crowd of nondescript youths, when she heard (with some envy) that description: "I wanted the nickname for myself. I asked him if *he* thought up the name. He said no, it was his father's idea—a punishment. I told my father I wished he had been quicker to get annoyed with me—and call me 'Lorna of the early spring wind.' I like the early spring, when it is beginning to thaw and suddenly a strong north wind comes, and it is angry and ready to give everything to frighten us. In the middle of the winter the wind is more relaxed; it knows it has plenty of strength, so it doesn't have to scare us by bragging and raising its voice so high we think the worst will happen. In the early spring the wind can fool people. They are ready to call its bluff. They are sure it is just a child, trying to show its big muscles. But it may be a strong winter wind that has been waiting in line very quietly until its turn has come—*and then!* I remember one time we were almost carried across the tundra, the entire village. My grandfather said we should stop using the word 'spring'; it is the white man's idea. We have cold weather and we have warm weather. We have darkness and light. There has to be something in between, the teachers say. They have many names in their suitcases, and they pull them out so that we will say thank you.

"The more Fred made people worry about him, the more I noticed him. At times he would say something or do something I wished I'd said, I'd done. I told him one day: You make me think we have the same spirit in us! He laughed. He said he is younger, so he is copying me. But he wasn't. I had my thoughts, but he spoke or used his legs and arms. Some of the older people called him a caribou, or a stubborn husky. I liked that; I liked his 'fits.' He would kick a snowmobile or shake his fist at it. He would take his dogs to the store and tell them to go inside, eat up all the bags and cans, then run away—and throw it up: a pile of dog's stomach stuff outside our village! Let them build a new store next to the pile! Some people thought Fred was being 'a little boy,' but I'd heard that before. They still say I'm the way I am because I had a good time as 'a little girl,' and I don't want to grow up. They also say my father taught me 'bad tricks.' His spirit went into me, and I try to be like him. I told him I'd heard that, and he said the Eskimos never used to worry about where spirits go, and they never used to tell each other that the spirits are running them and making them do 'bad.' It used to be that the spirits came and went, and no one was there watching and counting and saying *see, see, see.* My father says we have lost our own eyes. The outsiders tell us where to look and what to look at, and we obey. We learn their words and use them—to tell each other what came before our new eyes.''

She found herself noticing Fred more and more. She found herself, at eighteen, thinking of him when he was nowhere in sight. She found herself asking where he was—a question directed at herself, however. There was no one for her to talk with; and she had, in that regard, no regrets. She had learned to keep her own company rather well. But Fred had begun to threaten that accomplishment, and she was, in succession, surprised, bemused, annoyed, angered. She remembered a time when he was a child in her mind, one of many—yet another blurred face to her eyes, which were so anxious, anyway, to shun neighbors and relatives in favor of the surrounding landscape or seascape. She remembered when she began to notice him—but not to a degree that could be called personal. She remembered with considerable pain the first time she could not get the young man out of her mind. She had seen him tell off his friends. She had come closer, heard him talk about the "stupid Eskimos" and the "mean white people." She had stood spellbound as he lashed out at idle, drinking, increasingly welfare-conscious villagers who have been trapped by clever, manipulative, profit-hungry outsiders, always ready to make a joke out of the Eskimo's source of pride and dignity: survival against great odds.

It was Fred's clean, forthright, unqualified anger that caught her attention—trapped her. She used that imagery at the time: "I went home and I felt upset. I was breathing too fast, and looking at the ocean, and imagining myself with my father in his boat. But I couldn't go there. I couldn't fly across the land to one of the ponds inland. I wasn't a goose. I don't want to go in an airplane, ever. But I'd give most of my life if I could have wings and fly for a few days! We can't bargain with the world, though. Not even the outsiders can bargain with their God, though some of them would trade their children, if the right reward was offered. I kept wishing I could talk the way Fred did. I liked him a lot for being honest. I wondered if there was some way for me to become a friend of his. When I saw him the next day, I couldn't look at him. I'd been thinking of him too much, and I was afraid he'd know it—or maybe *I* knew it, and was afraid that I was beginning to like him. I was afraid I might be trapped. No wonder I was wishing so hard I could fly!"

Fred was going through a similar turmoil; he had begun to notice her, and he had his own reasons to feel envy, and a touch of awe. He was a friendly, outgoing person, but at the same time preferred to be on his own, to spend time by himself. In the winter, he loved fishing; he could stand for hours on the ice near a hole, holding his line. When his friends came to join him, he wanted to flee. Why did others not leave him alone? Why was he unable to tell them to do so? Where did Lorna find the extraordinary capacity to live her own life? How might he follow suit? And for that matter, how might he get to know her—not just to learn from her, but be with her? She was not only fiercely independent; she was a lovely young woman—slightly taller than most Eskimos, and rather thin and possessed of noticeable grace, yet obviously tough and knowing about the natural world.

They began to throw furtive glances at one another. Eventually the glances intersected; each of them realized the other's interest. Eventually, they started to talk, first with others around, then by themselves. Eventually, they became known as good friends and Lorna as a bewitching figure who cast a magical spell on a younger, somewhat vulnerable young man: "I began to hear that I was a bad woman. That was the first time I'd ever heard myself called a woman! They were calling me a 'strange girl' until Fred became my friend. Then they saw me in a different way. Who are 'they'? I'll tell you: friends of Fred—including cousins of mine, neighbors, everyone of our age. *I* don't have friends! I've always been off doing things with my father, or on my own. It bothered people that Fred began to take walks with me. We went and worked on the boats together, or on a house or two. Usually, we were with my father, but people didn't notice that. They missed Fred, and they saw him with me; so they turned on me, and I finally heard what I knew they thought about me.

"I don't want to *brag* about being unpopular! I don't enjoy feeling eyes on my back as I walk! I wish we'd all leave each other alone in this village. My grandfather told me, when I was younger, that when he was a boy no one worried if someone decided to be alone for a long time. He used to go to the edge of the water and watch the sea gulls, and they'd talk to him and he would talk to them. Now no one would do that. The teachers have taught us that sea gulls don't talk. I know they do! But I don't say so out loud. People would say I'm trying to be 'a special one.' That's what they called me for a while, until they stopped calling me anything. They forgot about me, thank God. When Fred became my friend, they started up again. I told Fred that I wasn't sure I could stand having him as a friend—not because I didn't like him, but because I didn't want to put up with those smart words of theirs."

Those "words" began to change after a few months. Lorna and Fred were no longer "friends." They were "always together." And Fred was her "shadow." In fact, they were not "together" all that much. They would go on walks, then separate—she in one direction, pursuing an interest in, say, watching birds, and he toward a pond or the river to do some fishing. They would meet at a certain place at an agreed-upon time, using the sun's trajectory rather than watches, which they did not own. They would enter the village as if they had been taking a long walk —but in silence. They hated to talk in front of others. And since Fred had always been fairly easy with words, his apparent silence with Lorna only confirmed once more the appraisal of his old friends—that he had been in some unfortunate manner transformed by his new companion. Certainly *she* showed no sign of being different in any respect.

She was becoming somewhat different, however. She found herself noticeably and, for a while, unnervingly dependent on Fred. If he was not around and if he had not told her where he would be, she became morose at first, then rather truculent. She kicked pieces of wood, hurled stones. She was indifferent to the dogs—a surprise to them, because they always counted on her as their dearest, most obliging, and considerate friend. And she failed to notice the details of the world around her—a lack of alertness she herself found surprising, confusing, and ultimately as enraging as the anger that prompted this lack in the first place: "I would begin to think I was as stupid as some of the teachers and some of the cousins and neighbors think. I would think very little of myself; and I would feel that Fred was to blame. I felt that he had me in his paws—as if he was a polar bear, and I was a fish grabbed out of the water. I know what 'they' thought—just the opposite. But 'they' always look for the easy way out. If there is a package of potato chips, they won't go hunting! If they can make me into a hunter and Fred into someone being hunted, they are very happy. When I got angry at them, I wanted to leave and never come back. But I thought of Fred, and I wanted him to leave with me. I would be angry at him, too—for not letting me know where he was going. I had bad thoughts: trapping him, instead of a caribou! I prayed, like the minister taught us, for God's mercy!"

She began to think of marriage as an answer to the dilemma. She couldn't imagine herself living without Fred. But was he ready for marriage? And did she really ever want to marry? She had always seen herself, when grown up, as a single, rather solitary figure—as cranky and eccentric at forty as at fourteen. Now, approaching nineteen, she no longer felt able to be alone and contented. Her mind wandered toward Fred, held on to a picture of him. She repeatedly sought him out, even if discreetly, sometimes furtively. For a matter of weeks, maybe a month or two, there was a distinct chance, a probability even, that she

would turn on him fatally, solve her difficulty by driving him off:
"I began to dislike him. The nicer he was to me, the more I
wanted to leave him. When he spoke pleasant words about me,
I pretended not to listen. I didn't like the way I was thinking of
him as the sun, the moon, the stars. I decided that I didn't really
like him. I decided that he was a mere child—and, like all the
other boys, anxious to tell me about his high opinion of himself.
When he chewed on the dried salmon, I told him to stop making
so much noise. When he brought the fish he'd caught, I told him
his smile was too big. (All he wanted was for me to smile back
and let him know how good he is as a fisherman.) When he fed
the dogs I called him stingy. They deserve all they are to get right
away. Why was he giving them a little, then a little more, then
the rest? When he walked, he was either being too fast or too
slow.

"Once, on a walk, I realized that it wasn't his fault at all. He
was trying to keep up with me. When I slowed down, he went
slower; then I speeded up—and blamed him for not thinking of
me! I decided to tell him I was sorry. He didn't know why I
should be sorry! I was sorry that I'd told him I was sorry. I knew,
right then, that I was either going to say good-bye to him and
leave the village and never see him again, or I was going to sit
down and tell him that I like him a lot, and already spend all my
time with him, day and night (in my thoughts and my dreams).
I decided to ask him if he wanted to sit down near the ocean and
listen to *it* talk. I wasn't sure I could say what I wanted to say,
so I was glad to have the ocean there, talking for me."

In the course of time she talked for herself. She told Fred that
she liked him—too much, perhaps. She told him that he had best
ignore her; that she might, one day soon, start walking and never
turn around; that she was saddened by the ribbing he was getting
from his friends; that she wished him well, and was, that day,
saying a personal good-bye, even if they would, of course, still
meet almost every day in the course of their respective lives as

young villagers. He was not as talkative as she. He drew close to her, put his arm around her, and told her, briefly and quite to the point, that he wanted to live with her. He made no effort to answer her questions or reply to her fears or ask that she reconsider her plans. He mostly stared at the ocean, and she mostly talked—a reversal of the usual way things worked out when they were together, or when each of them was with other people.

She remembered, some time later, how astonished she was, how singular the time turned out to be: "I became like one of those schoolteachers. I talked a lot. When I first started I thought something was wrong with me. I wondered where the words were coming from! I don't think I ever used so many words. I won't ever again, I'm sure. I repeated myself a lot—just like those teachers! I told Fred that he'd made me think of him all the time, but I didn't blame him. I liked thinking of him. I'd wake up, and there he would be—in my mind. His smile was always on his face. He wouldn't be saying anything. He'd be standing outside, and I'd go and say hello, and he would say hello, and then we'd walk. Every morning I'd have that same picture! I told him I didn't feel myself anymore; I felt as if I'd been caught, trying to run away, and now I was in his house. But I didn't like thinking of him as a hunter, and he didn't like hearing me say that I was 'caught.' He told me I'm different, and not to worry: I'm not locked up in his house or anyone else's. I was glad to hear him say so!

"We went for a long walk, and there was a warm sun, and there were no clouds, and we both loved the day. It must be like that a lot in the Lower Forty-Eight, but not in our village. We are far north, even for Alaska. Fred and I talked about going even farther north. He said he misses the snow and ice in summer, and so do I. But I don't think I'd like to live so far north that we had no summer. I'd miss the sun and the blue sky and the long, warm days. I'd miss the flowers and the birds that come to see us, even if for a short while. I told Fred that it would be nice if the two of us could become birds—and stay for a season, then go somewhere else for another season.

"I wouldn't want to fly with a flock, though. I'd like to fly with him. We see birds, two of them, four of them, flying off. They seem happier than the ones in a flock. I remember when I was younger seeing a duck trying to keep with a flock, but she couldn't. My father and I watched her, and I kept praying she'd let them go ahead, and stay behind and land near us. We would try to feed her. She did give up, and we saw her land. We rode toward her; we made the dogs work hard. There was snow already on the ground. We left some food and moved back. I don't know what happened to her. We never saw her again. But I've thought of her. I wished, even then, that she had found another duck, and that the two of them had stayed here. I told Fred: It's better to have two than one—but a flock is another story."

She told him much else. She worried that he used to be, in her mind, "a boy"; now he seemed to her much older than she was. He reminded her of her grandfather, no less. Like the old man, Fred was his own person, quiet when with her, though voluble enough when with others; and, above all, not one to try to impose his ideas, hopes, values, fears—his person—upon others in such a way that he became bossy, self-important, insistently judgmental. For Lorna, the Eskimos of her generation were developing such characteristics under the influence (she kept insisting) of missionaries and teachers and government officials from the Lower Forty-Eight.

For years she had chafed under the watchful "guidance" of various men and women who had come to her village for a year or two at most, and who wanted her and others like her to do this, behave like that, believe such and such. And she was especially tired of being given similar lectures or bits of advice from members of her own family, or from those who were her own age, or from fellow villagers. Stubbornly herself and scornful of the various categorical schemes others came up with, she proposed to Fred a club, no less: her grandfather, herself, him, and two or so other persons he would want to nominate for membership. The club was meant to be a haven for a handful of people who would strengthen each other by meeting occasionally in order to talk about and laugh at the pompous tyranny of everyone else.

Lorna was joking about the club at first, but after a few remarks about it, she managed to pique the interest of her friend Fred. He wanted to know what she meant, and how she had managed to come up with such a notion. She was able to explain: "Since I began to like Fred, I realized I didn't want to be by myself for the rest of my life. I asked my grandfather what I should do. I told him I wanted to leave the village when I was younger, but now I thought of staying. I told him I worried that Fred used to be just a boy, but suddenly he was grown up. I wondered if he would stay grown. My grandfather suggested the club. He said he and I could talk to my father and to Fred and to anyone Fred wanted to join; and we could build a small house, and sometimes we could go there. I worried that my mother wouldn't like the idea. She has always wanted me to spend a lot of time with my grandfather and my father, but for all of us to build a clubhouse would be to take a big step away from the home.

"My grandfather told me that years ago some of our people did that; they would decide to get away from other people and build a place outside the village. They went there to sit and be by themselves or with a friend or two. My grandfather's grandfather told him he had two daughters who were very good friends, besides being daughters, and the three would go to a log cabin, in the summer, and the father would tell the children stories. That was a long time ago. My father used to tell me stories when I was younger. He still does when I work with him. I'd like to keep doing what he does, fixing boats and working on the houses in the villages. My grandfather said that maybe if we became a club, and Fred joined, we could all keep doing the work, with my father.

"The trouble is, some people in the village say that it was all right for me to work with my father when I was little, but now that I'm big I should stop—I should 'grow up,' stop being different from everyone else. I think my grandfather hoped that if we became a 'club,' everyone would forget that I was in the club! I don't think he realizes that today the Eskimo people are like the white people from the Lower Forty-Eight. No one is supposed to be different. Everyone is supposed to listen to the ministers and the teachers and the people who come here from Fairbanks and Anchorage. I tried to explain to Fred what my grandfather said and what I said. I tried to tell him that maybe he would be happier if he stayed away from our 'club.' But I guess we *are* a club already; there's no need to start one."

Fred joined up—not the "club" (it never was formed), but as Lorna's husband. They were married by the missionary because Fred's parents, no fans of Lorna's, insisted that they be. Fred's mother almost didn't go to the wedding. She described her future daughter-in-law as a "bad woman," a judgment not as moralistic as it seems. For Fred's mother, Lorna would not be "loyal to the house," and so she was "bad" as a *woman*. As a *person,* it was quite a different matter: Lorna was thoughtful, polite, quite willing to be of help to people in need, and a considerable asset not only to her father and grandfather as a worker, but to the village as a whole, which received the benefit of the labor done.

In fact, Lorna heard from Fred's younger brother that her mother and Fred's mother had a rather agreeable conversation when they learned of their children's desire to marry: "I've never been close to my mother. She used to say that it was as if my *father* gave birth to me! She would look at me and say she doesn't know me, but at least my father does, and that's enough.

The only time in my life I talked with her, we lasted about five minutes together. It was last year. She asked me what I was going to do, now that I've been a woman for a few years. I said I'd do what I've been doing—help my father and grandfather. She shook her head. I knew why. I didn't know then I would be making friends with Fred. I said I'd be glad to leave the village. She said no, I should stay. But she wasn't holding on to me to save her life. If I'd told her I *was* going, she would not have shaken her head. She would have nodded! No wonder she told Fred's mother that I wasn't beyond all hope—that I could make good coffee, if my father or grandfather are around! I'll bet my mother was more upset about the marriage than Fred's mother. He says his mother is no big friend to him. She prefers his younger brother. It is no gift of God to be a favorite of your mother; it is like being a prisoner. I told Fred that when we talked about our mothers, and he smiled and told me I am as wise as my grandfather."

She didn't feel especially wise during that period of her life—the weeks before and after her marriage. She kept asking Fred whether they should acquiesce, get married in the small mission church, or follow her instincts: take a long walk and declare themselves married—speaking to the sky, the earth, the water, the nearby life of birds, animals, fish. It was an Alaskan spring, after all, and millions of nature's "marriages" were taking place abroad the land, she kept reminding Fred. Why make such a special occasion out of *their* decision? He always smiled as she came up with such questions. She is a rebel, he told her; she should have patience, go along with his family and her mother—settle for what the prevailing customs require. Later, when they would be a bit more on their own, there would be time for a more vigorous assertion of their individuality as a couple.

She would become even angrier and more defiant when Fred talked like that. She told him once that maybe they shouldn't get married, that he was "nice," and that she was indeed a "bad woman." She went on, spelled out the dimensions of her "bad-ness"—declared herself a "spirit" from the ocean, restless and fiercely private and generally impatient with the habits or beliefs of others. True, she knew that many Eskimos, despite the continuing presence of Christian churches, think of themselves as bearers, so to speak, of "spirits." But she was not as casual as others became when they talked about themselves—who they are, where they come from, where they are headed in the years to come. She not only listened to the wind, but talked with it, obtained messages from it, *relied* upon it as a means by which she connected herself with the surrounding world. She also found herself scrutinizing the clouds, the stars, the migrating birds—in search not of signs so much as *herself.* When there was no wind for a long time—a rare event in the coastal Arctic village—she complained of the stillness, suggested that Death might be stalking the community.

Her friend Fred found such an attitude, such fears, quite uncongenial to his temperament. Yet he took Lorna seriously, responded with quick attentiveness to her ideas. She not only excited him as a person, as a woman. She made him stop and think about things. He told her that, and she was touched. But she also worried. Was she "taking him away from himself"? She once put it that way as she talked about her future husband. They were to be married in a week, had come to know each other rather well: "He likes to go and hunt and fish, and forget about everything but catching all he can, then eating until he's so full he can't really move. That's the way our men are—except for my grandfather and my father. They're different. They've always eaten less than the other men. They don't worry about what the other men think of them. They change with the weather, the seasons; they will sometimes talk with the sea gulls, not go rushing after the seals. They are too 'patient,' one teacher said. Maybe she was right. But she didn't call me 'patient,' even though I was with them so much. She said I was the opposite: 'impatient'!

"I remember learning the word, and I remember her telling

me why she believed I was so 'impatient.' She said our *women* are 'patient'; they stay and wait for the men to bring home fish or caribou or seals—then the men do the cutting, the dividing up, and bring their share home, where the women are waiting to cook. But I was 'impatient,' because I went hunting or fishing with my father or on my own. Even if my father encouraged me to go with him, those teachers would still call me 'impatient.' I should have said no to my father, and sat at home and learned to eat potato chips and smile at visitors from the Lower Forty-Eight!

"I told Fred that he'd have to hear about me all his life, if we got married. I told him that I've become myself, and he's become himself, and I might end up taking him from himself—because his friends would say he should make me be like their wives, and I will never agree to give up being myself, and so there might be trouble. But he said no, I should stop being 'impatient'—with him! He said he knew what I'm like when he began to notice me and like me and follow me with his eyes. He went to talk with my father before he ever told me how much he likes me. He told my father first! He asked him if I would mind a husband who didn't try to make me into one of the village's 'regular wives.' My father knew what he meant. He told Fred that I can cook if I want to, but I won't cook just because everyone else thinks I should. Fred told him he liked to hear that about me. Then he told me, when we had our long talk, that he hoped I never gave in to anyone—including himself! I wanted to give in right then, and tell him I was ready to do anything he wanted! If he thought I'd make a 'patient' cook, I'd become one. We've joked ever since about my cooking. I don't do the best job; he is very helpful, and he usually finishes the cooking. I always start out, though. I get 'impatient' in the middle. I'll get to staring out the window or up the ceiling, and he will come up beside me and take over! Then I go feed the dogs or make sure the house doesn't need some work done."

They were married quietly, with only their immediate families
in the church. Lorna's grandfather insisted on giving them his
small house, near that of her parents. She, in turn, insisted that
he stay with them: her first child, she kept saying. He had always
eaten with her parents, but started taking meals with Lorna and
Fred, who declined the offer that they, with the grandfather,
continue to eat "next door," as Lorna would refer to her parents'
house. Lorna virtually stopped going there, as a matter of fact.
She regarded the tundra, the seashore, the ponds, and the river
bank as her home. She had never liked the land near their homes.
She laughed at the idea of private property, even as her grandfather did. The schoolteachers had never enjoyed her insistence
that the land is everyone's, that the world is a place for people
to share.

Her new husband would have his first difficult time with her
on just that score. He liked to walk the tundra, the shore, the
rising land up the river, but he stopped short of territory near
the village. He had learned about "property," as had many
Eskimos. Land here belonged to so-and-so; land there to someone else. Not that anyone possessed a deed; not that people had
built fences around their property. Nevertheless, Fred knew who
lived where, and he wanted to respect the rights of others. He
was not about to use land near the village for his own purposes
—walks, picnics, hunting, and fishing—without nodding to others, thanking them for their kindness. The villagers had not
become obsessed with the principle of ownership, but they did
look to one another for approval, sanction, encouragement.
And, especially, they tended to do certain things together—not
only hunting and fishing, but work on the rather simple roads
that connected the village's houses, or on the primitive landing
strip, a link with the outside world.

Lorna had no interest in such shared efforts. She pulled hard
on her new husband to stay away from others, to go on walks
with her, to contemplate even a further step—living more deci-

sively alone. She wanted the two of them to build their own home, to begin a life far from her parents. She wanted to take her grandfather away. He had always been a relative loner, anyway. Why not let him disengage, at last, from "the others." At nineteen that is what her family and neighbors were: "others." And she was not simply being fussy, willful, or aloof out of any resentment or hurt. She had her strong disagreements with her fellow villagers, but more important, she felt herself upholding sentiments which were not, actually, her own: "I feel our ancestors talking to me—the Eskimo women of this village who were here for a time, and long ago left. They were tough; they did not sit and wait for a plane to bring Coca-Cola, or for the men to bring food. They went hunting and fishing on their own. They were very proud. The women in some Eskimo villages were not proud at all; they were branches, their husbands the trunks of the trees. But in this village the women stood up and said yes, there is food out there to go find, and we will start out.

"When I look at the sky, I feel the women who once were here in this village. They push their opinions into my head. I talk for them when I say my thoughts to Fred! He laughs, and tells me there is no one up there except God. He believes the minister: one and only one God. I tell him I didn't say I was listening to any God; I just mentioned the other women of this village. They may be gone, but that doesn't mean they aren't somewhere, and don't remember the past, and don't have good advice for us. Fred says no; he says when we go, we go for good. We never come back. He has heard too much in church and at school. When I was in school I tried to keep my eyes on the sky. In church, it's best to think of the wind coming across the water!

"I don't like to walk near the village. I don't want to live so near everyone else. I don't want to ask people what they are doing. I don't want to hear them telling me what I should be doing. I don't want to hear them giving their orders to Fred. He will obey, and that is too bad. He will end up listening to the men he grew up with, and they will end up taking him with them everywhere: riding all day on the snowmobiles. I don't want to live like everyone else—not like the Eskimos of our village live today. I think the spirits of some of the Eskimo women who used to live in the village a long time ago are asking me to stand up and speak for them. They are unhappy at what they see, and someone has to be their friend in the village."

She almost lost her husband as a consequence of her loyalty to certain others, now dead, or as she saw it, departed. He took to leaving her, talking with his friends, going with them on snowmobile rides, chatting with them at the store. His wife did not want to acknowledge the importance of their company. She wanted to be on her own. She wanted him to be on his own. She did not mind a disagreement between the two of them; it was the constant presence of others in his mind that got her so fiercely upset. One day he failed to come home. She decided that he had left her, and told her grandfather that he should return to her parents' house. The old man refused. She became angry. She told him he must go; she told him *she* was going. Where? She would not answer. In fact, she did not at the time know.

Fred came back the next morning; he had been at home. He told her where he went. She pretended indifference. She also reversed herself—announced that she didn't care where he went, or for how long, and was even willing to go live with her parents, with his parents, with anyone in the village. He was surprised at her change of mind and heart, but quite happy, too. His wife was growing up, he said to himself—echoing wishes for that outcome he had heard from members of his family, and from his old friends.

She had decided to yield. Better to go along, she concluded, than lose someone she had, after all, married and become increasingly attached to. She began walking with him to the store; she began standing in the background with other young wives while the men talked and made their decisions: who does what, when, and where. He never really pushed her in that direction; he was far more respectful, guarded, even, with her than others he knew (and had grown up with) were with their wives or future wives. But she even seemed anxious to stop him from being solicitous or deferential. She stayed in the cabin more and more, cleaned things up often, cooked and cooked—and puzzled her grandfather, her father. She no longer wanted to go out hunting or fishing with them. She stopped taking her long, solitary walks, and discouraged her husband from suggesting that they both go out for a stroll.

Her father told her husband that this developing behavior was "strange." Her grandfather became so nervous he asked to move back with his son and daughter-in-law, Lorna's parents. When Lorna heard of that contemplated change of residence, she said nothing to her husband, her father, her grandfather. She took the old man's clothes and carried them over to her parents' house. No one was there. The entire village seemed deserted: a fishing expedition. Why shouldn't she go, too—go and stand and wait and talk? She walked, instead, toward the landing strip. She was musing, thinking back, wondering how it had come about that she was no longer the person she used to be.

Suddenly fate intervened—for her an invitation she could not refuse: "I thought I was hearing a noise, so I looked up at first and saw nothing; it was cloudy. Then, all of a sudden, I saw it: a plane. It was very low, and I thought it was headed for the ocean. But it turned around, and it landed on our strip. I couldn't understand why the plane was there. We know days ahead about a plane coming. We're all out waiting. No one seemed to know about this plane. I just stood there and watched. The pilot got out, and some other people. They were going to unload some packages, but they didn't know what to do because no one was there. They were having trouble with their engine. I heard them talking. I went nearer and they saw me, and they asked me if I'd

take care of a few boxes they were going to leave. I told them
yes, but I didn't really want to do that! The pilot heard me, and
he came over and asked me why.

"I didn't answer him at first. I didn't know the answer. Then
I spoke—and I was surprised myself to hear what I said. I told
him I wanted to leave our village, and I *was* leaving. I told
him I never come to see the planes land, but now I was there because
I was hoping to get a ride on it! He laughed. He said there was
plenty of room, but he didn't want me to come on just because
I said I wanted to come on! And anyway, he knew I wasn't there
waiting for the plane, because no one in the village knew he was
coming! He'd only landed so that one of his crew could check
out an engine. He had some packages for our village, but he was
supposed to fly over our landing strip, and go to other places, and
come to us much later. I told him I never know when the planes
are coming, but my friends told me this time. He asked me who
my friends are. When I told him the birds, he smiled. When I
told him my ancestors, he smiled. He thought I was another
stupid Eskimo woman! I've seen the same look for years on
missionary people and schoolteachers and others who come up
here from the Lower Forty-Eight."

She kept conversing with the pilot, however. She smiled, and
asked him personal questions. How long had he been in Alaska?
Where does he live? Where does he come from? She remembered the radio-telephone in the school. She decided to make up
a story. She told the pilot that she had a sister in Fairbanks, that
she wanted very much to see her, that she had tried calling her
on the phone, but to no avail. The radio-phone frequently breaks
down. If only the two could talk; better, if only they could see
each other again! The pilot expressed agreement: it is always nice
when people apart get together again. Within an hour Lorna was
on her way to Fairbanks.

She had no friends or relatives in that city. She had told her
story in order to get away, and she had succeeded. When the

plane landed, she got out, obtained a ride to downtown Fairbanks with a crew member, and ended up standing on a street corner, knowing no one and without a penny in her pocket. The man who gave her a ride had told her his name, and written his phone number on a piece of paper—so that she could ask him about the flights back home. They would be glad to take her back, he said. The pilot had, in fact, told him to say that. Lorna had overheard the conversation.

Meanwhile, she had other things on her mind: the sight of a large city. She walked a few blocks, stopped, stood on the corner of a street, watched intently the people walking, the cars passing. She lifted her eyes constantly, surveying tall buildings. She peered at store windows. The cars enthralled her—a steady flow of them, up and down a well-paved street. She wondered why they started and stopped, eventually figured out that the traffic lights were the clue to what she was noticing—and, so doing, remembered what she had long ago heard in school, even read there: "A teacher once told us about the colors red, yellow, and green—about traffic lights in cities. At first I couldn't understand where all the cars came from, and where they were going, and why they would suddenly start, then stop, then start again. Then I remembered the schoolteacher I once had, and the pictures she showed us of the traffic lights in the Lower Forty-Eight. There they were, before my eyes—and the cars, too."

There was a lot else before her eyes, though she would never be willing to talk at any great length about what she experienced during her brief stay in an Alaskan city. Once she spoke for a half an hour or so about Fairbanks, but not about its urban landscape: "Every day, until I die, a woman I met will come to visit me. I think of her, and I pray for her. I pray to the wind: go get her spirit, the woman spirit in her, and take her away—bring her to a river or a pond and let her rest there for a long, long time. A little while after I figured out what made the cars stop and go—the lights, the red and yellow and green stars of Fairbanks!—I

met a woman. She came up to me. She asked me if I was trying
to take over her territory. I couldn't figure out what she meant.
I asked her what she'd said. She told me I'd heard her the first
time. I didn't say anything, but she did. She told me to go away
and stop bothering her. I didn't even know her name.

"She was all dressed up. She looked like an Indian, maybe. She
was an Eskimo, though; I know it. Suddenly she became friendly.
She asked me where I came from. I told her. She asked me how
long I'd been in the city. I told her. She asked me why I'd come.
I tried to tell her. All I could say was that I liked to be alone, and
sometimes I didn't want to see anyone except my husband—and
sometimes I didn't even want to see him. She said she knew how
I felt. She warned me I'd better go back home, though. She said
the sooner I went back, the better. If I didn't I'd end up like her.
I told her she seemed nice—even if she wanted me to go away!
She laughed. She asked me how much money I had. I said none.
She wouldn't believe me. She asked me where I kept my money.
I said nowhere. She asked me where I was staying. I wasn't
staying anywhere. She wouldn't believe me. She asked me where
I was going. I told her I wanted to go back to the village. She
asked me how I'd get there. I didn't know how I'd get there—
but I remembered the name of the man on the plane.

"She took me back to her room, and she called him for me.
She was very nice to me. She talked to me a lot. I liked her. I
liked her better than a lot of women in our village. I only spent
an hour with her, but I thought I knew her. Maybe her spirit
came from around here. She told me she dreamed of leaving the
city and returning to the village where she was born. But she
didn't know the name of it. She was brought to the city when she
was a baby, and her mother died when she was little. She told
me she has dreams of an Eskimo village near the ocean. She told
me that in the taxi. She took me in a taxi to the airfield. She spoke
with the man. She gave me money. She took my name. She told
me she'd write to me. I told her she belonged to our village. I

know she does. I only saw her for a small amount of time, but I know she belongs to our people here. But I don't like to talk about her. I'd rather think about her; that way, I can bring her back here, and take a walk with her along the ocean."

She lowers her head. She is, in her mind, taking one such walk. She gets up, a few moments later, and looks out toward the ocean. She tells of a dream she had a day or two earlier, a daydream—the only way she really feels comfortable, a year later, talking about the woman she met in Fairbanks: "I was walking along the ocean by myself, and suddenly I saw my friend from the city across the water, standing on some ice, talking with a bear. They seemed to be friends, but then the bear moved toward her. She moved away, and I could tell that she was afraid. She fell in the water, and I thought she'd drown. But the wind picked her up and brought her over to the land, and she smiled at me, and we went for a walk, and I joked with her. I told her we could walk and walk, and there are no lights to tell us to go, to stop, to wait. That was the end; I saw my husband coming."

She had told her husband about the woman—had told him everything that happened during her brief, eventful trip. Her husband had won from her unforgettable respect and affection with his initial response: Why had Lorna not tried to persuade the woman to come to the village? Lorna had indeed tried to do just that—but once her woman friend and benefactor had placed the call to the pilot (who had just come home from the airport) a chain of activities had been set in motion. The two women went in a taxi to the airport; they were met by the pilot of the plane that had only a short while earlier brought Lorna to Fairbanks; he arranged for his erstwhile passenger to be returned home forthwith, and she was. The worst moment of her life, she felt later, was her time of arrival: all the village, there, waiting. But the best moment followed soon afterwards: her husband's expressed regret that she had not become better acquainted with the Fairbanks woman, had not even learned her full name or address, and so could not insist that a considerable display of hospitality and considerateness be reciprocated.

For Lorna, in the years that followed, the woman of the Fairbanks streets became a soul mate of sorts—constantly evoked, held in high esteem, considered a gift of providence. Her first name, Lorna knew, was Sally. Lorna's first child, a girl, received the name Sally. And though another girl followed, then a boy, then a girl, then a boy, Sally would always be her mother's favorite child. When Sally was about two years old, her mother began telling her who her namesake was—the first time in three years, Fred observed, his wife showed any interest in mentioning out loud her Fairbanks memories. It was then that the significance of an exceptionally brief trip became apparent to him, and no doubt, to his young daughter. It was then Lorna became more willing to share her friend with others: "I think of my trip to Fairbanks a lot, especially since Sally began to walk and talk. I hope my girl will be like the woman I met that day in Fairbanks. When I said that once to Fred, he asked me if I knew the woman Sally well enough to wish her life on our child. I knew what he was thinking: maybe she isn't so good all the time. We've never talked much about Sally, but I'm sure we both suspect that she meets men and brings them back to her place, and takes money from them in exchange for doing things for them. I told my grandfather about Sally, and he told me, before my first child was born, what he thought I would have learned if I stayed in Fairbanks longer.

"I think I would have found out a lot in a short time, if I'd stayed long enough. When she told me to get away from her 'territory' I knew what she meant. Men always think they are the smart ones. Even my grandfather, even my father, even my husband—three wonderful men!—make that mistake. They smile at me as if I am like my child Sally—a person who doesn't know, who has never learned how the world really works. One afternoon my grandfather told me he was going to explain 'the facts of life' in Fairbanks. He had been in the Second World War, he said. He saw cities. Well, I've been in no war—except the one I carry on here in this village! I told my grandfather I knew what he was going to say to me, but he didn't pay any attention; he went right on talking. At least Fred stops sometimes and smiles and says I'm right, and then he lets me speak and he listens. The other men in the village think he has 'surrendered' to me. They think I am a 'bad one.' They call me 'a polar bear with a bad mood.' Fred laughs at them. He says he is strong enough to hear their words, and to hear my words as well. He *is* strong, because there are days when I don't feel very good, and I *do* say the wrong words. I feel my stomach turning, and I want to run away, and I look at my husband and my children, and instead of getting better, I get worse. So I go outside and talk with the dogs, or take a long walk, and I get over my mood."

Her daughter Sally became increasingly important during those moods; she was the one who learned to help her mother get over them. The mother would suddenly begin to stare out the window or look fixedly at some object in the house. The children would ignore her, continue their play, go outside, keep on eating—whatever the particular rhythm of the day. For Sally, however, the time had come for action, for an initiative with respect to the mother. Eventually, the girl's father would seek her out—the only one, really, who knew how to reach Lorna and bring her out of herself, bring her back to the rest of the family. The mother eventually recognized the significance of her daughter's attentiveness to her psychological fluctuations: "I leave. I leave the children and cross the ocean and sit on an ice floe, far away, and think. I leave the children to go to Fairbanks and talk with my friend. She and I go for a long walk in the city. I leave the children and fly away with the ducks I hear passing over our village—the lucky ones. But Sally never lets me go far without coming after me. Sometimes we stay away a little longer, but mostly I go right back home with her. The children notice what happens; my oldest son will say: 'She's with us now.'

"One time I almost got lost. Sally says she was scared. It was the only bad walk we've had. I was surprised to see her; I thought I'd got away, and I didn't want to be followed, even by Sally. I was in Fairbanks—talking with my friend, telling her how lucky she is to have that nice room, and not to have a lot of people pulling on her all the time. She was telling me I could stay with her for a while if I wanted. (There are days when I wish she'd asked me to stay when I really was there in Fairbanks!) I was just about to thank her, and tell her I'd be glad to accept, and live there until I was ready to go back—when my girl showed up, and she put her hand into mine. I get upset when she does that. I feel like crying. I don't know why. That time, though, I didn't want to cry. I wanted to hit Sally, slap her on the face! I'd never in my life felt like doing that to anyone. I almost hit her, my child. I started crying. She squeezed my hands and I cried more.

"I still didn't want to go home. I asked Sally please to go away and leave me alone for a while. She said she would. I think she realized it was better not to argue with me then. I turned my back on her. I left the village and walked toward the ocean. The other children started to follow, but she kept them away. I remember hearing her tell them that they had to stop and turn around. She said I would be back soon. I think at the time I believed I would never come back. I had my eyes on one of the islands. I wanted to walk to it. I wanted to live there. I must have started walking in the water, because I noticed that when I was back in the house, cleaning up and making supper, my feet were cold and wet. Sally had trusted me. I told her the next day I'd never leave her again. Since then she always goes with me when I leave."

Does she know that she is upset, sad, angry—hence impelled to remove herself mentally from a given scene? Does she actually believe that she has "left," said good-bye to her children and/or husband for a brief spell? How does she herself regard her departures—as necessary interludes, as indulgences, as mad but unavoidable forays, as seizures that are nonetheless limited and on the whole beneficial? She is able, in her own way, to run through such considerations, and, also, in her own way, to come up with a concrete psychological analysis, along with a political, an ideological point of view, all clothed in the earthy, coastal Arctic experience of her people: "I am not the kind of woman my mother is, or Fred's mother is. I am a different woman. There are days—an entire season, even—when I wonder whether I am a woman at all! But I'm not a man either! Make no mistake about that! My grandfather has found that out, living here with us. He says that sometimes he looks at me, and he thinks I'm not a man and not a woman, but a spirit that doesn't like being either a man or a woman. I asked him why he thinks that. He says I'm too much by myself, and I don't join the women, but I'm not a man.

"He says I may have an Eskimo woman spirit locked up in my body, and the spirit wants to be let loose, but I'm still alive. I don't think that's the only reason I want to leave. Sometimes there may be a spirit in me, pushing or pulling; but I have my eyes and my ears, and they get me going. I'll see a woman in our village talking one way—like a child—to the men, and another way to her own children, and I want to go shake her. It's not my business to shake her, I know. Maybe she wants to shake me! I know that some women in the village think I once had a high fever or got a bad chill, and that's why I act so 'funny.' That's what their children tell my children, that I am 'funny' in the way I do things.

"I *am* funny, I guess. I think the women should stand up and say to the men what they whisper to each other. Maybe the women should start by talking louder to each other. I remember my mother lowering her voice when she wanted to ask my father for help. My father *raised* his voice when *he* wanted help. I always thought he was smarter, and I always wanted to be with him—because a strong voice is a lot of help when you're little and you don't know what to do. My husband and I are called 'the strange ones' by a lot of people our age in the village. They think there is a man inside me and a woman inside my husband. They joke with him about that; they are afraid to say anything to me, but I hear from him—talk of my strong voice and the attention he gives the children and me. If he didn't help cook and help the children learn to obey and learn to dress and learn to play with each other, I would not be here now. Sometimes I leave for a few minutes; I close my eyes and take a trip away! I am not the most patient woman in this village. But if I had to be a woman in this village like other women in this village, then I would be living in Fairbanks right now, with the woman I met there, my friend Sally."

Her friend Sally has become a lifelong companion of sorts, a person constantly summoned for encouragement, solace, and, even at times, outspoken conversation. Most Eskimos of the village haven't known that Lorna has been, for years, speaking with a woman from Fairbanks. They have not credited Lorna with having a particular person in mind when she has been seen talking—but alone. For them, it is a matter, again, of the strange, the peculiar, or if they are older, of a "spirit" coming over someone, possessing her. Lorna has not been unaware of her reputation. She has, in a way, cultivated it. She has tried hard to persuade herself that the woman she briefly met in a city hundreds of miles away may well have been a "spirit." And there are times when Lorna has succeeded—when she believes that to be a fact: the Sally met in a city as a "spirit" carried home. But Lorna also knows the exact nature of a quite real experience she had: "There are some women in this village who think I never went to Fairbanks. They think I walked far away, and tried to fight a 'spirit' in me, and didn't succeed. They think that since I came back, I've been under the power of that 'spirit.' Or they think I met a 'spirit' in Fairbanks, and that 'spirit' drove away my own 'spirit' and won me over. They are wrong; but they are right, I guess. I've never been the same since I came back from Fairbanks. I live here, but I live there, too. I think the woman I met there may have followed me back—a shadow.

"My grandfather said his grandmother always talked of a 'shadow' over her. The shadow was the spirit of an ancestor who wanted to come back here and see if there have been any changes. If I was an ancestor, I wouldn't want to return, not to this village. I'd rather take my chances with a polar bear—and be able to stretch out and enjoy the ocean and the ice and the sun, without the minister reminding me of my sins, and the schoolteacher reminding me of all the things I don't know. Of course, the polar bear has to watch out, too; those hunters come up here from the Lower Forty-Eight and shoot to kill, so they can go home with the furs and put them on their floors.

"Maybe a spirit made me go to Fairbanks. I never planned to go there. I just went. I've asked myself a lot how I got there. Sometimes I think it was an accident: the plane landed because of an emergency—and I happened to be right there. Sometimes I think I went to the runway because I knew the plane would be coming. And maybe Sally was pushed by some 'spirit' in her to come say hello to me. She herself told me that she didn't usually go out that time of day. She felt 'itchy,' and so she decided to take a walk. When I feel 'itchy,' it means I want to go talk with Sally, so I go. If someone sees me, I speak louder, hoping the person will be able to hear. That's the way not to be heard!

"Four women once started to follow me on a walk. They kept back, but not so far that I didn't see them. I turned around and walked *toward* them. I *ran,* actually; and I shouted. I told them I was the Devil—the one the minister mentions all the time and seems to know pretty well. They didn't think I was being very funny. They were back in the village pretty fast! I wanted to keep after them and make strange noises—like in the movies they used to show us in school: the ghosts. But I was so glad to be alone again, I did run—but further from the village. I laughed and I told Sally I wish she could have seen the four of them, like rabbits in the summer, jumping all over and running so fast they forgot where they were trying to go. One of them ran a circle and came back near me, so I raised my voice again. Then she disappeared."

As she became older, in her late twenties, she earned the title of a "woman spirit" from some of her husband's friends. She also started becoming more directly outspoken. She talked not only to herself, but with others—the friends of her husband, who occasionally came by, intent on a chat, a Coke, an exchange of news and ideas. She developed even stronger resentments against the Eskimos in the village who helped the minister and the schoolteachers. She also began to urge Fred to speak up, take issue with his childhood friends, the men of the village who were, by that time, as a group increasingly becoming the effective political authority. She wanted to know why, in 1974, with all the other changes taking place in the village, in all Alaska, she was regarded as a bit out of her mind because she behaved as an *individual,* because she questioned various customs, and, not unimportant, because she began to tell the men she talked with (those friends of her husband's) that they were "noisy bosses."

What did she mean by those words? Where had she obtained them? Why was she, yet again, confusing everyone—now by the use of words, rather than through some action she took? She had for years known what a "boss" is. The Eskimos had "bosses"— the white people who come up from the Lower Forty-Eight on various errands, the white people who have airplanes and armed ships and who run the state of Alaska. In school she had always remembered the stories of slavery and the South's turmoil. Now, years later, she was connecting her own people to another, far distant people—the blacks of Alabama or Mississippi. She was going further; she was distinguishing between those of her own people who rule and those who are ruled. She had begun to do so, in her mind, one day when she happened to be near the village's landing strip, and saw some of her fellow villagers waiting for the plane to arrive—the weekly intermediary between them and the outside world. She, too, wanted to see the landing, and did. But she saw more. She saw the men on the plane talk

with the men on the ground. She saw the women there with-
draw, become a huddled group of expectant, attentive, quite
respectful and certainly demure, individuals. They occasionally
giggled, but were mostly serious, even grave. The men, from the
plane or the village, were a contrast indeed. They were open,
expansive, friendly. They were enjoying the company of each
other. They kidded. They even played a few games: who can
throw a piece of wood farthest, or who can reach highest—
various points on the plane being a measure of achievement.

Lorna knew that she wasn't *only* angry; she was frustrated,
envious. She liked to throw—almost always by herself. She also
liked to show how strong she is, how able to exert her muscles,
her will, and thereby excel even her own expectations. And she
had learned to appreciate the airplane as extraordinarily valuable
—a means by which one can leave a village and, only hours later,
be standing far away on a relatively crowded city sidewalk. Why
weren't the women near the plane? Why hadn't they shown an
interest in it? Why were only men going in and out of the plane,
loading and unloading? She suddenly remembered the harsh
comments she had heard from her friend Sally in the Fairbanks
airport—to the effect that men run everything from airplanes to
businesses to governments. What would Sally say about this particular Eskimo village? Lorna asked herself that question as she
stared at a rather ordinary event. She would never stop asking
that question, nor would she keep her thoughts to herself, as had
often been the case before.

She broke her own meditative gaze after about five minutes,
and walked over to the plane. She made a point of passing the
women. She asked them if they wanted to accompany her, catch
a nearer look at the plane, even go aboard. They were stunned
by her sudden appearance, her summons of sorts. What did she
have in mind—another flight, this one publicly arranged? They
kept their eyes on her. She knew she had a certain control over
them as she walked toward the plane. She wasn't sure what she

would do, once at her destination. She walked fast, arrived at the plane with one purpose in mind—to mingle with the others, and doing so, show the onlookers what might be possible for them. When she came near the village's men, they frowned at her: Lorna, up to her old tricks. She was always a bit unpredictable, and certainly a known maverick. But she usually confined her iconoclastic behavior to the tundra or the ocean's edge, where she walked, talked to herself, seemed caught in moods that defied anyone's comprehension. Now she was turning herself into a public figure, and seemingly challenging a long-standing social custom—the way a particular Eskimo settlement comes to terms with outsiders.

For a moment or two the men glared at her, but said nothing. She walked past them, ready to look at the plane, then board it for a closer inspection. She stopped just short of the steps leading to the inside of the plane. One of the Eskimo men, an old friend of her husband's, approached her and asked her what she wanted. She looked at him intently, more curious than angry (so she later described herself). Why should he be asking her what she wanted? Why wasn't she asking him, in response, what *he* was doing—asking her what she wanted? She said nothing in reply. But she was deterred by the question. She had intended to go up the stairs, poke around a bit, return to the ground, and leave for the tundra and a good, long walk. Now she had other plans in mind.

She started up the stairs, turned around, looked across the field to the women, who were, as she had suspected, still watching her every move. She raised both her arms and with them beckoned the women. They were, for a second, puzzled and unresponsive. But soon Lorna was calling to them: Come here, come and see, come right away. They had rarely heard her speak at all, never mind approach them directly and invitingly. They were as much surprised by the sound of her voice and the phenomenon of her willingness to engage with them, pay them heed, as they were with the message. They responded to *her,* not to her more ideological interest on their behalf. They walked nearer, eventually were beside her. Lorna, for her part, brushed aside years of her own indifference, if not outright hostility, and smiled, even touched the shoulders of several women. Then she casually suggested that they all go up and look at the inside of the airplane.

She spoke in such a way that she was not really asking anything special of her newfound friends. She simply started up the steps. The other women seemed to sense that if they did not follow, they would be breaking a fragile bond, suddenly, surprisingly established. Up they went, oblivious of the men, who now had come together and were watching this development with surprise rather than annoyance. They were, in fact, an image of the group of women as it had existed until a few minutes earlier; that is, they were outsiders, if nearer at hand, and they were quite obviously interested in what would happen *next,* even as the women had hitherto stood patiently and wondered what they would see from minute to minute, as the plane's crew went through various rituals.

Soon enough the women had, for the first time, obtained a rather thorough view of the plane's interior. They had also met the crew, been shown the controls, even been allowed to sit, one after the other, in the pilot's seat. Each of them was permitted to use a pair of binoculars. They were given a brief lecture on distances: how many miles to various points in Alaska, and to the south. Then they descended, looking rather pleased with themselves and, of course, excited. The men broke out of their group, rushed to the women, embraced them, and started clapping at them: congratulations! They walked together back to the village, the first time that had happened. Always before the arrival of a plane had been an occasion for the sexes to separate and keep apart, until both the men and the women had returned to their homes or adjacent land, and the plane could be seen high in the sky, circling, or only be heard.

Lorna did not realize the significance of the occasion at first: "I was almost in tears, but I didn't know why. It was the first time I'd ever felt friendly with those women. I used to avoid them whenever possible. And I knew what they thought of me: the strange one, the proud one, the one no one knows how to figure out! I'd heard the minister's complaints about me years ago, and tried to forget them. I thought of the minister when I was walking back from the landing strip with my new friends. He is gone. We have a new minister. I wished that the old one was there. I wondered what he'd make of it—all of us walking together, the men and the women. He always gave us sermons about men having *their* work, and women having *their* work. It used to bother him that my grandfather liked to cook and would teach some boys how to prepare a soup. He'd learned how to make it from a white man, a hunter, but that didn't make any difference to the minister. He thought that my grandfather shouldn't cook; my grandmother should do that. No wonder my grandfather would leave and walk toward the ocean when the minister came to our house for one of his visits.

"When we came back to our village, we just stood there. We didn't seem to want to break up and go back to our houses. I got nervous for a second. I didn't know what to say, or do. I decided to say nothing, and do nothing. We just talked a little about the plane. Then I saw that everyone felt a little funny, so I spoke up. I said that now we should all go to the plane *together* each week, and have a good time there on the landing strip *together,* and then come back here *together.* Everyone laughed and said yes. Then we all hugged—and that was the end. We went home. I was quite excited, but I didn't really know why. I didn't know, then, what had happened—or what would happen."

She attributed her excitement, at first, to a more personal matter—her reconciliation, of a kind, with the people of the village. But they had not missed the point of her involvement in their lives. They began to realize that she had, in her own quiet but forceful way, asked them to make a break with their past. They got to thinking about not only Lorna's initiative, but their response—and its justification: "I heard from Fred, day after day, that I had turned into a different Lorna, and that probably another spirit had taken me over. That wasn't what happened, though. I'm still the same person I was. It's the people of the village who began to change a little. They really look forward to that plane coming; they have a party there now at the landing strip. They bring Cokes, and they all go together. The women love looking inside the plane. I take Sally with me; and Fred comes when he isn't fishing. Sally told me that she would like to be a pilot. She told the schoolteacher, too; and the schoolteacher didn't like the idea. She told my daughter to be more 'realistic.' My daughter didn't know what the word means, and I wasn't sure either. We found out: you're being 'realistic' when you do what the teacher tells you to do! When you think something she doesn't like you to think, you're not being 'realistic' at all! I hope Sally doesn't worry all the time about the opinion of others, even when it's me who's telling her to do something, and she wants to do something else. I hope she does become a pilot! I'd love to be one myself!"

She would never stop having thoughts about being a pilot. That was her inclination, her way—to have dreams of departure, travel; dreams in which she goes away, does the unusual, the difficult, the unconventional; dreams, it might be said by others, of transcendence. All her life she had been dissatisfied with the constraints, as she saw them, of her village's everyday life. All her life she had regarded herself (and been regarded as) a somewhat different person—elusive, strange, aloof, self-preoccupied, imaginative to the point of eccentricity in her wishes, ambitions, even activities. She would never become just another Eskimo villager. But after the incident at the landing strip she did change slightly, and her husband and children and relatives and neighbors noticed the change. She went with the others quite eagerly to await the plane's arrival. She laughed and joked while standing there, and often, when the plane first appeared, she clapped loudly, prompting others to follow suit. Eventually she became, by common consent, the group's leader—in the sense that she went aboard first and greeted the pilot. Later on, she was the one to say good-bye to him, on behalf of all present.

One day, when Lorna was thirty-five years old, a pilot took her and her daughter Sally up on a flight, showed them how to use the controls—as opposed to looking at them. The village from that time on regarded both mother and daughter as pilots, no matter how hard both protested the mere beginning of their experience. When Lorna came back home from that flight she predicted that Sally would surely one day become a pilot, and that she would, perhaps, get to fly with her daughter upon occasion. The mother also announced to her family that many "Eskimo women spirits," long silent, had begun to speak up. Those spirits were responsible for the slow but definite changes taking place in the village—the mixed group at the landing strip, the more casual mingling of men and women at the village store. When Sally asked her mother whether more "spirits" would arrive, and what changes they would bring, the answer provided was prompt and brief: "I hope more spirits will come; I hope they will help all the women of this village fly."

FIVE

CLASS
AND SEX

The "indefiniteness" George Eliot mentions in the prelude to *Middlemarch,* part of which we quote at the beginning of this book, is not only (she takes pains to indicate) a question of fate's arbitrary nature, but of the mind's astonishing range of responsiveness to any given condition or situation. For two decades we have tried to learn how certain women, faced with harsh and mean external circumstances, have nevertheless struggled fiercely to fashion particular lives for themselves. It has not been as easy as we might have hoped to come up with clear-cut generalizations about the various "attitudes" of those women. In a migrant camp, one finds women who all too readily and, it seems, enthusiastically, embrace a prevailing social, economic, and sexual exploitativeness. A woman sells herself, for instance, not only to the crew leader, as a laborer, but to a foreman or a grower, as a mistress; or indeed, to the crew leader as both an obliging "body" and a worker in the fields. Up the hollows of Appalachia, similarly, one encounters women who work hard outside on the land, and inside the house stand silent and servile, even when their husbands are themselves no tyrants—quite the contrary.

Nor are all Chicanos obsessed by machismo; some turn to their wives almost plaintively, only to receive in return an eager surrender of sorts: what you want, I will do. The same kind of ironic psychological submission obtains, occasionally, in the Eskimo settlements of Alaska—a woman almost provocatively self-effacing, despite her husband's inclination to welcome another kind of relationship with his wife.

This irony or ambiguity ought not be stressed too much. For many of the women we have come to know these past decades, the enemy is a given social order, yes; an economic system, yes; but also and quite distinctly—or as George Eliot might want us to say, quite definitely—a certain number of men. Not just *a* man; rarely have we met a woman who is unwilling to connect the serious and demeaning hurts of her life with the behavior of more than one person. Yet, when an unhappy and complaining (or protesting) woman begins to move her attention from the individual or idiosyncratic to a broader arc of humanity, a certain psychological "indefiniteness" will inevitably be the price, a sense of frustration and perplexity: where to begin with one's resentment and moral, personal outrage? Put differently, a specific denunciation brings more immediate satisfaction.

Moreover, social criticism is a risky venture indeed for the poor or the hard-working not-so-poor. Even those of us who are rather well off, protected by various privileges, and paid to observe and then write about our fellow citizens, do not always manage an unrelenting and forthright interpretation of the status quo. "Men are all alike," a factory worker from the Piedmont section of North Carolina remarked to us one day. She was hardly delivering herself of an exceptional conclusion; and she knew that we would not be overcome with surprise. She was quite willing to turn on herself, but also to explain her predicament—at once personal, social, and, despite her lack of pretensions, intellectual: "Men think they're so damn important. Even among ordinary people, the men will try to boss around the women, no matter that both men and women are being bossed by the bosses! It's always been like that, and I suppose God meant us to live like that—a strutting rooster and us hens, putting up with him. When that foreman comes in, he's not just someone over us who can fire you on the spot; he's a man, trying to show us women how big and important he is. I look at him, and I say to myself: You're on the lookout for someone to make you feel better. You're scared, and you want to see us looking even more scared. Then I think to myself that he's probably all right sometimes, when he's not scared. But when is that?

"I'll bet there are rich men who don't have a thing to be scared of—but they're still all full of themselves when it comes to the womenfolk in their lives. I can't figure men out. They're *not* all alike, I know that. My husband isn't like my three brothers. He's a little nicer to women. But push him far enough, and he'll stand his ground and say that he's glad I'm working because we need the money real bad, but he doesn't want me to go get any big ideas in my head. That's a joke! What big ideas can I get—and do something about? And that goes for him, too! We're in the same boat. He talks like a man, and I talk like a woman—because he's a man, and I'm a woman. But let me tell you, we're just plain people, without money, except for what we earn each week; and it all disappears fast, and we're always behind, always. And that's important, when you talk about the men and the women—what kind of *people* they are, working people or the well-off folks, who have a lot more time than we do to figure out what's happening in this world!"

She was not the first woman we met in the course of our work to connect sex and class, to point out that suffering or vulnerability or exploitation have a bearing on the way men and women think about each other, get on with each other. All along, in various parts of the country and from women of different backgrounds, we have heard angers and disappointments tied *both* to sex and class (and, of course, race) in such a way that to separate the "variables" or "factors," to insist upon sex or class or race as *the* important fact in a person's life, is to take a risk the woman just quoted knew rather well: "I will be feeling sorry for myself because I'm not rich, or because I'm not a man, but it's no good wishing you're a man who's as poor as my man is. He tells me he drives past the shopping mall where the rich women go, and he wishes I was one of them. With a few beers in him he'll joke with me and tell me he wishes *he* was one of them! I said once: 'You mean you'd become a woman for a few thousand dollars?' He said he would, he sure would! It's no good, talking like that. The reason we do is plain: too many bills to pay and not enough money to pay them. I told my husband I wouldn't be a man for anything, not for a million dollars. He said I was kidding myself. He said he wasn't talking about sex changes, like you see people on television tell about. He meant the dreams you have, when you stop and ask yourself why you're you and not someone else, and who you'd have liked to be if you could have your one and only wish—a chance to be somebody else, other than yourself. I remember my grandmother asking me to play make-believe with her: 'Make believe you're another person.' I still play the game sometimes while I'm working in the mill."

So it goes—childhood fantasies at work in a twentieth-century capitalist order among grown men and women who know little or nothing about names like Marx and Freud, but a lot about hard, mean labor and the mind's desperate effort to make sense of an obviously unfair world. There are in her and her husband other fantasies about sex and its relationship to a working life. She and he share daydreams of a privileged life. What would *she* do? What would *he* do? She is rather glad to imagine herself without a job. She would get up at seven-thirty, not five-thirty. She would see her husband off, her children off, maybe drive the latter to school herself, then have a quiet breakfast. She would delight in her aloneness—no one on either side of her, working the assembly line. She would watch television, meet a friend at a shopping mall, have lunch with her, come home and do some planting or weeding or "fixing" food or "just plain relaxing." That last option is the one she favors most when she evokes her daytime dreams while standing and inspecting an endless stream of towels.

As for her husband, she believes that if he had more money, lots of it, there would be no similar inclination to stay at home, or go shopping and meet a friend for lunch. Men are "different," she has come to believe. They not only have to work, most of them; they "need" to do so. She is convinced that her husband would go crazy if he didn't have a long and tiring job. How did she arrive at that conclusion? He told her that—and besides, men are full of energy, restless, and in constant pursuit of one challenge or another, however small. Women are better able to sit, to let the hours pass without feeling an urge to "prove" themselves. She is unrelenting on such distinctions: "I believe a woman isn't as fidgety as a man. Women like me go to work because we *have* to; there's no alternative but living poorer lives. None of my friends want to go to that factory. But my husband says he'd lose his mind if he didn't have a place to go to every morning. He says there are only so many days you can go fishing. He says it's in a man's nature to want to tackle the world, and it's in a woman's nature to want to be at home and take care of the house and children. He's right. I miss having a baby. My youngest is in school now. But I had to work before she went off. My mother helped me with the child. I'll probably help my daughter the same way, one day."

Not very remarkable or surprising stereotypes—and one hears them constantly, in home after home, despite the arrival of a women's liberation movement. But in which homes? And do such restrictive self-appraisals go unqualified? It takes years, sometimes, to answer that second question. Those who work long, hard days are not ready in the evening or on a weekend day to deliver themselves of extended, outspoken searchings of

236 WOMEN OF CRISIS

soul. Yet over time we have heard, in bits and pieces, strong-minded answers of a reflective and discerning nature—from women not especially "educated," but sometimes able in a flash to take not only their own measure, but that of others who belong to their sex, though not their class.

One encounter in particular threw these questions into focus. Each of the women's lives we have studied, including those in this book, gave us tentative answers—clues. But close to home we came to know a woman who expanded her own extraordinary insight into the relationship of class and a struggle for identity. Through her we were able to tether our abstract theories to the actuality of two lives: a maid and her employer.

A white woman from Somerville, a so-called "streetcar sub-urb" outside of Boston, has for a long time worked in the home of a prominent, quite well-off Cambridge family. Helen has cleaned for them, cooked for them. She has taken care of their two children. She knows them well—and herself, too; and knows the difference: "I come over there every day. When they go away, I stay. They've given me a room. They say I can live with them. They mean to be nice, but I get upset. They don't stop and think that I have a family, too. Yes, they 'know' I have a family, but they don't want to remind themselves of what they know, because they really would prefer that I live with them. They've been telling me for years that I should 'stay over,' and they'd pay me more. I say I'd love to do it, but I can't. What about my daughter? What about my son? They remind me that my mother is there to take care of my children; but *I* am their mother.

"I worry about my own children, while I take care of other people's children. That's the way it has to be, I know. I need the money. They have the money! I can't even leave this house when I go home. The place sticks in my mind. I'll think of what I did the day before, or what I'll be doing the next day. All those important people come here, and I serve them food. You get used to the way the rich live, and you go home at night, and suddenly you're poor again. I tell my husband he's lucky he works on a truck. He doesn't see what I do, so he doesn't miss what I do.

"I'll be working, and I'll hear them talk. The missus is a big talker. She goes gab, gab all the time, when she's home. She has a lot of money, but she works, too. She's in public relations, she tells me. She helps the museums. She writes articles. She calls a lot of people up and goes to see them. She has an office in Boston. She used to do volunteer work, a lot of it; but she said she should *work*, like men do. My husband thinks she's crazy, and so do I. If I had money, I'd quit this job, and go home and stay home for a thousand years. I'd be with my own kids and not someone else's. Does it make sense? The missus says that she has to get out and work, or else she'll 'stagnate'—her favorite word. She's always worrying about 'stagnating.' She says women are in danger of 'stagnating.' Maybe in her dictionary I'm not a woman!

"It's different being a woman like the missus, and being a woman in the neighborhood where my family lives. We were brought up to wait on our men, hand and foot. Here in this house, the missus is the equal of the mister. She speaks and he listens as much as he speaks and she listens. I think she runs the money, and she doesn't *ask* him for anything. She *tells* him: I'll do this, and I want to do that! In my family, my mother always let my father run things; and that's the way I am with my husband. He wouldn't have it any other way. He says women are getting out of line these days. Maybe he's right; I don't know. I don't envy the rich women I see over in that Cambridge house! A lot of them have husbands who are doctors or lawyers or professors, and they have more money than I'd know what to do with; but I'll look at one of them, a pretty lucky woman. I'll think for a second or two, and she's not at peace with herself—that's how I'd put it. The missus I work for—she weighs herself twice a day. If she gains a pound—*one* pound!—she tells her husband she's 'depressed,' another of her words. He asks why. She says she doesn't know. But I know. I've seen her face when she's been on the scale. I can tell what she'll say afterwards. Her husband never uses the scale. He's not fat. He looks thin and healthy to me. He doesn't worry about himself the way his wife does. She's always buying clothes and putting them on and taking them off and looking in one mirror and then another mirror. I can't figure her out. I guess she's a rich, spoiled woman."

Helen's observations, a maid's strenuous outpouring, turn out to be at once sociological and psychological—connected to another person's sex and membership in a particular class. She never graduated from high school, has no intellectual pretensions, and certainly no radical ideological polemics to urge upon others. She lost a son in the Vietnam War, which she upheld all along as "necessary." She is a faithful Catholic, and by her own, oft-repeated description, a "loyal American." She is not so sure that "a lot of those Harvard people" are as "loyal" as she is to the flag, to the nation's various traditions and institutions; but she has also learned (out of self-interest, perhaps) to live and let live. She doesn't care about politics, she insists. She may know that she disagrees with her employers and their friends, but she remembers that it's "a free country," and so differences of opinion are to be expected. She denies, at times, even an interest in how "they" live. At other times she is knowing and subtle in her observations, which she is obviously anxious to express.

Helen has noticed the changes in the views of her employers —their response to the world's events. She has noticed the changes in the way they get along as husband and wife. She has heard much talk of "women's liberation," has declared a real disdain for the idea—yet has kept careful track of what has been done in the name of this "movement." And despite her repeatedly avowed lack of interest in politics, she indicates by her words anything but indifference to questions of power, inequality, justice. She also claims to be "uneducated" and a "simple" person—though in a flash she can make evident her understanding and appreciation of psychological irony, social complexity, cultural ambiguity. When she referred to "the missus" as "rich," as "spoiled," she was making an obvious judgment—class against class. But she had more indirect but no less significant observations to make. She saw that a well-to-do, well-educated and vigorously "liberated" woman nevertheless was far more obsessed with her weight, her appearance than was the case, in either respect, with her husband. And, too, the maid never forgot her own importance: her work was an important prerequisite to a family's enjoyment of various interests, activities, hobbies. She was an indispensable presence; her efforts enabled others to proclaim the virtues of their hospitality.

The "missus" urged that women affirm themselves outside their homes; to do so herself, she had to bring someone into her own home—thereby taking that person away from a home hardly with the resources to welcome and sustain a person known as a "maid." The husband went along with his wife, urged her to move from charitable work on a part-time basis to full-time employment, whereby one becomes "fulfilled" and "committed." To enable that shift, Helen had to work longer, stay over sometimes, be aided by another woman called a "cleaning lady"— meaning that she was asked to do more menial work (vacuuming, cleaning the bathrooms) while the maid did sewing, answered the phone, ordered food and cooked it, sent clothes to the cleaner. The "missus" constantly thanked something abstract for her "liberation"—a movement, which had "raised" her "consciousness." But the maid had an occasional thought that such a development, such a movement, wasn't so far doing much for her.

One day Helen had been asked to come stay in the large Cambridge home for a week. The "missus" had to leave town for a three-day conference important for her work. Her husband also had a trip scheduled that week, and they had decided to meet after their professional obligations were ended, spend a few days together in California: "She came to me and asked me what I was 'doing' for that week. That's her way of talking. They're always saying that they're going to 'do' this and 'do' that—or 'take up' something, or 'take up' something else. I guess I didn't say *yes* fast enough for her. She looked at me hard for a second, and said: 'Do you mind?' Well, what was I supposed to say? What difference does it make if I mind or I don't mind? I hear her and her husband talking about the colored people, and how they should have their rights, and the women, and they should have their rights. But when the missus wants me to do something, or the cleaning woman to do something, or the man who works on her plants and trees to do something, she doesn't worry about us; she worries about herself.

"She tells her children that they should feel sorry for the poor, and if they ever see a colored person, they should put themselves in that person's shoes. The way those kids order me around, I know they're not fighting over who gets to try out my shoes! Once the girl asked me if I liked the colored. She was eleven, and I didn't want to get into a long talk with her. I just told her yes, I thought some of them are good people, and some aren't so good. She didn't believe me! She said she knew I didn't like the colored. I asked her where she got *that* idea. She said her mother had told her that a lot of white people who don't have much money are afraid of the colored people, and are prejudiced against them. I told her I was going to tell her mother *a lot,* the next time I had a talk with her! But I didn't want to get into a fight. I'd lose my job. I need the money. She pays a good salary. The house is an easy one to take care of.

"I hear them talk at the table. The missus is always worrying about something happening far away. She calls people up and gets them to sign their names, to protest this and protest that. I've never heard of all those 'causes.' She calls them that. She says to me: 'I'm working on a cause; we've all got to help.' I'm glad she never asks me to sign. I'm not an important person, so she doesn't want me. If she ever did ask me, I'd probably do what she wanted. I wouldn't want to cross her. She calls people who disagree with her 'stupid.' Her husband is even worse when he hears that someone disagrees with him. He calls them Nazis or Fascists. I thought we beat them and got rid of them a long time ago! Or he'll talk about 'right-wingers.' I can't figure out who they are. Maybe, if they heard my husband talk, they'd call him one! But I never talk at home about what I hear those two bosses of mine say at work. I'm glad to say *good-bye* when I leave work. On a bad day, I'll say *good riddance* instead of *good-bye* when I'm leaving. The worst days are when the missus has been talk, talk, talking, and calling up all those people, and being real nice to them, and worrying about the whole world—except me, and except her own children. She shouts at me. She tells me to get the children 'in good shape.' She can be a mean one sometimes, underneath her smile and her good causes."

One woman sizes up another woman. One person comes to terms with another person. Poverty bows to wealth, but not without an occasional moment of resentment. Liberation proceeds at full pace, but servants do not disappear—in fact, at least in certain neighborhoods, seem to multiply. A generous, compassionate interest in the oppressed and tortured of Latin America, Africa, Asia is not enough to prevent a baleful look in the next room—from a fellow citizen who has her own reasons to feel manipulated if not oppressed; insulted or looked down upon, if not tortured. That maid, in an outburst meant to be part of a confrontation that never took place, had not failed to notice the various ironies: "I come there, and the house is full of talk, even early in the morning. He's read something that's bothered him, and she's read something that's bothered her. They're both ready to phone their friends. The kids hear all that, and they start complaining about what's bothering *them*—about school, usually. They're all so *critical.* I tell my kids to obey the teacher and listen to the priest; and their father gives them a whack if they cross him. But it's different when I come to fancy Cambridge. In that house, the kids speak back to their parents, act as fresh and snotty as can be. I want to scream sometimes when I hear those brats talking as if they know everything. They have no respect for anyone, older or younger. They're taught to be in love with themselves—but they keep saying how much they love other people. They can dance like they do in Africa, and they can sing all those songs from foreign countries, and they love the one or two colored kids handpicked for their classrooms. But they can be so rude to me, and the cleaning woman, and anyone else who doesn't just run to them when they snap their fingers. And they have no God. They worship themselves—and their 'causes.'

"I almost quit the other day; I'd had enough. Their eleven-year-old daughter complained that I 'disturbed' her seashell collection! She said she was sure I'd broken one or two of those shells and thrown them away! The missus asked me if I'd been dusting in the girl's room. I said no. She asked if the cleaning lady had been there. I said no. We'd both been ordered to stay out by the girl! Her mother had agreed to do that one room. But the mother had more important things to do, of course. She told the daughter to take care of her own room. The daughter didn't do a good job—and they've been squabbling and arguing and fighting ever since. The mother tries to get the daughter to 'clean up,' and the daughter says she can't be bothered, because *she* has more important things to do! The mother says the daughter has to learn to take care of her own room. The daughter reminds the mother that she doesn't take care of her house, that we do—'the help,' the girl calls us.

"I hear them talking, and sometimes I want to walk in and quit on the spot, and tell them both what I think of them. But I'm not 'liberated.' They always talk about civil rights and liberation and freedom—but it's the people far away that they worry about. My husband says to tell them off and leave, but I have to make a living, and when they're all out of the house—and most of the day they are—it's a nice place to work in. I can watch some television or listen to the radio. I can check in with my mother. I can make myself a nice lunch. They never really check up on you. They don't count minutes, and they don't try to overwork you. They told me that some of their friends ask 'the help' to eat certain things, and not other things. But I can eat their avocados and lobsters and shrimp; in fact, she sometimes tells me to take some leftovers home. When they have a party, I tell my mother not to buy as much food as usual, because I know I'll be carrying some good food with me when I open the door and see her the day after the party. It's on those nights that I have to sleep over, for sure. They give me a real comfortable room. They can be very nice. They can be good to you, when they stop and pay attention to you. They are too busy, I think, with their 'projects.' Each of them tries to do too much; that's how I see it."

That is how Helen moves, back and forth, back and forth, with regard to her sentiments toward a family she knows well indeed. She is especially attentive to "the missus"—watches her, listens to her, thinks about her ideas and expressed convictions. They are the same age, the same race, and residents of adjoining municipalities. It is important to emphasize their mutual dependence, and the burdens such a relationship inevitably puts on the weaker (socially, economically) of the two. It is important to document the nature of those burdens, and the response to them by the party who feels injured—elements of hypocrisy and phoniness and arrogance and condescension, which in turn generate anger, sadness, scorn, and, yes, a prejudice that occasionally escalates into hate. It is also important to see what that maid and her "missus" may have in common, for all the differences they have to contend with, similarities they usually do not acknowledge to themselves, never mind others.

If rather often they appear to be protagonists who have reconciled an essential conflict just enough to live and work under the same roof, there are other moments when the two women, for one reason or another, come rather close to each other. The maid is not unmindful of those times, and their significance: "She drives home, goes to her room, and gets into a mood, and I have to tell everyone who calls that she's sick and she can't come to the phone. When her mother got sick, she fell apart herself. When her daughter was hurt in an auto accident, she got so upset, I worried they'd have to take *her* to a hospital. She had a lot of trouble with her husband then. He wanted her to keep up the schedule they had, and she said she didn't feel up to it, and he told her she was 'overreacting,' and she started shouting that word, and it took them a week to patch things up.

"She would sit and talk with me, and I began to see her side of things. I began to realize that she can't just stop and take it easy, because she *has* to keep going as fast as she does and she *has* to 'prove' herself. That's what she told me—that her father was a lawyer in a big firm, and later he became a judge, and he was always telling her and her sister to study harder, and do better in school, and be the best in sports and at cooking and at everything she did. I guess she felt bad, because she was pushing her daughter to be the best skier, and the daughter didn't want to go skiing that weekend; but the mother made her go, and that was when the girl got in the accident, coming home from Vermont.

"The girl broke her leg in several places, I think, and she had to be in the hospital, with her foot up in the air, for a long time. I felt sorry for her. She got hurt in the stomach, too. They did an operation. She needed a lot of blood. The parents kept fighting with each other. The father said that the mother was to blame because she was always sending the children away—on ski trips, and to camps, and to tennis clinics, and to go visit friends and relatives. He said she wanted to get rid of them. She said he never did anything in the house, but he wanted everything to be perfect all the time. She told him she was tired of hearing herself complimented when there was no trouble, but let there be trouble, and she's always the one to get blamed. I heard them shouting, and then I heard the whole story again—because she confided in me. She asked me one morning if I wanted to have a cup of coffee, and I said Sanka, because I'd already had too much coffee. We sat down, and she started being real nice to me. She asked me if I wanted some English muffins. Then she told me to sit in another chair, where I'd be more comfortable. I began to feel like I was a guest of hers, not the maid! She filled up my cup a second time, and she told me to relax—and she kept on telling me about all her problems.

"I couldn't help feeling sorry for her. She was about to cry several times. Then she finally did. She said she's in a 'rat race,' and she wishes she could go to their summer home and just stay there on that island, and not come back for a year or two. She wishes her husband would try running the house, and going to work, and having guests over, or going to the houses of other people, and then writing thank-you notes, and remembering to return the invitations, and all the rest she does, like being responsible for the meals and the appearance of the house—and *the children,* you can't forget them. I didn't say much, but when she came to the subject of the children, she asked me about *my* children. I told her that, thank God, my mother is around, or else we'd be a lot poorer than we are. She asked me whether I'd work if I didn't need the money. I told her no, I wouldn't. She said I'd change my mind once I was at home all day, sitting and waiting for people to come back from school and work, so that I could wait on them. I didn't know how to answer her. I guess I got flushed, and she could see I was upset. I didn't say a word. I just looked into my cup of Sanka. I swallowed all there was left of it, and got up. I started cleaning up. She must have figured out what was bothering me. For the first time, ever, she came over to the sink, and started to dry the dishes I was washing. There were only a few, and I didn't want to stick them in the dishwasher and let them stand there dirty all day.

"She was lost, trying to help. She didn't know where her own dishes belonged! I was in a bad mood; I knew I'd best not say anything, or else I'd say too much. Suddenly, she asked me please to stop what I was doing, so that she could say something to me. I obliged her. She told me she was sorry. I didn't say anything. I guess she wanted me to smile and say: 'That's all right.' I just stood there. She started talking some more. She said she knew I did a lot of work for her, and she hoped that she was paying me enough, and if she wasn't, I should let her know. Then she said she thought of me a lot, during the week—especially when she talked with her women friends about women. She was sure that I was as hard working as a person could be, because I had two jobs—at my home and at her home. But she wanted me to know that she is in the same boat: she has her job, and then she has to be in charge of the house, because her husband won't help out. I was going to answer her back, if she said anything bad about *my* husband. I was going to quit on the spot. But she stopped because the phone rang, and I realized she was late for a meeting, so I wouldn't have to worry about another talk with her after she hung up. When she did, it was as if she'd forgotten that we'd even had our morning-coffee talk. She said to herself two or three times: 'Where am I?' Then she went upstairs to change her clothes. She didn't even seem to remember that I was there in the kitchen. She just ran out of the house. When she came home, she had her usual list of questions—Who called? What time? Any message?—and errands for me."

Helen was bitter—but not only bitter. The maid was able to summon pity, even compassion, for her boss. The maid was always telling her husband and mother and children that she wished she had more money, but she emphatically did not want to live 'their kind of life'—the endless involvements of the well-to-do and socially active. Most of all, the maid defended her marriage—the bond between herself and her husband—from the charges she heard leveled against many marriages by "the missus" and her friends. Her husband is "hard working," is a "slave" to the needs of his family. If he had his way, she would not be working. That is a measure of his virtue, not his pride and conceit and prejudice and *chauvinism*. That last word has come to her attention in recent years, mostly from the girl who was injured in a car accident, but also from her mother. The maid is not about to call her husband perfect, but she sees only too clearly the differences between him and the man she has worked for. He is all too commanding a person. Her husband, like her, keeps his mouth shut all day at work for fear he will be fired. The man she works for has two secretaries; he tells them, all day, what to do. Her husband gives orders to no one. Her husband is deferential to women, and will never stop being so. She likes that quality in him—and does not want him behaving like the men she sees at work, who are all too casual, by her standards, in the way they address and get on with women.

Yet, Helen combines that conservative way of regarding men and women with another line of observation that is never declared in a formal or direct fashion. She would never say that she wants to qualify what she has previously argued—and then go on to make her point. Rather, she maintains her formerly stated views, and even defends them hard, but ends up showing herself a cannier and more astringent social critic than she really wishes to be—as she herself eventually comes to realize: "All I hear the missus talk about is how 'free' she thinks women ought to be. Her friends will come over—women who live nearby—and they say they're glad to have their careers, and they're glad they're not just 'housewives.' I guess I'm not just a 'housewife' either! It's crazy: they say they're glad to get out of the house, and all my friends, who work in supermarkets or factories, keep on wishing the day will come that they don't have to go to work. And they envy me for at least having the kind of work I do: housework!

"They ask me when they see me how they live here in this

neighborhood of Cambridge, and I'll tell my girl friends that it's not only a picnic. The woman I work for *thinks* she's so 'free' and 'independent,' and 'equal' with her husband, but I know different. I've heard her husband tell her off. I've heard her manipulate him. She's a clever one. She talks in a soft voice, but she's tough underneath. She pretends to be a little dumb—when she wants to get him to change his ideas. She's no different from any other woman; she uses her wiles when she needs to. My mother used to tell us girls that when you grow up and get married, you have to know how to talk with your husband, and if you don't know how to talk *with* him, you have to talk *around* him. I can remember my mother turning into a different person when she wanted my father to buy something or agree to do something she wanted us to do. She'd be as smart as could be with us; then she'd suddenly turn dumb with him. She'd say 'yes, dear,' until my sisters and I wanted to scream. We knew she was acting. Of course, my father was a hard-working man, and he'd come home dead tired, and I can see why he didn't want all our family problems dumped on him. There wasn't that much left of him by the time he came back to us at the end of the day. He was a janitor, and he had a lot of buildings to look after. I'll die smelling the garbage on him. Every time I empty our pail, I think of how my dad spent his days. And he never complained.

"My mother didn't either. He'd turn on her sometimes. He'd say, no, no, no—to everything she asked. Then she'd turn dumb on him. She'd yes him to death. She'd become a rug for him to walk on. The more she did that, the more he 'came around.' I remember her using that expression: 'I'll get your father to come around—just you wait and see.' And she did.

"It's not much different here in this big, fancy Cambridge house. They *think* it's different, the missus and that husband of hers. But I'll think of my parents a lot, when I listen to them talking and arguing. The missus talks one way with her women friends and another way with her husband. In fact, she talks with all the men who come for dinner differently than with the women. She's either very tough when she talks with men, or she becomes silly and sarcastic, and makes them laugh. With her women friends she relaxes; with men, she's always watching herself. I don't see how that's any different than what I saw go on between my mother and my father. When the missus has an argument with her husband, she speaks and he speaks. Neither gives in. Then she changes. She starts crying. Then he collapses, and says yes to her. I heard her tell one of her women friends that she has her 'final weapon,' if nothing else works. I think she stays away from him until he surrenders! What's so smart about that! Is she really 'liberated'? I'd never do that! I'd rather scream and shout and throw dishes than hold out on my husband that way. It's being sneaky and dishonest.

"The trouble with those two is that they think they're so honest with each other, and she thinks she's equal with her husband. But she acts like a woman and he acts like a man, and that's how they get through their troubles. She told me that herself one night; she had a few drinks in her, and she laughed at herself and said she talks 'a big line,' but in her heart she's just like me. I thought to myself that she was talking a big line right then and there! But the more I thought about it, the more I began to believe her. She's a woman who thinks she's no different from men, she keeps saying; but she *is* a woman and she'll always act like a woman part of the day—and at night!—and I suppose we *are* alike, because we *are* both women. I hate to be so hard on her and her husband. I hate to say bad things about them. I'm grateful to them; they help me out, help me see a lot that's going on in the world. They're smart about other people, but they don't look at themselves and see as much as they do when they look at their friends. I think they're afraid they'll see what they see when they look at their friends. I think they're afraid of their friends. I sense it in the air when they're having friends over—the fright."

Fright was a word she would also acknowledge as part of her own mental life, or that of others in her family. When Helen first came to work in that home, she assumed that a radical difference existed between herself and her employers. She especially observed how dissimilar the lives were—hers and that of her "missus." And when she heard, day after day, mention of the special problems women must face, she was inclined to agree—but to wonder why *this* woman, living in *this* home, and with *her* privileges should consider herself a member of a "minority" (the word she used) and tell her daughter that she also faced the hurdles of "discrimination." At first her interpretation was a simple one: the daughter is spoiled, vain, self-indulgent; the mother is all too sure of herself, is as petulant and smug as they come. Over the months, the years, the maid's opinion slowly changed. Not that she became an apologist for a family whose values, in certain respects, she found strange, unappealing, even abhorrent. She would never, she was sure, condone the talk she heard, or the espousal of various social, political and cultural viewpoints. Still, she began to realize that, deep down, there were troubles in this enviable household she helped keep going —and serious inconsistencies or contradictions of a psychological and ideological nature.

The more Helen thought about such matters, the more she recognized the ambiguities of the world she visited regularly, for pay; the more she turned on her own world, her own neighborhood, with critical intensity and candor. However, she found it possible to maintain this perspective only for brief periods of time. In the early afternoon, when the house she helped "organize" (the word used so often by the "missus") was at its most quiet, there was time for reflection, for an outburst of anger followed by a spell of self-scrutiny that was anything but self-serving: "I get annoyed at the girl and her mother—all their pretense that men and women are equal. They're not equal. My husband is stronger than I'll ever be. My father was stronger than my mother. I couldn't do the work my husband does. The trouble with these people is that they're *all* soft and weak, because none of them does much physical work. They sit and use their voices. They move around in their chairs. He says he's going to go jogging. Big deal: an hour every other morning! She does her Canadian exercises; I hear her going thump, thump, upstairs. Her biggest exercise is keeping her hands away from those butterscotch candies she says she buys for her husband; but he doesn't know the half of it—how many she's taken before he gets home. Then she says out loud, as if the cleaning woman and I are supposed to pay attention, that she doesn't know *where* all those candies go! I feel like coming into that study of hers and saying: 'Come on, lady, stop kidding yourself!' I don't like those candies; they stick to your teeth.

"A lot of things stick to my teeth! When I go home I need an hour to adjust to my own home. I'll hear my son talking with his friend about airplanes and spaceships. Both boys want to be pilots. They'll talk about 'reentry' problems—I guess spaceships coming back to earth. I think to myself: I have one of those problems every night. I'll hear something at work, and even when I'm really back in the swing of my own family, I can't get the words out of my mind. The other day I heard the missus talking to her daughter. The girl was throwing a fit over something, and I was glad I didn't have her as my child. Then I heard the mother trying to be nice, and the girl only got nastier. I wanted to go and give her a whack—but God forbid! In that house they don't believe in using 'physical force' on children. The missus once asked me if I used 'physical force' on my children. I said no, but I sure hit them when they get fresh or rude, especially when they act like spoiled brats. She looked at me for a while, and I thought I'd said the wrong thing. She seemed interested, though. She asked me where I hit the kids, and how many times. I told her anyplace, and the number depended on what they did and my mood. Then she gave me one of her smiles

—as if to say that *she* was *above* that kind of behavior! I thought of her daughter, and got snobby myself: I would never have a girl who acted like that one does!

"The girl came home the other day, and was upset. She spoke up in class, and the teacher didn't agree with her. It's a fancy school she goes to—a private school. The mother gets angry with the teachers in front of her daughter, and tells the girl she's going to get the woman fired. I don't understand how a woman who is always talking about the way women are unfairly treated can speak of a schoolteacher, a woman, as if she's dirt to be brushed aside. Maybe that's the way they talk about me and the cleaning woman, too—behind our backs. She's a great one, that missus, for being sweet to people, then turning on them behind their backs later on, with her gossip and her 'stories.' She always has a 'story' for her husband when he comes home. She's home an hour before him, and does she go and help prepare supper? No, she takes another shower (two a day!) and changes from one fancy dress to another, and does herself up, and goes into her study to 'think.'

"My husband still won't believe me when I tell him what she does *then.* She sits and writes things down in her 'journal.' She's been writing her 'stories' to herself for years and years. She says it helps her to 'think'! I peeked once. I've never done it again. She went on and on about herself—what *she* thinks, and how *she* feels, and what someone said to *her,* and what *she* planned to do. I remembered what the priest used to say about the sin of pride. That lady is the biggest sinner I know!

"The girl got her mother so angry about the teacher that the mother went to her study first, and wrote her 'story.' Then she took her shower, and all that. When the father came home, the mother was waiting for him. He had his drink and she had hers and she started in. I could hear their every word, because I was setting the table and then waiting for the food to be ready, and they were in the den, off the dining room. They talked loud, because they got to arguing. It turned out that the girl came home all upset because the teacher kept asking a *boy* to open and close the windows, and not her or another girl. So she spoke up; she told the teacher she was 'prejudiced' against women. The teacher got annoyed, I guess. She told the girl she had no right to talk without raising her hand. The girl got annoyed, and said she did. The teacher told the girl she could open and close windows at home all she wanted, but at school only someone asked by the teacher would do that. I think the teacher had been asking the same boy to do the job since the start of the year.

"The father told the mother not to make an issue out of it. He said that it wasn't a 'good case'—and that the girl should watch the teacher carefully and get more 'evidence.' I thought he was being smart—though I'd hate to have *my* daughter sitting in a classroom like a spy, trying to trick or trap the teacher. But on my way home I had these memories: the time I was in the third grade, and the teacher, 'Miss Rattan' we used to call her—she used one a lot—had the boys, always the boys, open and close the windows. It was an old school building, and the windows were long, and I can still see that pole she had leaning in the corner near her desk. She would pick it up and hand it to one of her teacher's pets—and they were all boys, too. He'd open or close the windows, depending on what she told him to do. We'd all watch, and we'd envy him, I remember.

"Once I came home and told my mother I had one wish—that before the school year was over, I'd be able to take that window pole and open and close the windows. I remember the catch on each window, and how the boys raised their arms and got closer and closer to the catch with the pole. It seems silly now, but to third-grade children it was a big moment in the day. The teacher made it that way; she didn't say a word while the boy was at work. We had three or four big windows, and she'd wait until they were all the way she wanted them, and that pole back in the corner, before she resumed her talking to us.

"I never would have dreamed of speaking up, the way that girl did. Of course, my parents weren't like her parents! And I wasn't going to a private school. I am convinced, after all these years of work among the rich folks, that they send their kids to private schools so that if there's any trouble, the mother and father can use their influence—wave a checkbook or something like that. Now that I think of it, my father used to get upset with the teachers. In my heart, I have to admit that I thought that Miss Rattan liked boys and didn't treat us girls fairly. I'll bet any girl could have opened and closed those windows with the stick. By the end of the year, she had us girls convinced we couldn't do it. And in the sixth grade we weren't allowed to be safety monitors either. I remember the teacher choosing them—all boys. They wore those white belts, and seemed so big and powerful to us.

"I never wanted to be a boy as much as I did those first few weeks of the sixth grade. I remember a boy I had a crush on; he became a safety monitor, and he never gave me the time of day. All he did was shout at me to stay on the sidewalk, and not take even a half a step off, until the light changed and he said 'go.' I remember when he and the other boys started opening their desks, and taking out their belts, and putting them on, a few minutes before the bell rang. I used to dream of stealing those belts, but of course I never did. Now girls as well as boys are safety monitors. I hope my younger daughter becomes one. My older daughter didn't; she wasn't tall enough. I can see why they want tall people—to impress the younger children.

"A girl is as good as a boy in a lot of those activities once allowed only the boys. After I remembered my own days at school, I wasn't so angry at that 'rich little girl,' my husband calls her. I actually felt sorry for her. And a few days after she had her trouble I told her about my own experiences at school. She listened to my every word. I've never had more of her attention. She didn't run out of the room when the phone rang, to see if it was for her. She didn't make up excuses, like she does a lot of times: Sorry, I have to do something. She didn't tap her right toe or keep fussing with her socks. She looked right at me, and I thought to myself, for the first time, that she could be a nice girl, and she isn't so different, when you get down to it, from my own girls or from me when I was a girl."

Helen is quick, naturally, to qualify that comment. There certainly *are* differences between her and the girl she had been speaking with, for once so candidly and with such rapport. Yet she had for the first time been prompted to link her own experiences with those of someone from quite another background than her own. And she had (with no great personal fanfare or protestation of psychological turmoil) made her mental association, of sorts, in such a way that she was able to glimpse for herself how girls and boys learn what a given world expects of them. She would never forget that moment in her life. She would never become a politically active spokesperson for her sex, but she would, from that time on, be more likely to take notice of who, *of what sex,* was saying or doing what.

When Helen told her husband what she had recalled of her childhood, he was not especially interested. But she made him become interested. She told him she had heard him, for years, tell his son how much he, the father, had dreamed of becoming a pitcher for the Boston Red Sox, and how sad he felt, to this day, when he watched a baseball game being played in Fenway Park. If she could feel not only his sadness, but her own, on his behalf, when they sat and watched those games on television, then he ought think of dreams and hopes and aspirations she once had, and may still harbor in her soul.

Helen has a notion of transcendence. She refers to her "spirit," or sometimes, her "soul." She will be talking about her childhood, and suddenly she laughs derisively at her "silly wishes," which she attributes to the "wicked spirit" that occasionally seized her, years ago; or to the "bad side" of her "soul."

Would she care to get specific? She is vague about details, she protests—but not a bit vague when she actually starts evoking them, one after the other: "I was a tomboy. What did that mean? I don't to this very moment really know. I never wanted to *be* a boy. I just was 'too much,' my mother said. She was the one who used to tell me that I had a bad 'spirit' in me; that I was mischievous, she said; that there was a 'devil' somewhere, out to get my 'soul.' I would get a little scared when she talked like that —I suppose she wanted just that to happen. But my mother was not a cruel person; and she always encouraged us to have 'heart-to-hearts'; so one day I came to her, and we had one.

"I told her that a boy had called me a tomboy. She asked me if I knew what a tomboy is. I said no—but I knew I wasn't a boy, I was a girl. My mother said that a girl should be a girl and a boy should be a boy. She said that when a girl starts playing baseball, like I wanted to do, and getting into a lot of fights with other kids —with boys!—and climbing up buildings and playing games on roofs, then she's got some of the devil in her, and her soul is in trouble. The nuns used to tell us about the devil, but I never really knew what they meant. My mother told us there's a struggle always going on between the 'wicked spirit' and the goodness in us. I think I began to believe when I was a little girl that if I did anything boyish, I was bad.

"There was a 'sissy' on our street, a kid I'll never forget. His name was Joseph, but the boys called him Josephine, and so did the girls. I was the worst offender! I guess he wasn't tough enough for our street! But now that I look back, all that boy did was read a lot and help his mother with the shopping. He didn't like to play our games, and we *said* he talked like a girl. I don't know now what happened to him. The poor kid, he had to wear glasses, and that's what got us going, to begin with. I'd be very upset if I saw any of my children treating a boy that way. But my mother never punished me for talking the way I did about that boy. She wanted me to be a 'nice,' pretty, dainty girl, and she wanted that boy to be a big he-man or something.

"The same with my father; he would laugh and laugh when we talked about 'the sissy,' and he would want me dressed in the fanciest dresses, even when it cost a lot to buy them, and it was work cleaning them. I wanted to wear my brother's dungarees, and my parents wouldn't hear of it. They didn't have any explanations for me. They just told me it was wrong for a girl to wear jeans—and act the way I wanted to act. After a while, I gave up. And now I try to encourage my little girl to be a *bit* of a tomboy, but my mother is with her more, and she has got her way. She's very much a little lady, my younger girl. So was my older girl, when she was seven or eight. I compare them with the girl I take care of, and I realize that girls may be girls—but it's different being a girl in a big Cambridge house near Brattle Street, and being a girl over in Somerville, where we live."

So much for an appraisal of the significance of social background upon a child's psychological growth—and sense of what sex has to do with class. As a maid Helen had her own reasons to be envious, resentful, even outraged. But she also had memories which urged her in quite other emotional directions. She is not one to turn her back on her own people, or to make a try at leading them politically or socially. She is, by her own description, "a devout Catholic" and "an ordinary housewife." She complains bitterly at times that she has *two* houses to care for; yet she insists that she would have it no other way. She loves the "kind of work" she does—"most of the time." There are moments, however, when she dreams of lying in the sun and being near food and drink, both brought by someone else. Who? She smiles, and blurts out an answer: a man. She is, immediately thereafter, embarrassed that she may have made a remark that identifies her as sympathetic to the cause "the missus" advocates. She adds a qualification and a further explanation. She meant "a colored man," *and* she wasn't being a racist or condescending or snobbish. She simply had in mind the television commercials she's seen—of utterly relaxed tourists stretched out on deck chairs near a pool or the ocean, with strong and smiling and attentive servants, always men, always colored men, standing nearby.

She admits, however, that she could not allow a woman, colored or not, to serve her. In that regard, she has a good deal of conviction: "I've waited on too many people to let someone wait on me—a woman. I'm a woman, and I'm the one who has been the servant. I wouldn't want a woman servant helping me out. I'd want to tell her that I'm a member of the same club—that we're on the same side in the 'battle of life,' my grandfather used to call it, the time we're allotted by God. If a man came and waited on me, it would be different. No man has ever done that, not while I've been around; so I'd be a little curious.

"I guess I shouldn't talk like that! It's no better that a man should be a servant than a woman. But it wouldn't get to me, a man bringing me food, the way it would taking a sandwich and a Coke from a woman. I don't know how the missus can allow me to be in her house, waiting on people all the time, when she says she's against women doing that. I thought of her ideas on women yesterday, when I brought her husband some steak, and he thought I'd 'burnt' it, so I had to start all over again. He was practically shouting at me. He eats his meat raw. They all do. They think they're so good—eating like that. When I go home, just thinking about that red meat makes me want to go vomit. They're like cannibals. When I came back the second time, he said I'd 'overreacted,' that he did *not* want steak tartare—raw meat, I guess. So, I went back and put the lousy piece of meat in the oven and said ten Hail Marys, and took it out. While I carried it to him I made believe, in my mind, that it was *him* I was carrying, and he was in Hell, and he'd just been roasted. He tasted the meat and said 'all right,' but I heard him tell his wife that 'from now on' he wanted *her* to make his steak.

"She didn't say a word. She knows when to be quiet! He was in a bad mood, and when he's like that, he becomes the man and she is the woman, and there's none of that talk they have about

CLASS AND SEX   259

how women should have more rights and men should act differently. She becomes like a mouse. She tiptoes around the house. He bangs his hand on the table, and he shouts. I think the daughter enjoys seeing him like that! I heard her talking to her girl friend later that night—I'd finished washing his plate; he left half the steak on it—and she was saying how 'exciting' it was, because her dad was 'on a tirade.' He never gets angry with her, so she can have her fun watching him! He gets angry with his wife, and with me, and with the cleaning woman—and with his mother. He'll call her up, and in five minutes they're fighting, even though it's a long-distance call, and the cost must be enormous.

"Once I heard him tell his son that he ought to be very careful about the woman he chooses to marry. He said that right in front of his wife. She didn't answer him back. I had some words on the tip of my tongue, but they never came out—naturally. His wife gets even with him the next day. I know her almost as well as I know my own self. The next day she complained of a bad headache, and said she was sick, and she had to stay in bed. He became worried. The more he told her he was worried, the more she complained. When I came there she was promising to call a doctor, and telling him to go to work and she would call him there later. I told my husband when I left that morning that she'd be 'sick.' She has her tricks up her sleeve like any other woman."

A rather unqualified generalization, and Helen knows it. In her own indirect or spur-of-the-moment way she can be bluntly political about women and their fate, so far, in this society. The polemics of "the missus" turn off the maid. But the maid has her own reasons, at times of her own choosing, to make a vigorous and even acerbic analysis of the various burdens a particular sex carries, and of the consequent maneuvers of mind and heart millions of women learn to execute. One such maneuver is, of course, hypochondriasis. Is there a nod of assent to be found from "the missus"? That is to say, does she acknowledge in her more offhand moods a continuing resort to the "tricks" the maid refers to—a conscious or not-so-conscious dependence upon bluff, guile, pretense, bodily complaints, even an occasional outright lie? If so, at what ultimate personal cost? And does "the missus" acknowledge, even to herself, the ambiguity of her responses—to men; to the maid; to those other women who are called "equals," friends, acquaintances, and, at work, colleagues?

Helen has, of course, come up with her own answers to such questions. From her vantage point as a largely silent member of a small group of people sometimes rather pompously called a "staff," she makes her continuing observations, and comes up with her conclusions. She would be the last one to answer with self-important authority, but when she commented upon the "tricks" used by "any other woman," she meant herself and every woman she has ever met. She certainly meant what she said about "the missus." She certainly meant what she said about her own moments of coyness, feigned exhaustion, carefully staged helplessness: "I come home and I see my husband in a bad mood, and I say to myself: Have you got the strength to outdo him? Can you make him feel even worse than you do? I know it's my only defense against him, when he becomes like that—a cock strutting around, my mother says. We become nervous hens! We become *sick* hens! If I don't have the energy to plead an ache or a pain, and if my mother doesn't start saying she thinks she's having a heart attack—well then, my little girl starts crying. She never says what she's crying *about*.

"My *sons* don't start crying. They've never cried when their father has a temper fit. If they *did*, he'd get worse, not better. They're *boys*, you see! But he melts when his little girl cries. I think he waits for her to cry! She's his last hope! She's the one who can protect him from the mean tongue he got from his father. He told the priest that one day in confession. Do you know what the priest said? He said that it was the Virgin Mary talking through the girl's tears! I liked that a lot at first. I could have cried myself! But the more I thought about it, and especially after I talked to my best girl friend about it, the more annoyed I became.

"My girl friend grew up in the same block I did, and her husband walked out on her. He's a no-good drunk. She's become tough. She knows the score. She gets very angry at some of the things she hears in church. She argues with the priest. She took her girl out of parochial school. She said she doesn't like what the nuns teach her—about how a girl should behave, and a boy. She may be right. I don't know what to think. I couldn't live without my faith. God means a lot to me; He gives me strength. If the priest or a nun says the wrong things, they're just human. You can't expect anyone to be perfect. I guess that's what it comes down to—that everyone makes mistakes. I'll get angry with the church; but like the priest tells us almost every Sunday, it's the anger that comes out of love. You mustn't forget that. There will be times I do. I worry about the missus because I don't think she believes in any religion, or even in God. I wonder if there's someplace she can just sit in, like I do at church, and collect herself and figure out what she believes *most.*"

An interesting and quite discriminating distinction: "the anger that comes out of love." She speaks with emphasis and obvious relief—as if she has both admitted the contrariness of her various sentiments, and affirmed within herself an intelligence at work, sifting and sorting and coming down, finally, here rather than there. Her speculations about her employer, also characterized by complexity and ambiguity, are not unlike some the employer herself has put into words on various occasions. Once, when the maid's life was the subject of discussion, "the missus" (as we said, about the same age as the maid) took pains to emphasize the problems a woman in her late thirties or early forties has, regardless of her position in society or occupation. Helen listened and agreed, but couldn't quite manage the relentless silence that was her wont. She said that "a little more money" would help her

—and many others like her. Immediately, "the missus" stopped their rather casual, if interesting conversation. She had to go make a few calls.

But Helen knew that her employer did not run to make a call. There were several phones in the house, and when one of the numbers was in use, a light went on. No light appeared for an hour, Helen noticed, as she worked away at preparing dinner in the kitchen. She was not reluctant to figure out a possible explanation: "the missus," an earnest, decent, fair-minded woman, had suddenly felt that a conversation went too far and ought to be ended abruptly—lest she be manipulated into giving an employee a raise. This was no exploited person, or so "the missus" honestly believed. Her friends paid their "help" less. She insisted on "the highest rates" for people who worked for her. She had no interest at all in squeezing a lot of "extra work" out of anyone. She was generous with vacations, and actively concerned with the families of those who have assisted her, her husband, and children over the years. She has even kept up with some who have left for one reason or another.

Helen knew all that, was hardly prone to unfair exaggeration or distortion. She could sound, at times, like the wise, objective social historian—like a twentieth-century proletarian woman who had learned Karl Marx's breadth of view, detachment, and capacity for irony: "She gets nervous because of me, I know. She has all these good wishes for the whole world, and she wants to 'liberate' everyone, so it's embarrassing when she has to stop and think about *me!* I'm not her slave, but I do a lot of her dirty work, and she knows it. But if I was in her shoes, I'd be doing what she does—I'd be hiring myself a maid or two and doing other things with my time. If I was rich, I'd swim in a swimming pool outside my house, and travel a lot, and I'd have a lot of flowers around my house—and I'd hire the gardener she hires. That man could turn a desert into a jungle; he's got two green thumbs and eight green fingers. I'd keep him working all spring and all summer!

"I don't hold it against her that she has money. Some have it, most don't. That's the way it is. What can you do? If it was the other way around, I hope I'd be as considerate of her as she (mostly) tries to be of me. She slips up every once in a while. She shows the bad side of herself. She forgets herself. She turns as sour as month-old milk. She starts shouting at all of us working for her, especially the cleaning lady and me. The gardener is a man! She forgets all that 'women's liberation' talk I hear her speaking on the phone, or during those 'dinner parties' of hers. She sounds like my neighbor, with her tongue that needs to be washed with soap once a week. She sounds like a 'male chauvinist pig.' I've learned that expression from her—and the morning talk shows. I watch them sometimes when she's out, and there's no great hurry in the house.

"Once she was so rude to me I wanted to walk out and never come back. Then I thought to myself: Why not remind her that I'm a *woman!* But she wouldn't have laughed! She has a real mean streak in her, and when she's under its spell, you better stay clear of her. Then she'll snap out of it, and she's full of sweet talk, and she's worrying about people everywhere in the whole world. I suppose if I was her, I'd be no better. I can go a little crazy myself—not a lot of times, but about once a month, I'd say. She's lucky to be in a family where there's money, so that when she gets upset, there are the rest of us to help her pick up the pieces. You can't *blame* someone because their parents were well off, or because her husband makes a lot of money. It's no one's fault— who her parents or husband are, and how much money they have in the bank. It's all decided someplace else—the roulette wheel of fate, my mother used to tell us when we were kids, and asked her the same whys that my kids ask me!"

One of her children, her younger daughter, asks questions that Helen isn't inclined, as *her* mother was, to brush aside with a fatalistic or religious explanation. The girl wants to know why God chooses to make certain people well-to-do, others quite poor; certain babies boys, others girls; certain people strong and

healthy, others in constant jeopardy, due to one or another illness. The girl's mother can't simply say that God's will is His and
no one else's—so we must accept what He, in His inscrutable
wisdom, has decided for us. She sees the will of various human
beings at work, and realizes full well that her children must learn
about rules and values and assumptions that were not handed
down from on high, but have come about because particular men
and particular women have behaved in particular ways. At the
risk of offending the priest and nuns she has known, she tells her
little girl repeatedly that when she grows up she should try to be
her own person; try to think for herself; try to get a "good
education"; try to avoid working as a domestic; try to find a
good-paying job that will also earn her self-respect; and, not
least, try to marry a man with good prospects. The girl listens,
says yes, yes.

The girl listens with special interest when marriage is mentioned. More questions tumble from her mouth. How does one
judge the future of a man? How might she best meet such a man?
Is there, right now, somewhere on this earth, a boy who is
destined to be her husband—and what if he is not one of those
most likely to get ahead and do well financially? And, God
forbid, what if no boy should want to propose to her, when she
is grown and eligible for marriage? Helen knows full well that
her daughter is not the only one who will ask herself various
questions in the course of her childhood and youth: "It's not
right that I criticize the people I work for. My grandmother
worked as a scrubwoman in a bank. I know she didn't like those
bankers, but she told us that as long as she was taking someone's
money, she wasn't going to call them a lot of bad names. My
mother worked for a family in Boston, on Beacon Hill, rich as
could be. She didn't like the way they ordered her around, but
what could she do? She told me a long time ago that if you're
going to go into someone's house and take orders from them all
day long, then you have to keep your mind on the work and not

the people. Otherwise, you'll tell them off, and quit—and then you'll be without the dollar bills you need for your own family.

"It's a little different with me, because my boss is a woman who worries a lot that women aren't getting all they should be. You can't help doing a lot of thinking, after you've heard her talk. You can't help asking yourself things. She goes to see a psychiatrist, and then I'll hear her telling her husband that she's the way she is now because of the way she was treated by her parents when she was a little girl. I don't know why anyone like her should go see a psychiatrist. She's got everything in the world, you'd think. She should be happy. I wish I had her life! But all I hear her talk about on the days she goes to that doctor is the bad trouble she went through a long time ago. I guess her father wanted her to marry a certain boy she'd known since she was a little girl, and she didn't like the boy when she was little, and she didn't like him when she grew up either. So the father didn't like *her*—I think that's what happened.

"Her mother was always on her father's side, so she didn't like both her parents very much. But they gave her a lot of money, so they weren't that bad to her. I guess they ended up liking her husband, but she says it all leaves a bad taste in her mouth. Why doesn't she use Listerine instead of going to a psychiatrist twice a week? I heard her tell her husband that she pays the doctor seventy-five dollars for each time she sees him. My husband wouldn't believe that someone gets that kind of money, just for talking to a woman for three quarters of an hour. That's all the time she spends there. I know, because I see her schedule. She's big on planning her day down to the last minute—like the doctor does, I guess!

"She worries too much about her daughter, and how she is spending her time. She's trying to get the girl to be like her— figure out everything in advance. I don't blame the girl for saying no a lot of times, and trying to go off on her own. That mother isn't any different than her father was. I hear her talking to her husband about who the girl should marry. They like a boy who lives nearby and goes to school with the girl. They keep on saying that they want their children to 'associate' with 'all kinds of people'—but you can tell, they won't want her to marry 'just anyone.' They talk a big liberal line, my husband says, but it's only skin deep.

"They're not always matching their son up with someone; it's the *girl* whose friends they keep their eyes on! Lord, I don't blame them. A girl's future is determined by the man she marries. I tell my daughter that all the time: watch out—and *never* marry a man who drinks a lot or is mean to people! It's no different with the people I work for; they'll talk a lot about marriage to their girl because she asks them questions, like what's a good age to get married; and then they get started, and before you know it, they're telling her more than the best age for her to march down the aisle in church! But they never have talks like that with their son. My sons have never brought up the subject, but my two daughters did, as soon as they were old enough to know what the word 'marriage' means! If you ask me, there will have to be a lot more changes in the world than the missus wants before girls stop planning their lives around the husbands they'll marry.

"I think the missus is right: everyone should be equal. She keeps on saying that. But then she has me working away in her house, and I'm not equal with her—and she doesn't want to be equal with me; and I don't blame her, because if I was her I'd hold on to my money just like she does. Maybe that's what the men are doing—they're holding on to their money. And the women are trying to get more money. And it's a big fight, like it always is about money. She should know. She doesn't go throwing big fat checks at her 'help.' She's 'fair'; she keeps on reminding us—but she's not going to 'liberate' us, anymore than the men are going to 'liberate' their wives or their secretaries or the other women working in their companies. That's the world for you. Look at our Lord, Jesus Christ—all the trouble He had, trying to convince people to be nicer to each other, and share their riches with the poor, and be equal before God. They killed Him for talking like that!"

It is impossible, Helen knows in her heart, to achieve a truly just society this side of Heaven. Yet she takes notice of various injustices, and would surely like to see them remedied. She appreciates quite clearly her own situation—and that of millions like her: the overwhelming majority of the world. She has little or no resources—less than five hundred dollars in savings. One major illness in her family, and her husband and she are not only wiped out, so far as "capital assets" go, but impossibly in debt. Who is she to take risks, to agitate on behalf of changes—to go challenging ideologies, bosses, a given social and economic system? And, too, she is observant enough to notice that her employers, self-proclaimed "activists," are not without their own considerable political inhibitions.

Like Helen, they worry about what might happen given one or another turn of events. Like Helen, they worry about their children and don't always practice, with respect to them, what they may well feel ought to be preached to others. The maid wants her daughter to be an utterly faithful Catholic, but she also wants her to be a realistic, twentieth-century citizen of the United States of America. The woman who employs the maid wants her daughter to have "a liberated woman's consciousness," but she also wants her daughter to know how to appraise her "net worth," to review statements sent by a trust officer of a bank, and, yes, one day to evaluate the "prospects" of a certain man: what kind of family does he come from, and what kind of work will he do, and how much money will he make, and where does he want to live, and how does he want to live?

No doubt some working-class women are more idealistic or politically energetic than this particular maid. No doubt some upper-class women are willing to be more vigorously, thoughtfully, consistently radical in their struggle on behalf of their sex than is the case with this particular person. Still, as Dorothy Day (hardly compromise prone) once pointed out: "In each of us there is a limit; beyond it, we personally can't go. The world faces us down every day. I have never wanted to shake my finger at others. I know how often I fall short of my own mark. We keep trying, though. We pray for strength to keep trying."

If there is anything that unites the women we have met these past years, it is their continuing determination to do what Dorothy Day suggests. They persist, these hard-pressed, relatively poor, constantly vulnerable women. No doubt the admonition to "keep trying" can imply for many a certain passivity. One keeps trying all right—adjusts to the powerful imperatives of the status quo. But Dorothy Day did not have resignation or acquiescence in mind when she used that expression, nor has apathetic surrender been the dominant psychological characteristic of many women we know in migrant camps, Indian reservations, ghetto communities, working-class neighborhoods, Eskimo settlements, Appalachian hollows. Moments, yes—moments of grim fatalism, of melancholy, of lacerating nihilism. No wonder so many revolutionaries have grown up in relatively comfortable circumstances—and become puzzled at, impatient with, even enraged by the failure of others, the victims of this world, to follow suit.

Still, even among those without apparent radical political zeal, one finds evidence enough of shrewd social analysis and personal courage—daily efforts, not without much pain, to get by and maybe obtain a slight edge over life. A migrant worker, a young woman with a bleak future indeed, manages to fight for her dignity. She resists temptations and blandishments which are the equivalent, for her, of the enormous wealth and power others succumb to—with the justification that it is inevitable that people "sell out," given the rewards a rich society like ours can offer. A woman from the hollows of Appalachia, now in a northern industrial city, dreams of a cozy, suburban life, and at the same time remembers with nostalgia and edification a valuable rural heritage. She never quite becomes a conquest of the imperial suburban sprawl, but she also knows poverty, Appalachian poverty, well enough not to romanticize it. She fights for herself and her daughter against dozens of daily corruptions, not the least of which is her own desperate willingness at times to surrender completely—wipe her mind clean of all previous loyalties, attachments, convictions, and yield to the demands of the next television commercial, the nearest billboard, the signs that line the upper walls of the buses she takes to and from work.

A woman from a *barrio* of San Antonio takes the measure of her people's misery and her own relative privilege. She could have more, much more—if she would sell herself to a prosperous entrepreneur. But she is, yes, privileged—enough so that she knows how to say no even before she is thoroughly aware of what she is refusing and why. She is fiercely independent in her own quiet and innocent way. She will not storm a barricade, will not speak out loudly and clearly for her people, her sex, but she proves herself—even if, in George Eliot's word, "indefinitely" —a *Chicana* of extraordinary intelligence, tact, and moral discrimination. And an Eskimo woman contends with psychological intensities and polarities that prove themselves almost mythic in nature—elusive yet powerful ghosts that push and pull upon her, seize her, direct her, and, very important, enable her to stand up, stand apart, stand for more than a community's consensus.

None of the women who speak about their lives in the foregoing pages will achieve the dramatic and historical importance of a St. Teresa. They are, rather, the women George Eliot knew to mention in her prelude to *Middlemarch.* Today some social scientists describe them as inert, as plagued by indifference or worse —*anomie;* or as a bundle of bitterness and frustration—*ressentiment.* For years, as we prepared ourselves to work in various parts of this country, we heard about the limitations and worse of such individuals. We were told they have been rendered not only complacent, but thoroughly malleable. We were told they are their own worst enemies. We were told they have been reduced to animals of sorts—grabbing at crumbs, at straws, at the coattails of any petty boss who comes along with some tinsel in exchange for lots of sweat. We were told they are "one-dimensional" and deracinated and brainwashed. We were told they are the lumpen-proletariat—or maybe a step above socially, economically: the pitiable, dehumanized, petit-bourgeoisie.

No doubt many thousands of women, like men, have succumbed irretrievably to the demands of a particular world. The maid quoted above, who helped us see rather a lot, was able to acknowledge her considerable flaws of character and judgment —her sins, she preferred to call them. She knew when the tides of her day threatened to drown her. She knew how to fight for air. She knew how to hold on to anything—no such desperate necessity for those perched safely on cantilevered porches with magnificent views of meadows or mountains or the ocean, the sky above, and, near at hand, plenty of food and drink, stocks and bonds. "I turn on the television set in the late morning at work," the maid once told us. She had let us know that fact of her morning life before. This time, however, she didn't watch quiz shows; and no, we weren't regular viewers of any soap opera. (She watched one while taking her lunch.) She had better things to do than justify herself to us—or to her "missus." Yet she also seemed to know, in her considerable intelligence as a social and psychological observer, that the problem, alas, was one of ignorance—ours—cloaked in the smugness of a self-serving illusion: that we are smart all right, and know a lot, whereas she is well meaning though not "educated," not "aware" of so very much —hence prone to things like quiz shows, soap operas.

In order to help us—more than we knew at the time—she gave us yet another moment of her life as a woman servant to another woman who is decent, knowing, politically alert, and socially sensitive: "I was watching a quiz show a couple of weeks ago. I thought she'd gone, the missus. She'd been talking on the phone, and then it got silent, and I heard the door open and close. I kept up my work until I was ready for a break, and I put on the television. She must have come back in. I hadn't heard her. She walked into the kitchen and she surprised me. She gave me a look—as if to say: caught you! I thought she'd at least be good enough to leave right away. I wasn't upset or ashamed of myself. I had no reason to be. She knows I watch television during the morning break I take. I guess the volume was up more than usual —but I thought no one was home. I usually keep the volume down because I don't want to disturb anyone who might be near the kitchen. I guess she was just in a bad mood, and needed to let some steam off at someone, and there I was.

"It didn't take her long to get her satisfaction. She didn't say much either. She just gave me a look, and gave the television set a look, and asked me if I knew what needed to be done that day. She knew I knew. She could tell from the look on my face that I was upset by the look on *her* face—and by that question of hers. So she tried to apologize by saying she was 'just checking.' You bet she was 'checking'! That's her privilege. I hear her talking about all of us women, who have such a 'poor life.' Then she comes and sees me watching a program on television, and she decides I'm not spending my time the way *she* does—and besides, she wants me to be doing all her work for her, so that she can spend her time any way she wants.

"I wonder whether she'd really like it better if I sat and read a fancy book from her husband's library. He doesn't read those books, and she doesn't either. They skim some new books, and then they tell people they've read them, and then they laugh and confess to each other how they 'fake it' when they talk about those books. Meanwhile, I'm 'wasting my time' watching those 'stupid' television programs. I hear her speak like that to her children: Don't watch the 'stupid' TV. I'm one of her children,

I guess! I'll tell you what she doesn't know about the world—
that because of who she is and who I am, we're not just two
women, the way she pretends we are sometimes when she tries
to be nice to me; we're something else—the boss and the one
who's being bossed. Sure, I'm 'wasting my time' watching her
television set; but I wonder if she knows how I feel when I get
up before the sun does, and start getting myself over to her
house. I'll be drinking my coffee, and I'll say to myself: another
day down the drain, and all for *the almighty buck*—my dad's
words. I remember him saying over and over: *the almighty buck.*
He said *the almighty buck* is the lord and master of everyone—
except those who have lots and lots of bucks.

"When I sit and watch those quiz shows, I figure I'm gaining
a few minutes—and I can see someone win a few dollars without
being made to get up at five or five-thirty, and without getting
a dirty look for taking a break after working pretty damn hard,
I'll tell you. Who wants to read a lot of heavy stuff—and then go
back to the washing machine and the vacuum cleaner and the
stove and the refrigerator, and none of them mine! I'd like her
to come and work in my house every day, and see what she'll
want to do with her coffee break and her lunch hour! After doing
that, she might end up glad to go home—*and stay home.*"

She is a social commentator and occasional polemicist who
knows how to use the tentative "might" rather than the more
certain "would." She is not one to be all too sure of herself. She
is not one to tell others what they ought to be or do, or what they
will, in any case, end up being or doing. Still, she possesses a
strong sense of justice, a continuing perception of wrongdoing.
Moreover, she not only rouses herself from an early morning,
delicious sleep in order to start her working day, but asks her
mind to stop, to look carefully at what happens on her own side
of the tracks as well as the other side. And she keeps going; day
after day she does—holding herself together in the face of the
tension that accompanies the traveling back and forth, the en-

trances and exits that amount to a daily cultural journey, not to mention one person's membership in something called "the work force." She and others, millions of others—American women who all the time try to get by, get along, get ahead, and, not least, get. Get what? They ask that, too; ask what they work so hard for, and what in a better world they might be obtaining —in the way of respect, sanction, approval, and, not unimportant, position or money. They ask so very much, or as Lillian Smith, writer and brave, early integrationist from Georgia, wonderful friend to us, once put it in a note we received shortly before her death: "The Negro people of the South want to stop living for other people. They ask themselves often why for so long they haven't had the most important possession in the world, the right to live their own lives. I hope, one day, that the two of you will stop and think about *women*. They also are oppressed; they ache for a similar victory in their lives. They ache to find their lives."

We have heard in words the aching—the daily battles, the losses, the small victories, the long, burdened marches across time and space. In a moment of mixed faith and doubt the maid told us one blustery autumn afternoon that she hoped she would live to see her "people" have a better day. We thought she was being "ethnic"; we thought she was speaking of class and race, of neighborhoods and cities, of income levels and church affiliation and occupational status; but no, she explained when we asked: her "people" were "all the women of the world." She smiled faintly. She was being, perhaps, a little evasive with us, or maybe taunting us with a rather large generalization—a fine reply to a question meant to narrow things down, confine her, maybe lock her into one of our many categorical niches. A bit weary of ourselves and our self-appointed purposes, we did manage to restrain ourselves, if not shut up completely—and appreciatively. We nodded and said yes. And she nodded back and said her own strong, exceptionally audible and resonant *yes*.

part

SIX

REFERENCES

Georffe Eliot's "wisdom," often remarked upon by critics over the decades, was not confined to any particular range of humanity. She was interested in the poor as well as the well-to-do, the rural life as well as that pursued in cities; and, of course, she tried to understand both women and men. Her observations have constantly come to mind as we have done our work; and her way of regarding the world has for us been a constant source of encouragement. She lived comfortably with irony, ambiguity, inconsistency, complexity, paradox—not because she necessarily wanted things to be as they were, but because she refused to allow a conviction of what she believed ought to be (ideology) to enforce itself on her mind to the point that she blinked the truth of what actually happens in the world. Over and over again in our work her observations and reflections, especially those offered in *Middlemarch,* have come to our minds as we have tried to make sense of one or another person's life. We have both had occasion to work with her novels, to teach them in classrooms, to learn from her a second time around, so to speak, through the eyes of students who are themselves asked by a novelist to see

the particular without shunning those broader, impersonal, social, and historical "forces" that come to bear upon all of us, no
matter what our level of "consciousness" with respect to them.
We find it hard to imagine how we might have thought about so
much of what we saw, had it not been for those novels of George
Eliot—a woman whose spiritual richness and generosity we acknowledge ardently, to use a word she favored, but not much in
current use.

Nearer to our own time, we were fortunate in the first years
of our Southern work to get to know and spend time with Lillian
Smith. She was a brilliant and strong-minded woman who dispatched wonderfully informative and cautioning letters to us.
We remember a weekend in 1962, spent in Clayton, Georgia,
with her and Paula Snelling. We were living in Georgia then,
trying to understand how black and white schoolchildren of both
sexes were managing the pioneering effort of school desegregation—against substantial, sometimes fearful odds. She knew out
of her own experience what it meant to take on the segregationist
status quo. She told us much about herself—and was the first
person to suggest that we begin to make connections between
race and sex, between the ways white people treat black people,
and men of both races treat women. Her book, *Killers of the
Dream* (New York: W. W. Norton, 1961), meant a lot to us. We
read it when we lived in Vinings, Georgia, and carried it to New
Orleans; Greenwood, Mississippi; Burnsville, North Carolina;
Harlan County, Kentucky; and Belle Glade, Florida, as we became involved in the civil rights movement, and in an effort to
comprehend the lives of migrant farm workers, sharecroppers or
tenant farmers, and the mountain people of Appalachia. One of
her novels, *Strange Fruit* (New York: Harcourt Brace Jovanovich, 1948), explores the subject of miscegenation with tact and
intelligence—an especially noteworthy accomplishment for a
Southern white woman writing in the 1940s on such a subject.
Her personal advice to us was of enormous value; we keep a
strong memory of her vital, knowing, searching mind.

We also want to mention a woman still alive as we finish this book: Dorothy Day, eighty years old in early November 1977. We have been privileged to know her, have recommended to many students her edifying autobiography, *The Long Loneliness* (New York: Harper & Row, 1952), an important book, indeed, by an American woman and political activist. We read her monthly *The Catholic Worker,* and one of us has written a book about her and her work: *A Spectacle Unto the World: The Catholic Worker Movement* (New York: Viking, 1973). Though she would no doubt prefer Dostoevsky and Tolstoy to George Eliot, she has what all three of those novelists possessed in such abundance: a capacity to cross railroad tracks, look everywhere for evidence of the human spirit at work affirming itself, and, not least, entrance us with stories. In her case they happen to be stories based on real events and people—the mystical labor of the Holy Spirit, which has (one believes) hovered over the various Catholic Worker hospitality houses for nearly five decades. Her letters to us we keep near—a constant message of affection, but also an admonition that the sin of pride is devious, unyielding.

Another strong influence on us and our work has been the three autobiographical volumes of Lillian Hellman: *An Unfinished Woman* (Boston: Little, Brown, 1969); *Pentimento* (Boston: Little, Brown, 1973); and *Scoundrel Time* (Boston: Little, Brown, 1976). She has been a warm and thoughtful friend for over a decade; her mixture of social perceptiveness and psychological subtlety has continually served as a standard for emulation. A few words from her, on most subjects, and we're back at the beginning, wondering how we managed to get so far astray. Her courage and candor and highly ethical sensibility have been refuges of sorts for us, as we have struggled with the thorny issues of observation and participation—the obligations of the student or writer, the responsibilities of the person who sees injustice abroad a land and wants very much to work for concrete social and economic changes.

We came across Tillie Olsen's stories (*Tell Me a Riddle,* New

York: Delta, 1960) when we were beginning our work in the South—riot-plagued New Orleans, Louisiana, in the autumn of 1960. We have both come to depend upon her enormously. Her stories have touched our students unforgettably. Her novel *Yonnondio* (New York: Delacorte Press/Seymour Lawrence, 1974) evokes the reality of working-class life of the 1930s in a way some of the women we have met also manage to do when they pour out their memories and "old, stale, thoughts," as one elderly woman from Georgia kept calling her rather intelligent reveries, sustained over the years, she would always remind us, by "two shots of whiskey in the evening." We have also admired, and urged upon some of the women we have known, Tillie Olsen's biographical interpretation that accompanies the Feminist Press reissue of Rebecca Harding Davis' *Life in the Iron Mills,* originally issued in 1861 (New York, 1972). Her most recent book, *Silences* (New York: Delacorte Press/Seymour Lawrence, 1978), includes her two penetrating literary essays, "Silences: When Writers Don't Write" and "Women Who Are Writers in Our Country: One Out of Twelve." These pieces are full of shrewd judgments about both individuals and the respective and quite different workings of culture upon men and women. For students of social history, and for those interested in learning of the vicissitudes (and hard-won triumphs) of working-class life, Tillie Olsen is a special resource—immensely gifted as a writer, constantly interested in looking back as well as struggling to make the future different, and, very important, able to convert an understandable rage at the injustices of this world into well-constructed, illuminating, sensitive, almost fragile, stories. One of us (in *The New Republic,* December 6, 1975) has tried hard to examine the range, limited but penetrating, of her published work, not to mention the nature of her moral and political convictions. To have corresponded with her and met her has been a special privilege, indeed.

While we lived in the South, we came to know and admire the

writing of Eudora Welty and Flannery O'Connor. To see Mississippi, say, through Eudora Welty's eyes is to be offered freedom
from dozens of stereotypic notions and exposed to the suggestive
but vexing layers of psychological truth that are concealed by the
social norms and rituals of a rural society. And to see Georgia,
or any part of the South, through Flannery O'Connor's eyes is
to be reminded that any segment of human experience—described by words like "race," "sex," "class," "regional affiliation"—ought in some way to be given its place in a larger scheme
of things. Flannery O'Connor could take sociological matters
like "segregation" and show them to be shadows created by the
flames of hell. We met and talked with her when we lived not
far from her. She was sick, dying. She spoke quite frankly of her
illness—and of her native South. She warned us not to become
so caught up in a region's special (and then urgent) difficulties
that we lost sight of what she referred to, the several times we
spoke, as "the larger human drama, in which all of us have our
parts to play."

She was not by any means trying to evade the specific chal-
lenges (and outrages) of a particular "way of life." She knew in
her heart how wretched and stunted various people could be in
her native land. But her eyes scanned the sky, in pursuit of God's
judgment—and also poked about various stretches of red clay in
the sure knowledge that the Devil would be found at work in
many guises. Her bitterly vivid portrayals of the evil creature in
us are meant to shake from us a bit of the vanity and conceit that
are, of course, inevitable companions of each human being—no
matter the person's skin color, occupation, sex, citizenship, religious affiliation. We found a talk with her unsettling, perplexing,
distracting. There was so much to see and do in the South of the
early 1960s, so why get caught up in her exceedingly strenuous
scruples, admonitions? Over the years, though, her words, her
point of view, her advice have weighed heavier and heavier on
our shoulders. "You will find here in rural Georgia fallen angels

by the thousands," she told us, a twinkle in her eye, but only the thinnest of smiles on her hurt and saddened face. It was a nice way to give us one of those "contexts" that get mentioned so often these days by social scientists, no great friends of hers. We have carried her *Everything That Rises Must Converge* (New York: Farrar, Straus & Giroux, 1965) and *A Good Man Is Hard to Find* (New York: Harcourt, Brace and World, 1955) around with us for years, and would strongly recommend *The Complete Stories* (New York: Farrar, Straus & Giroux, 1971).

If one wants to put women writers like those we have just mentioned in a larger historical tradition, Ellen Moers is of great help in her *Literary Women* (Garden City: Doubleday, 1977). An interesting way of regarding "literary women" is to be found in Ann Douglas' *The Feminization of American Culture* (New York: Alfred A. Knopf, 1977). The author suggests that at a certain point in nineteenth-century American history, the views of women writers became an important means by which a new social vision was forged and disseminated. Hurt, angered, curbed, denied women became strangely, ironically influential, if not prophetic.

One moves from American "literary women" and their influence to a broader assessment of American women contained in *Notable American Women,* a three-volume biographical dictionary issued by the Belknap Press, a division of the Harvard University Press (Cambridge, 1971). These volumes cover the years between 1607 and 1950. Each of the volumes reads like a history book—a brief narrative presentation of the particulars of one woman's life after another. In sum, the books tell an enormous amount about how this country was settled and developed—by those, in large measure, not ordinarily acknowledged in history books or, for that matter, a number of biographical dictionaries. The introduction by Janet Wilson James is a model of scholarship, yet accessible to the general reader—as is the case with the entries.

Another, more conventional way to look at the American woman's experience is through the eyes of a sensitive historian. William H. Chafe's *The American Woman* (New York: Oxford, 1972) is an exceptionally readable and lucid account of the decisive changes American women have had to confront during this century. The author begins his account with the year 1918—the end of the First World War and a time of the approaching franchise for women, requested that year by President Wilson. Chafe's book offers a sensitively sustained mix of social history, economic analysis, political interpretation. No wonder so many courses devoted to a survey of the contemporary woman's movement begin with *The American Woman*.

Two books that are concerned more specifically with the woman suffrage struggle, both exceptionally well written and organized, are *One Half the People: The Fight for Woman Suffrage*, by Anne F. and Andrew M. Scott (Philadelphia: Lippincott, 1975) and *The Ideas of the Woman Suffrage Movement, 1890–1920* by Aileen Kraditor (New York: Columbia University Press, 1965). Both books remind their readers how long and hard women had to strive for the most obvious and basic of all rights. The parallel with the civil rights movement is obvious. In the early 1960s we heard even so-called "moderates" utter dismay at the thought of the vote being extended to black people. As one goes through the Scotts' account, or that of Aileen Kraditor, or the sections of Dorothy Day's autobiography that tell of her suffragette days, one realizes how hard it is for one generation to realize the anguish, frustration, bitterness, or fear of another, preceding generation. Even now, a mere ten to fifteen years after the major thrust of the civil rights movement, one meets with incredulity on the part of *both* young blacks and whites—that in a time when they were children or, indeed, not born, about a third of a region's population could not vote. And one hears formerly strenuous segregationists, willing a decade earlier to equate black suffrage with something called "communism" (the

sinister, the corrupt, if not apocalyptic), now smile and say that
of course *everyone* should vote—that, yes.

As always, one wonders what succeeding generations will
think of what today is considered by many undesirable, contro-
versial, if not unthinkably radical. In this regard, a valuable and
instructive book is *Seven Women: Portraits from the American Radical Tradition* (New York: Viking, 1977). Judith Nies is the author, and she has selected an impressive cadre of women—from
Sarah Moore Grimké and Harriet Tubman, who fought *both*
slavery and the prevailing biases against women; to Elizabeth
Cady Stanton and Mother Jones, strong advocates of political and
social reform; to more recent pioneers—Charlotte Perkins Gil-
man, the economist; Anna Louise Strong, the journalist who
watched the Russian and Chinese revolutions so intently and
carefully; and, not least, Dorothy Day.

Those interested in Mother Jones, perhaps the most radically
activist of the above group of women, ought go to her autobiography, now reprinted and edited by Mary Field Parton, with a
foreword by Clarence Darrow (Chicago: Charles Kerr, 1974).
The book offers an interesting bibliography—sixty-two references that, in sum, offer a history of the labor union movement
in this country. Fred Thompson compiled the list, and also wrote
a first-rate introductory essay to a book about one of the most
unusual, impressive, and long-lasting of American lives. A fine
biography of Mother Jones also appeared in 1974: *Mother Jones:
The Miners' Angel,* by Dale Fetherling (Carbondale: Southern
Illinois University Press).

By no means were the suffragette or labor union struggles the
only ones to engage the activist involvement of women. *Woman's
Body, Woman's Right: A Social History of Birth Control in America*
(New York: Grossman, 1976) gives a chronicle, by no means
over, of an effort by women to have more and more personal and
social and legal say in a matter that men have concerned themselves with all too much. Linda Gordon has written a thoroughly

documented study, and her "reference notes" lead the reader here, there, and wonderfully all over—to questions of economics and politics, but also social ethics. And in the field of political history, we mention two critically significant and eye-opening books by Sheila Rowbotham: *Women's Consciousness, Man's World* (Middlesex, England: Penguin, 1973), and *Women, Resistance and Revolution* (New York: Vintage, 1972). The author connects the struggles of women to those of others: men, of course, and, often enough, children of both sexes caught up in the various exploitative economic systems that exist and persist on this planet. Of related interest is Harry Braverman's *Labor and Monopoly Capital* (New York: Monthly Review Press, 1974).

We are especially anxious to point the reader toward a number of books which take for their chief concern the ordinary, working-class women of this country—whom we, too, have come to know fairly well these past decades. A good historical account is offered by Rosalyn Baxondall, Linda Gordon, and Susan Reverby in *America's Working Women* (New York: Vintage, 1976). It is a documentary history, and starts in the seventeenth century and continues to the present time. The book offers essays, excerpts from diaries, old union records, letters and songs and photographs and various kinds of so-called "hard data": numbers, statistics, reports, compilations. Other books by and about women have approached their working life in a variety of ways. We especially like and recommend *Women at Work,* edited by William L. O'Neill (Chicago: Quadrangle, 1972), including the fine personal essay by Elinor Langer, "Inside the New York Telephone Company." In a similar vein, and of equal value, is Ann Oakley's *Woman's Work: The Housewife, Past and Present* (New York: Vintage, 1974). Also, *Nobody Speaks for Me: Self Portraits of American Working-Class Women,* wonderfully assembled and edited by Nancy Seifer (New York: Simon & Schuster, 1976). We would not have written our own book if we had not, upon reading those books with much admiration, concluded that our particular work made known still more voices and experiences in their tradition.

Three more helpful books that try to convey the way ordinary women try to make do are *Worlds of Pain: Life in the Working Class Family,* by Lillian Breslow Rubin (New York: Basic Books, 1976); *Working Mothers,* by Jean Curtis (Garden City, New York: Doubleday, 1976); and *Pink Collar Workers,* by Louise Kapp Howe (New York: Putnam's, 1977). A more historical approach is offered by Barbara Mayer Wertheimer in *We Were There: The Story of Working Women in America* (New York: Pantheon, 1977). And issues of class and sex are taken up theoretically as well as concretely in Ann Oakley's *The Sociology of Housework* (New York: Pantheon, 1974).

Quite another "level" of existence gets discussed in *The Managerial Woman,* by Margaret Hennig and Anne Jardim (Garden City, New York: Doubleday, 1977). High up as well as lower down on the ladder the biases, arrogance, condescension, and wrongheaded or simply pigheaded attitudes persist, so far as women are concerned. And higher up, as well as lower down on the ladder, one encounters thoughtfulness, courage, and considerable toughness of spirit—documented with striking, introspective candor by a number of women in *Working It Out,* by Sara Ruddick and Pamela Daniels (New York: Pantheon, 1977).

We by no means want to disregard here the well-known polemicists who have in recent years fought so hard and well—Friedan, Millet, Firestone, for example. For us, the most powerful statement has been Robin Morgan's *Going Too Far* (New York: Random House, 1977). The essays in that book are brilliant, lyrical, compelling. She provides a marvelous analysis of fear connected to one's sexual "condition," titled "Paranoia." There is also an excellent reading list, which is anthropological and philosophical as well as polemical—the last a term we in no way intend as pejorative. Speaking of that reading list, we want to mention four volumes listed in it that have meant a lot to us

over the years, and are of obvious importance in the "literature":
Simone de Beauvoir's *The Second Sex* (New York: Knopf, 1952);
Margaret Mead's *Sex and Temperament in Three Primitive Societies*
(New York: Morrow, 1935 and 1963); as well as her *Male and
Female* (New York: Morrow, 1949); and very significant for us,
because of our work in the South, Gerda Lerner's *The Grimké
Sisters* (New York: Schocken, 1971), an account of the develop-
ment of abolitionist sentiment, under by no means favorable
circumstances, in antebellum South Carolina. Another book that
has constantly helped us, and many others, too, also came out in
1971: Elizabeth Janeway's sensitive and vigorously thoughtful
Man's World, Woman's Place (New York: Morrow).

An increasing number of books try to convey the special situation of women who belong to particular cultures, communities,
or regions within a nation. Four such books have caught our
attention: *Indian Women of the Western Morning: Their Life in Early
America,* by John Upton Terrell and Donna M. Terrell (Garden
City, New York: Doubleday, 1976); *A Street in Marrakech,* Elizabeth Warnack Ferrea's account of the lives of Moroccan women
she has come to know (Garden City, New York: Doubleday,
1975); *Women in the Kibbutz,* by Lionel Tiger and Joseph Shepher
(New York: Harcourt Brace Jovanovich, 1959); and for us an
extraordinary book indeed, Ann Cornelisen's *Women of the Shadows* (Boston: Atlantic-Little, Brown, 1976), which includes portraits of the women she has lived near, year after year, in the
south of Italy, and some sharply suggestive critical comments on
social science research. One of us tried to evaluate the considerable merits of her book in *The New Yorker,* April 12, 1976.

There is no cause for great satisfaction with the contributions
of psychology, psychiatry, and psychoanalysis to an understanding of the various and particular ways women think and feel and
attempt to shape their lives. Too often, ideological narrowness,
a plague of sorts institutionalized in various "schools" or "ap-
proaches," has prevented the "direct observation" Anna Freud

keeps calling for, but to no overwhelming effect. It would have been helpful, one supposes, if the well-to-do men who so predominantly practice psychiatry and psychoanalysis and contribute to the journals in those fields had taken the time to acquaint themselves firsthand with the "actuality" (Erik H. Erikson's word) that informs the lives, say, of working women, before being so eager to write conceptually about their sexuality— to abstract it, after all, from lives being lived. In any event, distinct afterthoughts and helpful reconsiderations are now being given us. Ann Seiden has written a long "overview" of "Research on the Psychology of Women," published (with many bibliographical references) in *The American Journal of Psychiatry,* October, 1976. Jean Baker Miller's *Toward a New Psychology of Women* (Boston: Beacon Press, 1976) offers an important examination, based on clinical evidence constantly interpreted and discussed, of the so-called "masculine" and "feminine" psychological characteristics, *and* their origins in the lives of children who live in a given culture. She is especially sensitive to the complicated relationship between sexual attitudes or inclinations, on the one hand, and a person's sense of worth, competence, success, approval by others—in short, the stamp of sanction or disdain a community offers as a response to a manner of acting, talking, being.

Jean Strouse has pulled together an interesting collection of essays intended primarily to cast a second look at the various psychoanalytic theories of how women grow up, and what happens at various points in their emotional development: *Women in Analysis: Dialogues in Psychoanalytic Views of Femininity* (New York: Harper & Row, 1976). Many ideas in the book are quite speculative—that is, are not connected to empirical observation or even clinical illustration. Some of the authors are highly theoretical, capable of sweeping generalizations, not unlike Melanie Klein. It is, of course, always hard specifically to refute psychological theorists—and harder the more ambitious and grandiose they are. One thinks of oneself as an irritant, if not a bore, in the face of grand ideas—visions of astonishing breadth and ambition.

Still, we have not witnessed enough efforts to follow up assertions handed down—the pursuit, again, of Anna Freud's "direct observation"—over the years required to fasten down theory with the sustaining sanction and corroboration of evidence. We have not, for instance, always seen the shrill, angry inner state Dorothy Dinnerstein attributes to mothers, many of whom (from the so-called working class) keep telling us that they want more, not less, time with their children. Are they resorting to "denial" or "reaction-formations"—psychoanalytic ways of suggesting that people say one thing and mean in their hearts quite another? After years of work with those women, our answer has to be no. They say what they mean, and mean what they say. Others may well come up with different conclusions. It would be helpful if there were a substantial body of "longitudinal research"—the kind that takes, no doubt about it, a long time to do, because one is confronting a hodgepodge of (often contradictory) expressed sentiments or underlying emotions—William James' "blooming buzzing confusion" of the mind. But how can we rely on the dramatic and (for some, appealing) assertions of Herbert Marcuse or Norman O. Brown (also mentors of Dorothy Dinnerstein) with respect to the "one-dimensional" nature of twentieth-century "man" or "woman," if we haven't yet examined in real depth and with continuing tenacity the way particular men and women live in a given society?

We have good cause, therefore, to appreciate Mary Jo Bane's *Here to Stay: American Families in the Twentieth Century* (New York: Basic Books, 1976). An activist in the women's movement, she is also a painstaking scholar, without any inclination to offer conclusions that lack a grounding in the reality of day-to-day events, not to mention the findings of various social observers, social scientists, demographers, officials of the Bureau of Census, and so on. Her view of what men and women want for themselves—family life, at best with modifications—does not at all emphasize the psychological negatives so starkly evoked by Dorothy Dinnerstein. Nor does Herbert Gutman's *Work, Culture and Society in Industrializing America* (New York: Knopf, 1976) show Americans to be quite as psychiatrically jeopardized as they would seem to be if we are to accept the formulations handed down in *The Mermaid and the Minotaur.* Gutman is a shrewd social historian, especially in touch with today's working-class life—and its antecedents in our nation's past. Though not always concerned directly with the issue of *women's* work or position in our society, he has a way of showing how Americans of both sexes, from ordinary if not humble backgrounds, have managed to get along and survive, often against great odds. An interesting complement to his book is Sheila Collins' "Socialism and Feminism: A Necessary Ground for Liberation," published in *Cross Currents,* spring of 1976. The author argues persuasively that woman's special exploitation has to be connected to that of the larger exploitative patterns of the modern industrial state. She gives her readers a valuable bibliography.

As for bibliographies, references, and efforts to connect the experiences of women to those shared by various others (men, children, the elderly, the unemployed, the citizens of one or another nation—on and on the categories go), we should like to mention a brilliantly constructed and (for us) continually evocative special issue of *Southern Exposure* (Volume IV, No. 4, Winter, 1977); it is devoted to the women of a region we know and love: "Generations: Women in the South." There are wonderful essays, photographs, biographical portraits, and, not least, an exceptionally remarkable bibliography. We were drawn, in particular, to Jo Ann Robinson's fine tribute rendered Lillian Smith. Somewhere in the universe one dares imagine a smile—her spirit's acknowledgment of a Southern magazine's affectionate, respectful look at its "womenfolk." If we may be so bold as to suggest a particular way of responding to this volume of *Southern*

Exposure, there is a record that might be played as one goes through the pages—called "The Working Girl: Women's Songs from Mountains, Mines and Mills" (Voyager Recordings, VRLP 3055). Kathy Kahn organized the musical presentation, playing with her Cut Cane Ramblers Fiddle Band. Kathy Kahn's book, *Hillbilly Women* (Garden City, New York: Doubleday, 1973), is, for us, another source of constant grace, a literary and ethical achievement both—and perhaps mention of it is a fitting way for us to end this section of this book.

ROBERT COLES, M.D., who has published over 25 books and more than 500 articles, reviews and essays, won the Pulitzer Prize for *Children of Crisis*. He is Professor of Psychiatry and Medical Humanities at the Harvard Medical School and a Research Psychiatrist for the University Health Services. Dr. Coles is a consultant to the Rockefeller and Ford Foundations, a trustee of the Robert F. Kennedy Memorial, and a member of the Institute of Medicine of the National Academy of Sciences. He is the recipient of many national prizes for his writing, and of over a dozen honorary degrees.

JANE HALLOWELL COLES graduated from Radcliffe College in 1959. She has taught English and history in public schools in Georgia, Louisiana, and, most recently, Massachusetts. The Coleses are the parents of three sons.